MW00886151

Apologia Diogenes

An Analysis of the Character Diogenes Pendergast in the
Fiction of Preston and Child

by

Elizabeth Thomas

Michigoose Books

©2016

Austin, Texas

USA

Cover art is a work in progress by Rosalie Everts

Cover design by Tiffany Stafford

Dedication

This book is dedicated to the late John C. Steinmetz, whose own dedication to his administrative duties on the Team Pendergast Facebook page is now legendary. He and I were discussing some of the things I have committed to these pages one day, when he said, "Someone could write a whole master's thesis about all of this." Without him, I might never have done it.

Of course, it is also dedicated to the authors of the Pendergast novels, Douglas Preston and Lincoln Child, extraordinary writers and truly wonderful human beings, whom I must thank for so many good friends I have made in recent years. I hope you two have some idea of what a force you are for good in this world.

Acknowledgements

I would like to thank all of the members of Facebook's Team Pendergast site, for all the lively discussion and ideas. In particular, however, I want to thank Rosalie Everts for letting me use her wonderful painting on my cover; Tiffany Stafford not only for the cover design but for the tedious work of looking up hardcover page numbers for me; Elyse Salpeter for writerly commiseration; and my children for putting up with the time spent working on this.

Preface

Anyone who has read more than one book in Preston and Child's *Pendergast* series and looks at the title of this effort will perhaps ask, "why not an analysis of the *main* character, Special Agent Aloysius X. L. Pendergast himself?" That, to me, seems like a much larger task. A writer could fill volumes with a careful study of Preston and Child's most illustrious creation; as of this writing he has taken center stage in thirteen novels, has been an ensemble character in two others, and has been featured in two short stories. Even though the authors have shown us his family and several of the dramas that have come with it, he still remains something of an enigma. His younger brother Diogenes, by contrast, has only appeared in the flesh in three novels (for certain) as of this writing, and the first of those very briefly. Since his trilogy ended with *Book of the Dead,* however, he *has* appeared in some of Pendergast's memory crossings. Even so, he remains a less immense analytical challenge than his elder brother, more easily covered in a manageable number of pages.

Yet, of course, the scope of this project is in some ways just an excuse. For me, there has always been something utterly fascinating about Diogenes. Like many readers, I was intrigued by Special Agent Pendergast from his first appearance in *Relic,* and by the time he truly came into his own in *Cabinet of Curiosities,* I had fallen in literary love. In *Dance of Death,* however, I realized I had read some of the most beautifully bleak prose I had ever experienced when the authors wrote from within Diogenes' mind and spirit. As perverse as he was, his sharp wit seemed perhaps even more whimsical in some ways than that of his elder brother. When I picked up *Book of the Dead,* with all of its lurid warnings that only one brother would survive the conflict, I was terrified for Aloysius. By the time I had reached the point in that novel at which the exact nature of The Event is revealed, I feared for them both equally, and dreaded losing either. As I posted on Preston and Child's Facebook page, "I never understood women who wrote to serial killers in prison until I met Diogenes."

Though I have searched, there is a dearth of literary criticism or even substantial reviews on the Diogenes trilogy. Therefore this analysis will depend primarily on a close reading of the actual novels (and short stories) in which Diogenes plays a part. In titling this *Apologia,* I am jesting to a certain degree—as much as Diogenes both amuses me and grabs at my somewhat highbrow reader's heart, I can never truly defend serial murder or even animal abuse. It is also useful to draw a line between reality and fiction. While criminal profilers may tell us that some real-life serial killers, like Ted Bundy, are intelligent and charming, I doubt any of them are multilingual Latin scholars. And if there is any safe place to explore affection, understanding, and admiration of such personality types, it is within the context of fiction. I intend to assert here that, partially due to being a fictional creation, Diogenes is less crazy and vicious than many readers of the series believe him to be. Less crazy and vicious even than the authors of the books portray him in their statements and interviews. He also manages to maintain an element of the New Orleans-bred Southern gentleman, one of the very characteristics that makes Special Agent Pendergast so appealing. Notwithstanding all of the horrendous mental damage and sociopathology with which his creators have endowed him, he is a more than worthy *frater minor* to his brother. Diogenes Pendergast is one of the most complex and interesting literary villains ever to grace the pages of popular fiction.

One last caveat: it is not usually necessary in works of literary analysis to give spoiler warnings. Given the immense popularity of the Pendergast series, however, and the fact that Preston and Child have been blessing us with new additions to it at a yearly rate, I do feel as though I must note that I will be discussing the novels involved in great detail. Climaxes and denouements will be "given away" as a matter of course. Future possibilities will be fodder for speculation. If this distresses you as a reader, and you have not finished any one or more of the Pendergast novels, please come back after you have done so.

A Note on References and Bibliography

Most of the works I refer to are the novels in Preston and Child's Pendergast series. I quote portions of some of these novels so frequently that I do not always stop and include the page number. I do so often enough, however, that the reader may assume that any quotation that doesn't have a parenthetical title and page number after it, falls between the last one that does and the next one that does. I have included all the Pendergast novels in the bibliography, as well as a few other books and web sites. Absent from the bibliography are some of the poems and other literary works quoted by Preston and Child themselves, though I often address these as important parts of Diogenes' thought processes. Also absent are some works referred to that have many different versions and publications, notably books of the Bible and the Apocrypha. I hope that the citations I make in the text will be clear and adequate for understanding.

###

Aperitifs

Little is said in *Relic* and *Reliquary,* the first two novels in which Agent Pendergast appears, about his family background. He appears angry when Agent Spencer Coffey tries to insult his Southern identity by telling him to go "eat that catfish sandwich your wife put in your lunchbox" (*Relic,* p. 215); later we learn that he did have a wife, and she is dead (at least, she appears to be in the earlier novels). Pendergast's late wife apparently enjoyed hunting big game in Africa, and was an excellent shot—better than Pendergast himself.

In *Cabinet of Curiosities,* however, Preston and Child introduce us to other Pendergasts. In the course of investigating a mass burial of murder victims from the 1800s, discovered on the building site of a new apartment complex, Pendergast decides that he needs to review some old family history with his Great Aunt Cornelia. The reason he finds this necessary is that he fears yet another Pendergast ancestor is behind these crimes. To converse with his great aunt, Pendergast must visit her in the Mount Mercy Hospital for the Criminally Insane. What she did to warrant confinement here is only hinted at in *Cabinet of Curiosities;* later, readers learn that she poisoned her own children, husband, and brother— but fortunately not the brother who would become Pendergast's grandfather.

Aunt Cornelia is wheeled in on page 329 of *Cabinet of Curiosities,* and she is bound into her wheelchair with five-point restraints. The personnel at Mount Mercy consider her to be still quite dangerous, and Dr. Ostrom reminds

Pendergast of some seemingly violent incident that happened the last time he visited his elderly relative. Cornelia is clad in "a long, old-fashioned black taffeta dress, Victorian button-up shoes, and a black mourning veil." She asks the orderlies to raise her veil, and seems generally to be under the impression that they are her servants, explaining their lack of willingness to do her bidding: "The service here has declined dreadfully these past few years. It's so hard to find good help these days."

Despite Cornelia's status as the inmate of a mental institution, she is able to provide Pendergast with some information about the ancestor in whom he is interested—her own great uncle, Antoine Leng Pendergast. Presumably, Cornelia hasn't met him in person, because she tells Pendergast he moved to New York City "[l]ong before I was born" (*Cabinet of Curiosities*, p. 329). She also tells him almost immediately that Antoine "inherited the family tendency to madness," and that "even as a boy he developed certain dreadful obsessions." Nevertheless, Cornelia describes their relative as "quite a brilliant youth, you know: sarcastic, witty, strange." She notes that he "had inherited his father's interest in elixirs, restoratives, chemicals. And poisons" (*Cabinet of Curiosities*, p. 330). She attributes Antoine's actual descent into madness to "the tragedy with his mother," which readers later learn is her death being caused by the very patent medicine with which his father Hezekiah replenished the Pendergast family fortune.

Cornelia goes on to recount that Antoine "poisoned the six family dogs in an experiment," and had a possibly sexual relationship with a voodoo practitioner named Marie LeClaire despite her being roughly sixty years older than he was. "Then there was that unpleasantness with her tomb, after she died," recalls Cornelia on page 331. "The interference with her grave, the violated body and all those dreadful little cuts." Apparently, Cornelia reveals, "he believed he was going to bring her back to life. There was the question of whether she had put him up to it before she died, charged him with some kind of dreadful after-death assignment."

Later in the course of his investigation, Pendergast feels that he needs even more insight into his ancestor Antoine, and readers are treated to the first of the special agent's "memory crossings." These are a blend of the "memory palace" technique used by Arthur Conan Doyle's famed Sherlock Holmes, with Zen Buddhist "Chongg Ran" meditation—a practice that is the creative invention of Preston and Child. Pendergast's personal memory palace is a mental re-creation of his childhood home, the family's New Orleans mansion, Rochenoire. Pendergast's memory palace is all that remains of Rochenoire, because it "had been burned down by a mob shortly after Pendergast left for boarding school in England" (*Cabinet of Curiosities,* pp. 391-392). We learn a great deal more about the family as a whole merely from the following sentence: "He remembered the day, many years ago, when he had first been inducted into the family secrets: the hidden panel in the library, the stone chambers beneath, the room with the crest" (*Cabinet of Curiosities,* p. 396). The whole family, not just Cornelia and Antoine, has an air of rather Gothic mystery.

By the time Pendergast undertakes the memory crossing, seeking to learn more about Antoine, he has already discovered the body of "his great-grand-uncle tortured and murdered" (*Cabinet of Curiosities,* p. 393). More importantly, "the corpse of his ancestor *was only recently dead*—the state of the corpse suggested that the death had occurred within the last two months." Antoine Pendergast had indeed succeeded in his quest to prolong his own life. Of course, Pendergast had suspected this possibility when copycat murders similar to those from the 1800s had started taking place.

During the memory crossing, Pendergast realizes that Antoine's mansion on Riverside Drive was a deliberate recreation of the ancestral home, Rochenoire. This discovery aids him in discovering a way to defeat the copycat murderer, the man who killed Antoine while trying to learn his formula for lifespan prolongation. The reader, however, learns more about Antoine's history—how he performed "experiments on small animals," (*Cabinet of Curiosities,* p. 398) and how there had always been "rumors of certain hideous things found in the deep shadows of the tombs [in the basement of Rochenoire]; rumors of the real reason behind Antoine's permanent banishment from the house on Dauphine Street" (*Cabinet of Curiosities*, pp. 398).

In the midst of these revelations, however, Preston and Child subtly drop a bomb—their very first reference to the character later to be introduced as Diogenes Pendergast. At one point in Pendergast's meanderings through his memory palace, "he continued down the hall. The next door—the door that had once been his brother's—had been sealed by Pendergast himself, never to be opened again. He quickly moved on" (*Cabinet of Curiosities,* p. 393). Until this point, late in the third book in which Special Agent Pendergast appears, readers are completely unaware that he has ever had a sibling. After this quick allusion, this "brother" is never mentioned again in the novel. The stark fact that Pendergast has purposely sealed his brother's room in the house that forms his memory palace, mentioned in the midst of descriptions of the overwhelming Gothic misdeeds of his ancestor Antoine and coming after readers have already met scary old Great Aunt Cornelia, can only leave them wondering how utterly irredeemable this brother must be. After all, Pendergast visits Cornelia and even asks her advice, despite her insanity. He fearlessly plunges into his memory palace seeking information and understanding of his ancestor Antoine, who is a serial killer guilty of the vivisection of human beings. But his own brother? Not only is the room sealed, it is "never to be opened again." What could Pendergast's brother possibly have done to put himself beyond the pale?

Of course, with only these few words to go on, a reader might speculate that Pendergast's mysterious brother is dead, and the grief of this is so profound for Pendergast that he had to "seal" that particular door in his memory palace. Possibly, but that doesn't sound much like Pendergast. He can speak of his wife to people he respects without visible distress, after all. No. This brother must have done something of a spectacularly heinous nature to merit this special treatment even within the privacy of Pendergast's own mind. The understated dexterity of the authors' technique in bringing readers to this conclusion and preparing them for Diogenes' later introduction is nothing less than masterful.

Before leaving the discussion of *Cabinet of Curiosities,* I wish to posit one more possibility: Diogenes has probably already left a faint trace upon Pendergast's investigation. Later we learn he has been in New York since after the events of *Reliquary;* still later we learn he has done one better than Pendergast and actually spoken with Great-Uncle Antoine. The sense that Pendergast and Nora have that someone has been in the Museum's archives ahead of them is explained when Fairhaven is exposed as the new Surgeon, but perhaps Fairhaven had not been the only one to explore these resources. How else would Diogenes have known how to find his fascinating relative?

Preston and Child treat us to another singular and ephemeral mention of Pendergast's brother in the next novel in the series, *Still Life With Crows.* After three murders plus a dog killing have been discovered and attributed to the same perpetrator, Pendergast calls his bibliophile friend Wren, asking him to locate an old hand-written journal he thinks may have a bearing on the case. During the course of the phone call, Wren comments about the crimes Pendergast is investigating: "And from what I understand, such a strange set of murders, too. In fact, they're so unusual as to seem almost familiar. Your brother isn't vacationing in Kansas, by any chance?" *(Still Life With Crows,* p. 173).

Pendergast's "voice was chill, distant," in response. "I have told you, Wren, *never* to speak of my family," *(Still Life With Crows,* p. 173) he says. This, however, is all readers get in this fourth novel, as far as Pendergast's brother is concerned. We have learned that he is either a serial killer like Antoine, or that at least Wren feels he has the potential to have become one—and a bizarre one, at that. What readers have never learned as of this writing, is how Wren knows anything about

Pendergast's brother at all, especially given how reticent the special agent is in speaking of him.

Before moving on to a novel in which Diogenes Pendergast actually appears, it is worth mentioning another preview of his character. *Brimstone*, the first book in the trilogy that bears his name, and the fifth Pendergast book overall, saw print in 2004. In 2002, however, Lincoln Child's solo novel *Utopia* (now republished as *Lethal Velocity*) came out, featuring a rather interesting villain. Known only as John Doe, his "eyes were two different colors. The left was hazel; the right, an intense blue" (*Utopia*, p. 80). This, of course, is a distinguishing feature of Diogenes, though his blue eye is dead and sightless. Doe's heterochromia is apparently natural. Readers learn later that Doe also has a "closely trimmed beard" (*Utopia,* p. 273) as does Diogenes. Doe also has an elegant, silky, yet sinister way with words, quite similar to that of Pendergast's younger brother. When speaking with a team member who is having second thoughts about the crime they are committing, Doe says:

"I warn you, don't sport with my intelligence. Expressions of altruism make my gorge rise. *Everything* we do, we do out of self-interest. You, my friend, are no exception. Assertions to the contrary would be mere self-delusion. Need I remind you whose idea this was to begin with? Who contacted *who*? Need I remind you, *again,* of the consequences of developing an eleventh-hour conscience?" (*Utopia,* pp. 236-37). I like to think, however, that Diogenes would have said "who contacted *whom.*"

Of course, there are differences between the two characters.

In some ways, it is difficult to imagine Diogenes Pendergast working as part of a team, even in a leadership capacity. Yet, while masquerading as Hugo Menzies, Diogenes manages to be one of the most competent museum department heads known to the series, and manages to win the respect and affection of many of his colleagues. The resemblance between John Doe and Diogenes is certainly strong enough, however, to have been noticed by many readers. There is an entire thread on the Preston and Child fan site *Stormhaven* devoted to this issue. It is fair to speculate that the writing team decided to incorporate aspects of the character Child created and killed off on his own into the sibling/nemesis they were preparing for Pendergast.

###

Première Course

Diogenes Pendergast first appears in *Brimstone*, but Preston and Child take their time in introducing him. *Brimstone* centers on crimes with which Diogenes has absolutely nothing to do; Pendergast and his friend Sergeant Vincent D'Agosta are investigating a series of incidents that resemble spontaneous human combustion, but are actually murders. Interestingly, the perpetrator turns out to be a villain whom Preston and Child have borrowed from nineteenth-century novelist Wilkie Collins' *The Woman in White*, Count Fosco. Pendergast and D'Agosta are just about to fly to Italy in pursuit of one of the associated bad guys when Pendergast receives a message on linen paper embossed with the family coat of arms which he concludes is from Diogenes. "At first, D'Agosta thought the sheet was empty. But then he made out, in a beautiful, old-fashioned script, a small date in the middle of the page: *January 28.* It appeared to have been written with a goose quill" (*Brimstone,* p. 262). Pendergast also reveals to his investigating partner that this is actually the second time he has received such a message: "The first had the same date on it," Pendergast tells Vincent. "I wasn't sure what it meant. It arrived exactly six months ago—and now this. The meaning is now obvious" (*Brimstone*, p. 263).

Merely from the inscription of a date and the stationery he uses, we learn some things about Diogenes. One, he considers himself a Pendergast, through and through. Two, he has a similar elegance to his elder brother. Three, he is playfully eccentric—a goose quill? Pendergast, however, is determined to quickly color Vincent's (as well as the reader's) impression of Diogenes. It is interesting to note here that *Brimstone* is also the first novel in which Preston and Child provide us with a first name for Special Agent Pendergast: Aloysius. Jumping into the realm of pure speculation, I can imagine the writing team brainstorming a name for Pendergast's younger, villainous brother and realizing they had not come up with a given name for their protagonist yet.

Pendergast takes a bit of time, however, in deciding to confide in D'Agosta. "Perhaps I *can* tell you," he says at last. "In fact, if any other living person is to know, I suppose that person should be you" (*Brimstone,* p. 261). When Pendergast reveals that the note is from his brother, though, Vincent responds: "I thought he was dead." This seems to imply that Pendergast has mentioned his brother to D'Agosta previously, but this would be out of character for him, and does not appear earlier in the series at all. It is more likely that Vincent has inferred this from Pendergast's previous assertions that he is the last surviving member of his family, but it seems as though it would have been just as easy to imagine his uniquely brilliant friend as an only child.

Once Pendergast explains that he doesn't believe his brother to be dead after all, he begins painting Vincent (and readers) a dark portrait. D'Agosta notes, moreover, Pendergast's reticence: his friend's "sentences had grown hesitant, almost broken, as if he found the subject intolerably repellent" (*Brimstone,* p. 262). Pendergast first confesses that "a line of madness has run through my family for many generations now," then makes a startling assertion. "Diogenes is at once the most insane—most evil—and yet the most brilliant member of our family ever to walk the earth" (*Brimstone*, p. 262). Coming after meeting Antoine Leng Pendergast and Great Aunt Cornelia in *Cabinet of Curiosities*, this perhaps impacts readers more than it does Vincent D'Agosta. D'Agosta, after all, was away in Canada for the events of that novel.

Pendergast goes on to relate what to him at this point must appear a typical developmental progression for a serial killer. "As a young child, Diogenes was content with certain … experiments. He devised highly complex machines for the lure, capture, and torture of small animals. Mice, rabbits, opossums. These machines were brilliant in a horrible way. Pain factories, he proudly called them when they were ultimately discovered" (*Brimstone,* p. 262). At the time Pendergast is speaking, he has no recollection of what will later be termed "The Event"--the happening which, among other things, produces Diogenes' great hatred for Aloysius. Many readers have speculated whether Diogenes had already begun his journey to the dark side before The Event took place, but given that these "machines" which Pendergast describes sound a lot like the old family box in which The Event happened, I believe he had not.

Though regrettably Diogenes graduated to "first cats, then dogs" (*Brimstone,* p. 262), Pendergast is apparently unable at this point to offer D'Agosta any examples of his brother harming human victims. Diogenes did, however, spend "days on end in the portrait gallery, staring at paintings of our ancestors … especially those who had met untimely ends" (*Brimstone,* pp. 262-63). While this last may well be a symptom of his mental disturbance, it is also further evidence that he completely identifies as a member of the Pendergast family. According to Aloysius, as Diogenes "grew older— and as he realized he was being watched with increasing vigilance—he abandoned these pastimes and withdrew into himself. He poured forth his black dreams and terrible creative energies into a series of locked journals" (*Brimstone*, p. 263).

Pendergast goes on to tell D'Agosta that Diogenes kept these journals hidden, and that it took him "two years of stealthy surveillance as an adolescent to discover them" (*Brimstone*, p. 263). In many ways, this tells readers just as much about Aloysius as about Diogenes. While still a teenager himself, he feels the need to find his brother's journals—a brother who by Aloysius's own admission has *stopped* killing animals. At this point in *Brimstone*, the age difference between the two Pendergasts is not revealed, nor has Aloysius specifically mentioned to Vincent that Diogenes is his *younger* brother. With knowledge of the rest of the trilogy, however, we know. The words used lead me to speculate whether the "increasing vigilance" with which Diogenes was "being watched" refers only to Aloysius, and whether the Pendergast parents were even concerned about Diogenes' behavior.

After finding his brother's secret writings, Aloysius read only one page and then "immediately burned all the journals." He assures D'Agosta that the one page "was enough," and that "the world was never quite the same for me after that." Pendergast also adds that Diogenes "had hated me before, but this act earned his undying rage" (*Brimstone,* p. 263). On the one hand, Aloysius's being sufficiently shocked by one page of his brother's journals can be viewed as another example of

Preston and Child's knack for building horror through exaggerating the terribleness of something without ever actually revealing what it is. On the other, his stopping reading at one page can be seen as poor investigative technique which can only be excused by his adolescence. What if the other pages had been relatively normal? Or even sixty percent of them? What if they contained a few brilliant ideas that weren't necessarily diabolical? If viewed from Diogenes' vantage point, his anger is understandable. This journal is the one thing that helps him *stop* the behavior his family (or at least Aloysius) objects to, and his brother destroys it.

Pendergast and D'Agosta are too far committed to investigating the spontaneous human combustions to do anything about Diogenes' mysterious communications yet. The Special Agent's intent is to "wrap up this current case ... as quickly as possible," and then turn his attention to his brother. He vows that "the situation will be addressed with appropriate finality." Of course, Pendergast says this before he has remembered The Event he has repressed for so many years. Could it be possible that the one journal page he sampled recounted this Event, and Aloysius refused to entertain the possibility of its accuracy?

Diogenes is dismissed for almost the rest of the novel, and it is only in hindsight that readers know that he finally makes an appearance. Pendergast has just sacrificed himself to Fosco's pursuing henchmen so that D'Agosta can make his escape with Fosco's microwave gun. D'Agosta has reluctantly decided to make sure that Pendergast's sacrifice is not in vain, and is making his way down the hillside, away from the area where his friend is being surrounded. He sees a man standing in a sheltered area of the hillside, and at first thinks he is part of Fosco's group, and that his own escape is being challenged. Interestingly, he contemplates using the microwave gun on this man, but decides against it, not seeing any weapons on his person. Still, D'Agosta is about to attack the man to get past him, but: "Then he hesitated. Though the man was dressed in peasant garb, he seemed different from the rest of Fosco's men. He was very tall and slender, perhaps four inches taller than Pendergast, and he wore a closely trimmed beard. There was something strange about his eyes. They were different colors: the left was hazel, the right an intense blue" (*Brimstone*, p. 457).

After noting that "the man had turned calmly away from him, uninterested," D'Agosta decides that he is not a threat, and continues his escape. It is interesting that D'Agosta judges Diogenes to be "perhaps four inches" taller than his brother; in interviews Preston and Child have gone back and forth on the issue of both Pendergasts' heights, and usually settle on Aloysius being about 6' 1" and Diogenes about 6' 3". D'Agosta's estimate would put Diogenes at 6' 5", but perhaps Diogenes wore lifts in his peasant shoes that day, for reasons known only to himself. It is also telling that while D'Agosta does not appear consciously aware of a family resemblance between the stranger on the hillside and Agent Pendergast, Pendergast is the first person who comes to mind when he is making a mental calculation of the man's height.

Pendergast himself recalls his brother a little while after this incident. He has been sedated with phenobarbital, and Fosco is walling him up in his ancestral castle, *a la* Poe's "The Cask of Amontillado." After protesting that Fosco "must not do this," Pendergast explains: "There is something I must do. Something unfinished, of great importance to the world. A member of my family is in a position to do great harm. I must be allowed to stop him" (*Brimstone,* p. 468). Given Pendergast's drugged state, it is probable that he is sincerely motivated by fear of what Diogenes' terrible crime might be, and what effect it may have on an untold number of people. He may even be sincere when he promises Fosco to return and allow himself to be killed after he has finished the task. Fosco does not believe Pendergast, however, and the entombment proceeds.

Again, it is only with hindsight that readers know that Diogenes appears in *Brimstone*'s epilogue. Preston and Child manage this glimpse of him without revealing whether or not Pendergast is conscious to perceive it, without even revealing that their protagonist is still alive. They describe the painstaking tapping and gradual removal of a brick in the wall imprisoning Pendergast, and then the view through the place where the brick had been: "A moment later, two eyes appeared in the glowing rectangle, gazing in with curiosity, perhaps even anxiety. Two eyes: one hazel, one blue" (*Brimstone,* p. 497). The possibility of anxiety is interesting to note. Does Diogenes only care whether his brother is alive merely because death would foil his plans to torment Aloysius? Or would it actually touch him at a deeper level?

Despite the advantage Diogenes ultimately takes of Aloysius while he is helpless, the fact will always remain that he saved his brother's life. Yet we do not know enough about the timing of this rescue, aside from the fact that Diogenes is just barely prompt enough to prevent Pendergast's death. Did he wait as long as he did to be sure that Fosco was no longer around, or that D'Agosta had given up on finding his friend? Or did he wish his brother to be in as weakened a state as possible, so as to lessen the chance of resistance or escape spoiling his magnificent plans?

I also wonder what Diogenes would have done if D'Agosta had not taken Fosco out with the microwave gun. Personally, I think he would have given Fosco an even nastier death, if possible. Diogenes may hate his brother, but I think in some ways their relationship is just a more severe, more dramatic version of the stereotypical siblings who love to torment each other but will come down hard on any outsider who would dare to harm the other. Further, I believe this explains why Diogenes never actually tries to harm D'Agosta. He verbally insults him later in *Dance of Death,* and threatens Aloysius with killing the Lieutenant, but never actually moves to carry out the threat. In Diogenes' mind, he owes D'Agosta a debt of honor—for killing the man who tried to kill his brother.

It is even possible, given that we know he was in the vicinity, that Diogenes made Fosco's excruciating demise possible. The microwave gun did not work the first time D'Agosta attempted to use it, embarrassing himself in front of Colonnello Esposito. No doubt D'Agosta kept the weapon close to him at all times as he questioned the villagers living near Fosco's estate, but even as distraught as he was over what he assumed had been done to Pendergast, he surely slept at some point during the night. Diogenes, like his brother, is an expert at lock-picking. He could have slipped into D'Agosta's hotel room to repair the machine after having followed him around and observing him long enough to ascertain his intentions toward Fosco. Not that I do not think D'Agosta capable of achieving his triumph unaided; if the microwave gun truly was not damaged in its descent from the cliff, he could have figured out how to make it work on his own, just as he told Laura Hayward on page 492 of *Brimstone*. If it *was* broken, it might have taken a genius to fix it. If that were the case, however, why would Diogenes let Vincent have all the fun? Because genius or no, perhaps he might have been unsure of how well he had fixed it, and could not be sure it would not backfire and melt its wielder. Diogenes cannot afford to die in an accident when he is so close to putting his lifetime of planning into motion.

###

Deuxième Course

The first chapter of *Dance of Death* features not Diogenes,
but one of his murders, seen through the eyes of a random
college student. Interestingly, the professor who is murdered
is giving a lecture on T.S. Eliot's *The Wasteland,* and later
Eliot's poem features in the mad muddle of Diogenes' inner
thoughts. Technically, the reader does not *know* he is
witnessing a crime committed by Pendergast's brother, or
even a crime at all, though given the momentum of the series
to this point, it is not a difficult guess.

Dr. Torrance Hamilton at first stops mid-lecture, and
according to Dewayne Michaels, the aforementioned student,
"he noticed the professor was standing motionless, a strange
expression on his face" (*Dance of Death,* p. 3). After a few
moments, "Hamilton slowly withdrew a handkerchief,
carefully patted his forehead, then folded the handkerchief
neatly and returned it to his pocket" (*Dance of Death,* p. 3).
The professor recovers quickly and continues the lecture for a
few more minutes. When he stops the second time, Michaels
notes that "his face went slack again. He looked—what?
Confused? Flustered? No: he looked *scared."* Then,
Hamilton's "hand fluttered up to his handkerchief, fumbled it
out, then dropped it as he tried to bring it to his forehead. He
looked around vaguely, hand still fluttering about, as if to
ward off a fly. The hand sought out his face, began touching
it lightly, like a blind person. The trembling fingers palpated
his lips, eyes, nose, hair, then swatted the air again" (*Dance of
Death,* p. 5).

The professor's ordeal is far from over. Hamilton "took a small, lurching step forward, bumping into the podium. And now his other hand flew to his face, feeling it all over, only harder now, pushing, stretching the skin, pulling down the lower lip, giving himself a few light slaps." Then he asks the students in the lecture hall: "Is there something wrong with my face?" (*Dance of Death,* p. 5). He is met with silence. He recovers once more—or tries to. He starts to resume the lecture, but his hand will not stop, and he succeeds in emitting only a few more words. He scratches his own face, drawing blood, and demands to know: "Why will no one tell me what's wrong *with my face!*" He goes on to plead: "Get them off me! They're *eating into my face!*" (*Dance of Death,* p. 6). To observer Michaels' shock, the bleeding increases, "and now one finger hooked up and … worked itself into one eye socket." After that, "there was a sharp, rotating motion that reminded Dewayne of the scooping of ice cream, and suddenly the globe of the eye bulged out, grotesquely large, jittering, staring directly at Dewayne from an impossible angle" (*Dance of Death,* p. 6). By the time a horrified Michaels manages to flee the lecture hall, Hamilton has also broken his drinking glass and jabbed its shards into his own neck, but he is also receiving assistance from others in the hall despite his own resistance to it.

Readers only find out what actually happened to Hamilton through Pendergast, who has returned, incognito, from Italy. He tells D'Agosta that Hamilton had been one of his tutors, and that he was murdered, "poisoned by a rare nerve toxin, placed in his water glass. It's a synthetic toxin, very similar to that produced by a certain spider native to Goa. An ancestor of my father's died of a bite from that same spider when he was a minor functionary in India during the Raj" (*Dance of Death,* p. 77). It is the link to a Pendergast ancestor that convinces Pendergast that Diogenes was the perpetrator. Though I feel Aloysius overreacted to Diogenes while still a teenager, he is undoubtedly correct in concluding that Diogenes wishes not only to kill people his brother cares about, but to ensure that his brother recognizes that Diogenes himself is the one who has done the deed.

Interestingly, either Pendergast has some incorrect information, or the authors have made an error. Later in *Dance of Death,* through the investigative work of Captain Laura Hayward, we learn that the poison is actually placed in Professor Hamilton's coffee, which he drank before beginning the lecture, rather than the water glass he has with him at the lecture podium.

The first actual mention of Diogenes in *Dance of Death,* however, comes several pages after the description of Professor Hamilton's reactions to the poison. D'Agosta is summoned by Pendergast's chauffeur and right-hand-man, Proctor, to the house at 891 Riverside. There, Pendergast's ward, Constance (inherited from Antoine and properly introduced in *Brimstone*), hands him a small box, which he recognizes from having seen Pendergast putting a paper into it on the night the agent told him about his brother, Diogenes. Indeed, the note inside the box concerns Diogenes, and is Pendergast's request (seemingly from beyond the grave) that D'Agosta take his place in hunting his brother down and preventing whatever great crime he is planning. From the note readers learn that Pendergast believes Diogenes is plotting something that "will be infamous. It will make the world a darker place." He warns that "Diogenes is a man with exceptional standards. He would not settle for less" (*Dance of Death*, p. 19). It is also in this note that we are told for the first time that Diogenes "contrived his own false death some years ago." Though Pendergast reminds D'Agosta of Diogenes' missive bearing simply the date January 28, and feels that is the day on which the act of infamy will take place, he cautions: "I would not, however, make any assumptions—the date could mean nothing at all. Diogenes is, if anything, unpredictable" (*Dance of Death,* p. 19). He also states that his brother "is an expert on forensics and police procedure, and any information left at the scene of the crime—assuming, God forbid, you are not in time to stop said crime—will no doubt be cleverly contrived to mislead the police." Pendergast advises D'Agosta to visit his Great Aunt Cornelia for more insight into Diogenes, and ends by reminding his friend that his brother is "consummately dangerous. He is my intellectual equal, but he was somehow formed without the slightest shred of moral conscience. In addition, a severe childhood illness left him damaged" (*Dance of Death,* p. 20).

It is interesting that Pendergast calls Diogenes his intellectual equal in this passage; in *Brimstone* he told D'Agosta that Diogenes was the "most brilliant" member of the Pendergast family, implying that his brother was smarter than himself. As for being "formed without the slightest shred of moral conscience," I must argue that Pendergast, still suppressing his knowledge of The Event at the time of writing the note, is making that judgment in a subconscious attempt to avoid any feelings of guilt in relationship to his brother. Also, this is the first mention of the familial lie—which Pendergast at this time believes—that Diogenes' increased wickedness and alleged insanity is due to a contagious disease caught during childhood (later identified by Great Aunt Cornelia as scarlet fever).

D'Agosta follows Pendergast's instructions, and when he goes to see Cornelia Pendergast, readers learn more about Diogenes—or at least they learn what his great aunt believes about him, at this point in her somewhat confused existence. Incidentally, it is while en route to Mount Mercy that now Lieutenant D'Agosta reveals to Captain Laura Hayward that Cornelia "poisoned her whole family," including her "mother, father, husband, brother, and two children. She thought they'd been possessed by devils. Or maybe the souls of Yankee soldiers shot dead by her father. Nobody seems to be quite sure" (*Dance of Death*, p. 33). Nevertheless, Cornelia at least seemingly accepts D'Agosta as Ambergris, the very brother she poisoned. It is certainly possible, however, that she just plays along for the entertainment of being allowed visitors.

Great Aunt Cornelia tells D'Agosta that "from the day he was born" Diogenes "was different" (*Dance of Death*, p. 36). She falls back on the familial belief that "the Pendergast bloodline has been tainted for centuries," and reiterates that "young Diogenes was *touched* even from the beginning" (*Dance of Death*, p. 36). She notes that "none of the other children would go near him. They were all scared to death of him. The illness made it so much worse" (*Dance of Death*, p. 37). While Cornelia admits that "the illness" (or The Event) did make Diogenes worse, she seems to corroborate Pendergast's view that he was more or less born disturbed. Fans of the series who argue that Diogenes was destined for evil at birth point to these descriptions, and to Great Aunt Cornelia as an authority, but other evidence presented later in the Pendergast series (and thus later in *this* work) points in a different direction. In any case it is worth mentioning that Cornelia never seems aware of the truth of The Event; she seemingly accepts the scarlet fever explanation. Knowing through hindsight that The Event takes place when Diogenes is only seven years old, however, leads me to postulate that Diogenes' actions and attitude from the point of his physical recovery until he leaves the family at least ten years later could have been so memorable as to have colored Cornelia's perception of his life as a whole. Even if Antoine Leng Pendergast is cited as an example of the family "taint," Antoine, too, had a trigger point which tipped the balance and sent him down the path of evil—the death of his mother.

Great Aunt Cornelia is the first one to tell us that Diogenes is younger than Aloysius, and she is the first one to mention his heterochromia, adding that Diogenes cannot see out of the blue eye. She reveals that "Diogenes never cared for anyone but his mother, of course, but he seemed to put Aloysius in a special category altogether. After the illness, particularly" (*Dance of Death,* p. 37). Cornelia also tells us the story of Aloysius's pet white mouse, Incitatus, and the mouse's crucifixion on a wooden cross, "beautifully and lovingly made." While implying that Diogenes had indeed been responsible for this horrible act of cruelty, his great aunt admits: "Nobody had to ask. Everyone knew who'd done it." This, coupled with Diogenes' own very different retelling of the story later in the trilogy, leaves room for doubt. Yet we probably must lay this crime at his door. It is not so much Cornelia's declaration that this was "just the beginning of his, ah, *experiments* on animals" (*Dance of Death,* p. 38), but the fact that Diogenes tends to leave gifts in lovely carved wooden boxes which helps implicate him. Too, Diogenes' choice of crucifixion is not just bizarrely sacrilegious. It is significant that this is a Roman punishment; the brothers were competing at Latin translation right before The Event happened.

Cornelia also makes more personal the story of the fire that destroyed the Pendergast family home, first alluded to in *Cabinet of Curiosities.* She calls it "the dreadful, dreadful fire that destroyed the family and convinced my husband to bring me and the children up to this drafty mansion" (*Dance of Death,* p. 38; Cornelia alternates between believing she is currently residing in the New York mansion Ravenscry or the New Orleans home; she is referring to Ravenscry here). She cries out against the arsonists as "that superstitious, hateful, ignorant mob," and tells D'Agosta that "Diogenes was home that night. He saw his own mother and father burned alive." Some readers have speculated that Diogenes may have set this fire himself; again, I don't believe so. Other evidence later in *Dance of Death* points to Diogenes having positive feelings towards his mother, and a mob is mentioned several times in the series in connection with this fire. If, indeed, it should be revealed in a future novel that Diogenes *did* cause the conflagration, his mother's death will have been an unforeseen and undesired consequence.

From interviewing Great Aunt Cornelia, D'Agosta moves to

examining all the materials and documents pertaining to Diogenes that Pendergast has collected, including letters that Diogenes has penned himself. The ages of the Pendergast brothers, even in relation to each other, are somewhat ambiguous. Whether this is author error, character error, or deliberate vagueness in keeping with Preston and Child's desire to keep Aloysius Pendergast perpetually in his late forties, is difficult to determine. Cornelia Pendergast tells D'Agosta that Aloysius is twenty years old at the time the fire that kills his parents takes place. The brothers' ages are given as being two to three years apart at various places in the Diogenes Trilogy and elsewhere in the Pendergast series; this would make Diogenes seventeen or eighteen when it happened. While examining a letter Diogenes wrote to Aloysius, however, D'Agosta notes that after the younger brother stormed out on the elder, "for almost a year, there was no word at all" (*Dance of Death,* p. 42). Then a request for $100,000 from an attorney on Diogenes' behalf arrived, and this request was granted. "This was followed a year later by another, similar letter," this time asking for $250,000. This time, Pendergast refuses, prompting the letter that D'Agosta is examining. The lieutenant "glanced once again at the spidery, meticulous script, so curiously inappropriate for a boy of seventeen" (*Dance of Death*, p. 42). Except, by the time two years have gone by, Diogenes can be at the youngest *nineteen* at the time he wrote it. Even the portion of the letter mentioning that Diogenes "will come into [his] inheritance in a few years" would fit with this, meaning that in two years he will be twenty-one. Is it D'Agosta forgetting to add the years to Diogenes' age, or the authors?

The greeting of the letter, *"Ave, frater,"* is Latin for "Hail, brother." Though Diogenes goes on to express his dislike of Aloysius, as well as threaten him, the letter begins and ends with an acknowledgement of their kinship, since it concludes with "Good-bye, brother. And *bonne chance*" (*Dance of Death*, p. 43). Given what readers later learn about Diogenes' feelings about The Event, this emphasis on their familial relationship is probably part of a general accusation—how could a brother have done such a thing to him? In consequence, Diogenes writes: "I find it disagreeable to write you on this subject, or any other for that matter." He reminds Aloysius that he will be coming into his inheritance, and states: "Until that time I shall now and then require certain trifling sums such as I requested last month. You will find it in your best interests, and in the best interests of others you may or may not know, to honor such requests" (*Dance of Death*, p. 42). Diogenes alludes to their parting in Baton Rouge, more or less confirming Pendergast's claims to D'Agosta that his brother is planning some infamous crime. He then goes on to mention: "I am very much preoccupied at present with various lines of research and study and have no time to earn money in the conventional manner." It is interesting to note that Diogenes both considers sums up to $250,000 "trifling," yet believes he is perfectly capable of earning them "in the conventional manner" without yet having obtained a university degree, if only he were not so "preoccupied." He threatens that "if forced to do so, I *will* obtain the funds I need—in a manner amusing to myself." Diogenes is intelligent enough to keep his threats vague, so that Pendergast cannot possibly guess his intents and thus protect his potential victims.

Finished with Diogenes' letter, D'Agosta moves on to note the amount of the younger brother's inheritance (eighty-seven million dollars) and the circumstances surrounding his faked death. "Two months later, he was reported to have been killed in an automobile accident in Canterbury High Street. Burned beyond recognition. The inheritance was never found." (*Dance of Death*, p. 43). Unfortunately, a discrepancy quickly follows; on the next page it states that *four months* elapsed between Diogenes claiming his inheritance and staging his own death (*Dance of Death*, p. 44). Perhaps D'Agosta is fatigued and his mind is going in circles after examining all of the evidence Pendergast has left for him concerning Diogenes.

Among this evidence are records from an English private school, Sandringham, at which Diogenes managed to get himself accepted "on the strength of several forged documents and a phony set of parents hired for the occasion." Though he completely outshone his fellow students academically, he was expelled after only a few months. Pendergast's questions to Sandringham regarding the reasons for the expulsion were met "with evasion, even agitation," but he does eventually learn that Diogenes' roommate there had to be institutionalized "for acute catatonia." Again, this is an example of Preston and Child's building dread and fear by withholding information. Whatever they could have come up with for Diogenes to have actually done to his roommate would not have the power for all readers that the scariest thing imaginable will have for each individual member of their audience.

Pendergast has also collected some newspaper clippings,

mostly from European papers, that he felt might pertain to his brother's activities over the years. Though he has provided translations of each article into English, he has left D'Agosta no notes explaining why he felt any of them might be about Diogenes. "There was an entire family in Lisbon, killed by botulism, yet without any trace of food found in their stomachs." This is plausible; Diogenes later proves to be quite skilled with poisons and drugs. Another article records that "a chemist at the University of Paris, Sorbonne, was discovered with radial arteries of both wrists severed and the body carefully exsanguinated. Yet there was no blood at the murder scene. Files on several of the chemist's experiments were found to be missing" (*Dance of Death*, p. 43). Unless Preston and Child choose to go back and fill in these incidents in later works, readers will never know whether or not Diogenes actually committed these crimes, or "still other deaths, more grisly, in which the corpses seemed to have been victims of various tortures or experimentation" (*Dance of Death*, p. 43). We do not even know Pendergast's own level of certainty about them. Though it is admittedly difficult to imagine Diogenes patiently lurking around Canterbury funeral homes just waiting for someone of the appropriate build to be dropped off, we do not even know for sure that he killed his own replacement in the car crash of his staged death. It seems Pendergast also had a few ordinary obituaries in his pile of clippings; presumably he felt Diogenes had some connection with these deaths as well. The uncertainty only serves to make his younger brother seem even more sinister to readers.

D'Agosta observes that "there were a variety of thefts, too," among the clippings (*Dance of Death*, p. 43). These include "the robbery of a freezer full of experimental drugs" as well as "a collection of diamonds mysteriously vanished from a vault in Israel." Both of these mesh well enough with what readers will know of Diogenes by the end of *Dance of Death;* interestingly, there are also reports of "a rare, fist-sized piece of amber containing a leaf from a long-extinct plant lifted from a wealthy couple's apartment in Paris" and "a unique, polished T. rex coprolite, dating precisely from the K-T boundary" (*Dance of Death,* p. 44). Given that by the end of the novel we learn that Diogenes had discovered his relative Antoine Leng Pendergast's continued existence before Aloysius had, it seems probable that these last two items might well have been gifts to win himself an audience with his venerable ancestor. It would not be surprising if Pendergast eventually found them among the collections at 891 Riverside.

Lastly, D'Agosta examines a photograph. The novel never states whether this photograph is something Pendergast himself saved, or whether it was delivered with Diogenes' "January 28" note. It only describes "a single black-and-white photograph, scuffed and creased with age," that features Aloysius, Diogenes, and their parents. D'Agosta guesses that "the boys were perhaps eight and five" (*Dance of Death*, p. 45). D'Agosta also determines that the young Diogenes has ginger hair—I doubt he could do this from a black-and-white photograph, so it is seemingly an editing error. However, it is the first time Diogenes' hair color is described to the reader. D'Agosta notes that "both eyes looked the same—this must have been before the illness." He seemingly senses something unusual about Diogenes' eyes, all the same. "They weren't looking at the camera, but at some point past it if they were looking at anything at all. They seemed dull, almost dead, out of place in that childish little face" (*Dance of Death*, p. 45). This would appear to be more evidence on the side of Diogenes being destined to be disturbed even before The Event, but D'Agosta has been prepared to see him this way by both Pendergast and Cornelia. Who among us has not been caught by the camera in an unflattering light, when we were looking away, or blinking? Not to mention there are other pieces of the Pendergast stories that may explain this look of the young Diogenes that gives D'Agosta "an uncomfortable sensation in the pit of his stomach" (*Dance of Death*, p. 45).

The novel moves on to another random viewpoint to witness Diogenes' next crime. This time the unlucky voyeur is a seller of machine parts from Iowa, meeting with a client in New York City. From a glassed-in restaurant, the salesman first sees a man dangling in mid-air with a rope around his neck, struggling in the agony of being hanged. Then the rope snaps, and the man crashes through the glass ceiling, spattering the diners with gore and being killed upon impact. It is not until a few chapters afterwards, however, when Captain Hayward is investigating the crime scene, that readers learn just what a quirky piece of work it is. Firstly, the door lock of the victim's apartment (from the window of which he was hanged) "was expertly picked," according to Hayward *(Dance of Death,* p. 66). It is interesting to note that Diogenes shares his brother's skill with locks. Secondly, the initial assault on the victim involved "a blunt instrument of some kind," although "the body was so badly damaged by the fall that it might be difficult to determine the weapon the attacker used" (*Dance of Death*, p. 66). One of the oddest details Hayward is able to reconstruct, however, is "that the attacker then dragged the stunned victim to the sofa, where—and this is strange—he tended the wound he'd just inflicted." Captain Hayward elaborates for the precinct captain, Singleton, that the perpetrator "dabbed at it with gauze pads from the medicine cabinet in the bathroom. Several empty packages were found next to the sofa, some bloody pads tossed in the trash" (*Dance of Death*, pp. 66-67). Again, with hindsight we know that the victim is a friend from Aloysius's youth, and that Diogenes is trying to frame his brother for the crime, so it is interesting to speculate on why Diogenes tended the head wound. Did he think this would demonstrate the kind of remorse Aloysius might show if he actually were killing a friend, and therefore add to the weight of evidence against his brother? Or is it just a senselessly strange gesture on Diogenes' part, something that gives him more satisfaction in terrorizing his victim?

Hayward also notes that "the rope he was hung from was cut partway through with a sharp knife, maybe a razor, at the center of its length," and that it "was *supposed* to break the way it did" (*Dance of Death*, p. 69). This, the reader later learns, is to help replicate the strange death of another Pendergast ancestor—seemingly Diogenes' preferred way to let his brother know who did the deed, but also in keeping with implicating Aloysius himself in the crime. Diogenes also uses distinctive rope tied in strange knots later found to be associated with a Buddhist monastery in Bhutan. Of course this is to help frame Aloysius, but it is interesting that

Diogenes has followed his brother into yet another area of study in addition to lock-picking and forensics.

Almost as odd as Diogenes' tending his victim's wound, however, is the evidence that he somehow managed to persuade the man, Charles Duchamp, to take a running jump off a desk out of a twenty-fourth floor window with a noose around his neck. Hayward goes over the facts with Singleton: "Duchamp walked through his own blood on the way to the desk. See how, in the first set of prints, he's standing at rest? As the others lead toward the window, the distance between them grows larger. And look how, in this last print before the window, only the ball of the shoe hit the desk. These are *acceleration* marks" (*Dance of Death*, pp. 67-68). As Singleton puts it in reply, "What could somebody say that would induce him to take a running leap out his own window?" What, indeed. Again, Preston and Child are using *lack of information* to build up the fearful reputation of Diogenes Pendergast. Does Diogenes know of a strong phobia that Duchamp has? Does he have some information about the artist that would devastate him if the world—or even his friend Aloysius Pendergast—found out, something so devastating that the mere sight of Diogenes in his apartment scares the hell out of him? How could such a thing happen? Was the blunt object he hit him with first a flamethrower?

Meanwhile, between the out-of-town salesman's observations and Captain Hayward's crime scene investigation, the reader learns that Lieutenant D'Agosta has tried to follow up on the information Pendergast has left for him about Diogenes. Vincent learns that the old roommate from Sandringham managed to kill himself, and that all the old banks and lawyers involved in the monetary transactions between Diogenes and Aloysius report that their involvement with the younger Pendergast brother ended many years ago.

Incidentally, on page 20 of *Dance of Death,* in between the summons of D'Agosta to Riverside and the visit to Great Aunt Cornelia, comes the first mention of a certain Hugo Menzies. Dr. Menzies, of course, is the alternate identity Diogenes adopts to use the Museum of Natural History as an instrument in his quest for revenge upon Aloysius. Menzies comes up in the thoughts of Margo Green as having "asked solicitously after the subject of her panel discussion for the forthcoming Society of American Anthropologists meeting."

By the time Captain Hayward is investigating the murder of Charles Duchamp, Pendergast himself returns to provide D'Agosta with information about this case and that of Professor Hamilton. He reveals that Diogenes is patterning the murders after historic Pendergast deaths; more interestingly to D'Agosta, he also reveals that Diogenes is the reason he survived Fosco's castle. D'Agosta then realizes he has seen Diogenes before, "on the hillside there, above Fosco's castle," he tells Pendergast. "He was standing in the shadow of a rock ledge, watching the proceedings, as calm as if it was the first race at Aqueduct" (*Dance of Death,* p. 75). Perhaps subliminal memory of this is how D'Agosta deducted that the boy in the black and white photograph had ginger hair.

Pendergast goes on to explain to D'Agosta: "If I had died, I would have ruined everything for Diogenes. You see,

Vincent, *I* am the primary object of his crime" (*Dance of Death*, p. 76). Later, he elaborates: "That's the real reason he rescued me from Fosco's castle. He doesn't want me dead, he wants me alive—alive so he can destroy me in a far more exquisite way, leaving me filled with misery and self-reproach, torturing myself with the knowledge that I was unable to save those […] few people on earth I truly care about" (*Dance of Death*, p. 78). Incidentally, he also tells D'Agosta that after Diogenes rescued him from entombment, "he transported me to a private clinic outside Pisa." Though he doesn't realize it yet, it is while Aloysius is recuperating in this clinic that Diogenes obtains the hair and blood samples he uses to frame his brother for these crimes, as well as some unlooked-for information that will make his vengeance even sweeter.

The next time Pendergast summons D'Agosta, it is because he has received another message from Diogenes. It contains references to tarot cards, and causes Pendergast to explain to D'Agosta that "Diogenes always had an interest in tarot. As you may have guessed, those cards involve death and betrayal." Diogenes links Professor Hamilton to the Nine of Swords, and Duchamp to the Ten of Swords, but more importantly, he lets Pendergast know his next intended victim by linking Michael Decker to the King of Swords, Reversed. "Diogenes is telegraphing his move in advance. Baiting me" (*Dance of Death*, p. 93), Pendergast tells his friend.

Michael Decker is "highly placed in Quantico," and he is the one responsible for drawing Pendergast into the Federal Bureau of Investigation. In fact, Pendergast reveals, "he's been invaluable in clearing the way for my somewhat unorthodox methods. It was thanks to Mike that I was able to get the FBI involved so quickly on the Jeremy Grove murder last fall, and he helped smooth some ruffled feathers after a small case I handled in the Midwest prior to that" (*Dance of Death*, p. 93).

In threatening Michael Decker, Diogenes is not just attacking another person Aloysius cares about. He is going to kill the person who has made Aloysius officially into someone who seemingly could never co-exist with his brother. Decker has made it so Aloysius would be officially obliged to turn his brother in for his crimes. Decker's is also the murder that would most likely bring the death penalty—for killing a federal agent—if Diogenes succeeds in his intent to pin his own crimes upon his elder brother. For it is at the scene of Decker's killing that Pendergast realizes this deeper dimension of Diogenes' plan.

Pendergast knows that in revealing Decker his next victim, Diogenes intends for him to attempt a rescue. Aloysius feels he has no choice but to oblige. When he arrives at Decker's home, he finds that he is too late to save his friend, but just barely. After deducing that Decker had only been dead about three minutes by the time Pendergast found his body, he determines that "the precise time of death was irrelevant. What was far more important was Pendergast's realization that Diogenes had waited until Pendergast entered the house *before* killing Decker" (*Dance of Death*, p. 100). Examining his friend's body, he notices something clenched in his hand, which turns out to be "three strands of blond hair," apparently deliberately placed there by Diogenes. Hairs he had taken from Pendergast during his recuperation from the ordeal with

Fosco; hairs he plants to help frame his brother for Decker's murder and the others. Pendergast manages to remove these hairs from this particular crime scene, and escape from it before the authorities arrive—authorities that Diogenes probably summoned himself by having "deliberately tripped the burglar alarm *while leaving the house*" (*Dance of Death*, p. 100). This timing tells us that Diogenes is willing to have Aloysius captured at this point in his plot against his brother; if need be, he is willing to hold the number of crimes he frames him for at three.

As Pendergast later tells Constance, "the modus operandi" of Decker's killing "was a nod to a distant ancestor of mine, who died in a very similar fashion as an officer in Napoleon's army, during the Russian campaign of 1812" (*Dance of Death*, p. 123). More importantly, however, Pendergast recognizes the bayonet Diogenes used to kill Decker as one he inherited as part of Antoine Leng Pendergast's collections at 891 Riverside. Diogenes has been inside his own home. That Diogenes is able to do this without being discovered by Pendergast or Proctor reinforces his elder brother's assertions to D'Agosta about his intelligence.

Pendergast feels his brother "no doubt immobilized Decker with some kind of drug" (*Dance of Death*, p. 100) before driving the bayonet through his mouth, neck, and the chair in which he sat. A drug was probably necessary both for the precise timing that Diogenes desired, as well as because of Decker's assumed superior physical training. Yet one must not discount Diogenes' personal strength. Not only would it take a fair amount of force to pin someone to a chair with a bayonet in this manner, Diogenes has also broken the neck of

Decker's Weimaraner in two places. It is interesting to note here that although the dog was still twitching when Aloysius found him, this was a reasonably clean kill with no intent to torture. True, Diogenes was limited by time, and completely focused both on replicating his ancestor's death and framing his brother, but he killed the dog only because it was necessary to get to Decker. Although, too, his brother is no dog torturer; drawing out the Weimaraner's death might have cast doubt on the forensic evidence Diogenes planted to point to Aloysius.

At this point, however, it is time to turn our attention to Diogenes' alter ego, Dr. Hugo Menzies. We meet him at a Museum anthropology department meeting held to discuss Margo Green's editorial position on a key piece of the upcoming Sacred Images show. At this juncture in the story, the reader does not know Menzies is Diogenes. Not only has Diogenes managed to get an important position at the Museum under a pseudonym, we learn that Menzies has been "chairman of the Anthropology Department since the untimely death of Dr. Frock six years before" (*Dance of Death*, p. 103). This means that Diogenes has been working in New York City all this time, unknown to his brother— working at the Museum while Pendergast was closely involved with the institution during the investigation detailed in *Cabinet of Curiosities.* He did not, apparently, inherit Dr. Frock's office space immediately; this was occupied for the duration of *Cabinet of Curiosities* by the ill-fated Roger Brisbane. Brisbane was the Vice President of the Museum who tried to discourage Nora Kelly from assisting Pendergast; coincidentally, he shared Diogenes' lust for precious gems.

Margo Green suspects that Dr. Menzies "had also been instrumental in her hiring" (*Dance of Death,* p. 103). I do not doubt it. While Diogenes would have been willing to have Pendergast apprehended at the scene of Decker's murder, he probably also made sure he had plenty of Pendergast's friends and associates available with whom to continue the spree should his brother evade capture. Though Diogenes uses the Menzies persona to help lay the groundwork for his vengeance against Aloysius, this persona also tells us a great deal about the man behind it. For one thing, he knows how to make an entrance; at this initial meeting, he is "the last to arrive." He is an individual among the Museum's higher-ups; "Menzies carried around a classy canvas shoulder bag by John Chapman & Company" while "everybody else on staff … favored lawyerly briefcases" (*Dance of Death*, p. 103). Yet Diogenes as Menzies seems completely at ease riding herd on the anthropology department, while simultaneously manipulating them towards his own ends. In presenting Margo's position in favor of returning the Great Kiva masks to the Tano Indians, he announces that while it is his "job to make a recommendation to the director on this matter" and that "we are not a democracy," he does tell them that their "opinions will carry great weight with me" (*Dance of Death*, p. 104). He also does not hesitate to "insist upon *civility*" when Margo and Nora fall into sharp disagreement during the meeting.

Menzies renders his decisions on two issues at the end of the departmental meeting. The first is that he will allow Margo to publish her editorial in favor of returning the masks to the

Tano Indians. This serves two purposes; one is to encourage Margo to like and trust him. Diogenes is probably not sure at this point whether Margo will be one of his victims, or if so, just how it will transpire. Her relationship with Menzies can only make it easier for Diogenes to do to her whatever he wishes. The second purpose is to stir and increase the level of controversy and thus media focus upon the Sacred Images exhibition, therefore decreasing the relative amount of attention given to the Hall of Diamonds that he intends to rob.

The second decision Menzies makes is to recommend to the Museum's board of trustees that the masks actually be given back to the Tano people. Again, this helps strengthen Margo's positive regard for him. It also is a win-win situation for Diogenes. Either the board accepts his recommendation, and this creates publicity that distracts from his intention of stealing the diamonds; or the board refuses, and there is publicity nonetheless. When Menzies later reveals to Margo that the board has indeed overridden his recommendations, he warns her that the Tano Indians are coming to sit in and pray about their masks during the opening gala for the exhibition. It is certainly possible that he has written to the Tano chief himself (probably using a pseudonym) to suggest this, although I do not wish to imply that the Tano chief would be incapable of making such a decision on his own. It would just be a way for Diogenes to attempt to ensure greater distraction from his own intended crime.

One can only speculate about how—or if—Diogenes feels about the Great Kiva mask issue. Does he actually sympathize with the Tano Indians, and does he feel a certain rightness in forwarding Menzies' recommendation to the

Museum Board? Or is he incapable of preferring the ethical claims of one group of gut and blood bags to those of another? I suspect he at least enjoys spiting the more pompous members of the anthropology department, such as George Ashton. Though Menzies cites "the first responsibility of an anthropologist" as being "to the people under study" (*Dance of Death,* p. 109), I would postulate that Diogenes' truc opinion would run closer to that of Nora Kelly, who argues that the Great Kiva masks, like other great works of art, have transcended their original religious purpose and now belong to humanity as a whole. I think this because of things Aloysius says in a later book in the series, *Wheel of Darkness,* while he is under the influence of the Agozyen. This evil mandala changes a person to his worst self, drives him to madness, and leaves him vulnerable to certain evil spirits. In this state Pendergast tells Constance: "The one thing my brother Diogenes and I always agreed on was there could be no more odious a discipline than anthropology: imagine, devoting one's life to the study of one's fellow man" (*Wheel of Darkness,* p. 286; this is particularly ironic when the authors have published an "interview" with Pendergast in which he states this is what he got his degree in at Harvard, and when Diogenes has studied it in perfecting the alter-ego Menzies as part of his revenge plot against Aloysius). The elder Pendergast then goes on to discuss with Constance *Saint Matthew and the Angel,* a painting destroyed during World War II. He concludes by asking her: "If I had to choose between this painting or the lives of a million useless, ignorant, ephemeral people—the humanity you say is so important to me—which do you think *I'd* choose to perish in that conflagration?" (*Wheel of Darkness,* p. 287). It is reasonable to assume that Diogenes, who is a murderer, but as a Pendergast has been raised to appreciate the finer things in life, would feel the same way. Perhaps this is why, as Menzies, he is compelled to scold Margo for attacking Nora's position—it is too close to his own true feelings. Yet in every other way, he sacrifices these feelings to the greater cause of revenge upon Aloysius. This may not be the only time he does this.

Diogenes' next move in *Dance of Death* is to send Pendergast a calling card with his own name engraved upon it, with a message written "in rose-colored ink" that he intends his next victim to be William Smithback, Nora Kelly's husband. When Pendergast puts his plan to protect Smithback into operation, Diogenes is seemingly there to try and foil it. I say *seemingly,* because the authors never say definitively that Diogenes is behind the wheel of the black Mercedes that pursues the taxi Pendergast uses to kidnap Smithback. Pendergast believes it is him, but tells Smithback that "the high-speed chase and the use of firearms were uncharacteristically crude of him" (*Dance of Death,* p. 132). The crudeness is because Diogenes wants to ensure his brother's distraction from his true intention and true choice of next victim.

If Diogenes is indeed driving the black Mercedes, he is amazingly skilled. Though he loses the taxi Pendergast is driving—or feigns losing it, so that Aloysius feels prematurely relieved that he has "saved" one of his brother's potential victims—he does so while still managing to evade capture by the police the chase attracts. It is more likely that, while still achieving the remarkable feat of predicting when and where his brother will attempt to "rescue" Smithback,

Diogenes has hired someone to drive the Mercedes in pursuit of Aloysius and even take a few potshots at him. Whoever this driver is, he has probably agreed having no clue about Aloysius's skill level, and not realizing how much attention the chase will attract from law enforcement. If the driver of the Mercedes is not Diogenes but a hireling, he is probably apprehended by the police but can give them no useful information about the man who hired him.

In either case, Diogenes remains free to concentrate on his true next intended victim, Margo Green. And giving an excellent performance as Hugo Menzies is an important part of that victimization. Nora Kelly describes him during preparations for the Sacred Images exhibition: "He was shaking hands, nodding in approval, encouraging as he went along, knowing everyone's name, from the carpenters to the curators. Everyone got a nod, a smile, a word of encouragement" (*Dance of Death,* p. 137). "How different from Ashton, chief curator of the exhibition," Nora notes, "who felt it beneath him to talk to anybody lacking a doctoral degree." Nora goes on to recall that "after the meeting" she "had been furious with Menzies for coming down on Margo Green's side. But it was impossible to stay angry with a man like Menzies; he so clearly believed in what he was doing, and she'd personally witnessed so many other ways, large and small, in which he'd supported the department. No, you couldn't stay mad at Hugo Menzies" (*Dance of Death,* p. 137).

I do not mean to suggest that Diogenes, raised as a Pendergast, is admirably egalitarian in his outlook. He knows, however, that for whatever nefarious purposes he may end up having, useful people come in all classes and levels of society. He is wise to cultivate as many potential friends for Menzies as possible. Not to mention that the man whom everyone likes is the man whom no one suspects. While I personally see something of Diogenes' creepy quality foreshadowed in Menzies' telling Nora that the jade mask she is placing arrived at its proper thinness because its makers "polished it down by hand with blades of grass," Nora observes that Menzies "moved on through the chaos, leaving in his wake people who were working all the harder, if such a thing were possible." She "had to admire his people skills" (*Dance of Death*, p. 138).

In the next scene featuring Menzies, readers learn what he has done with Frock's old office after Brisbane's exit. Margo recalls that during Frock's tenure, "it had been stuffed with Victorian furniture, fossils, and curiosities," but that with Menzies occupying it, "it seemed more spacious and pleasant, the dusty fossil plaques replaced by tasteful prints, the heavy old furniture retired in favor of comfortable leather chairs" (*Dance of Death,* p. 161). Menzies' desk is mahogany. I doubt the décor says anything about Diogenes' own personal taste; only about what he believes will help museum personnel feel at ease with his alter-ego. His action of leaning back into the sun coming through his office window, which causes "his unruly white hair" to be "suddenly haloed in gold" (*Dance of Death,* p. 162) is probably deliberate as well—he wishes to seem angelic to Margo, above reproach.

Menzies has called Margo to his office to tell her about the board of trustees' rejection of his recommendation to give the Kiva masks back to the Tano Indians. For Diogenes, it is both an opportunity to increase Margo's trust in him, and observe his next victim more closely. As Menzies, he laments that most of the trustees "are lawyers and bankers who have as much knowledge of anthropology as I have of writs or currency futures. Unfortunately, the world is such that they can presume to tell us what to do, and not vice versa" (*Dance of Death,* p. 162). Though Diogenes appreciates the arts—and by extension the artifacts of anthropology, despite what his brother says in *Wheel of Darkness*—he is probably equally well-versed in financial matters, considering his vast inheritance. I suspect there is at least a portion of Diogenes' actual opinion in this statement, though with Diogenes, even his own opinion takes a backseat to his overriding purpose.

Margo believes that Menzies is "nettled" while delivering this statement. This is evidence of Diogenes' acting chops. No matter his actual opinion, he is certainly not going to let the issue bother him. He is using the opportunity to study Margo; Menzies "lean(s) on the table, looking at her intently" before stating: "This puts you rather more in the hot seat than before" (*Dance of Death*, p. 162). He reiterates that she will be under even more pressure not to publish the editorial in favor of returning the Kiva masks, though he also reiterates his complete support for her doing so. It is at this juncture that he tells her of the planned protest and "all-night religious ceremony" (*Dance of Death*, p. 163) by the Tano Indians. Menzies gives her more advice, telling her not to "speak to the press—*at all*" because the Museum will "be looking for another reason" they can use to fire her, since apparently they cannot do this on the basis of the editorial alone (*Dance of Death*, p. 163).

l

Diogenes' bid to get Margo to trust and feel indebted to Menzies works well; upon leaving his office, she says, "I thank you more than I can say." Menzies, in turn, calls her "a brave woman." Diogenes is probably sincere in this opinion, but his judgment of Margo as brave only whets his appetite for a worthy opponent. It also affects his treatment of her as one of his victims.

By telling Margo about the intended protest, Diogenes increases the chances that she will take a turn through the exhibit to make sure the Kiva masks are respectfully presented, in hopes of giving the least offense possible to the Tano Indians. Of course, given what we later learn of his skill with electronics in *Book of the Dead,* it is also possible that Diogenes has rigged various parts of the Museum with hidden cameras (or hacked into feeds from cameras already in place) so that he can actually see that Margo has gone into the Sacred Images exhibition. He probably has a way of seeing her badge in to the security system protecting the exhibition as well.

Knowing he is about to attack Margo, Diogenes wishes to make her good and frightened first, and causes a board to fall in the room next to the one holding the Great Kiva masks. No doubt he knows Margo's history, and knows of her adventures with his older brother. Thus, he suspects that the Museum itself holds some residual spookiness for her. He manages to elude her in the darkness, causing another board to drop in another room. She calls out, and he does not reply. Diogenes allows her to make it almost as far as the entrance to the exhibit, then turns off the exhibit's lighting. The emergency lights do come on, and stay with Margo for one more dropped

li

board before going out as well. When Diogenes finally chooses to answer Margo's demand to know who it is, he replies in a voice she's never heard before: "It's just me" (*Dance of Death*, p. 194).

Diogenes shortens it to "me" when Margo repeats her query; when she persists and adds a demand to know what he wants, he gives her a clue: "I'm looking for an honest man...or woman, as the case may be" (*Dance of Death*, p. 199). Margo may understand the philosophy reference, but she has never heard of Pendergast's younger brother, and so remains unaware of just how deadly a person she faces in the darkness. She does, however, sense "instinctively that this man was dangerous."

Margo also makes the observation that "the voice was small and almost effeminate in its exactitude" (*Dance of Death*, p. 199). I cannot help wondering exactly what statement Preston and Child are trying to make here. Do they consider enunciation to be somehow *girly*? Is there somehow something just a shade unmanly about Diogenes? After all, Aloysius has drawn his fair share of speculation from minor characters about his sexuality, a fate anyone as cultured and metrosexual as a Pendergast is bound to share. Even as Menzies, his voice is described as "reedy" (*Dance of Death*, p. 103). Yet I believe the authors are making a different point. Without going into too much detail about The Event, which I shall discuss more thoroughly later in this work, I think Preston and Child are cluing the reader in to the nature of the brain damage Diogenes has. The area of his brain that has been injured probably affects the quality of his voice. Though elsewhere in the trilogy it is apparent that Diogenes has the ability to sound any way he likes, it is presumably because he has overcome an injury-induced deficit through intelligence, practice, and sheer force of will. He leans toward over-precision in his enunciation, because otherwise the damage he has suffered would leave him with a tendency to slur his words—as do some of his later victims in *Book of the Dead.* His voice also tends to be higher in pitch because of this damage, but again, this is something he has learned to control if he wishes, and the reader sees it primarily in unguarded moments. In the course of his attack on Margo in the Sacred Images exhibition, Diogenes' voice is subsequently described as "thin" (*Dance of Death,* p. 200), a "gentle whisper," "whispery," "evil" (*Dance of Death,* p. 201), "a low, breathy chuckle," "another dry chuckle," "whispered," and "a final astringent chuckle" (*Dance of Death,* p. 202). Nevertheless, Margo does think of him as definitely male, in her previous conclusion that "this man was dangerous."

Diogenes may also, however, be attempting to prevent Margo from recognizing anything of Menzies in his voice. Though being attacked by a trusted mentor and colleague is horrifying in its own right, Diogenes apparently prefers Margo to be uneasy from the beginning, slowly building to terror. Though he has a sense of her integrity from knowing her as Menzies—and if he has followed his brother's adventures as closely as I suspect, he must surely realize she has courage—Margo still shows far more fight than he expects from her. She threatens to slash him with a box cutter she has picked up in her passage through the exhibit under construction. He tells her that she does not want to do that, and reveals more of himself in adding: "The sight of blood leaves me faint …

faint with pleasure" (*Dance of Death,* p. 200).

This comment is interesting, especially as accompanied by the paean to blood that closely follows it. The reader finds out only a few chapters later, when the authors finally let us in to Diogenes' head, that he is colorblind. He cannot actually see the redness of blood, though the way he continues to speak of colors throughout the rest of the trilogy gives the impression that he treasures his memory of them—he *could* see color until the age of seven, the age at which he allegedly contracted scarlet fever. It seems to me that Diogenes deliberately tries to hide his colorblindness from others; not so much because it is an identifying characteristic that could blow the cover of his various alter-egos, but out of pride. He simply does not want others to be aware of this deficit.

I do not doubt, however, that the sight of blood *does* thrill Diogenes. Even if he does not color it through the power of his considerable memory—and I strongly suspect he does—he knows what it is and what it represents. It is "so teaming with life, packed with all those red and white cells and antibodies and hormones. It's a living liquid. Even spilled on a dirty museum floor, it lives on—at least for a time," he tells Margo. What he does not mention but leaves to hang in the air between them, is that if left unchecked, spilled blood carries the very life force out of a victim.

Of course, Diogenes is exercising his warped sense of humor, and toying with Margo as well. By saying that the sight of blood makes him faint, he is offering her hope. Hope that she has, after all, been accosted by a man who is indeed weak, who is no real threat to her. He quickly snatches that hope back with the ironic twist of "faint with pleasure." These words signal to Margo that she is not only in the hands of a dangerous man, but in the hands of a dangerous man who really enjoys the damage he inflicts upon the human body.

Yet Diogenes continues to be impressed by Margo's courage. When she manages to follow the sound of his voice well enough to take a swipe at him with the box cutter, she elicits "a stumbling noise" and "a muffled sound of surprise" (*Dance of Death,* p. 200). Diogenes even praises her, saying "Brava" and admitting: "I'm impressed. Why, you've ruined my greatcoat." But then he chides her, saying her name thrice to belittle her and adding: "You really didn't think you'd *cut* me?" (*Dance of Death,* p. 201).

Diogenes applauds her second attempt to slash him, though he chuckles. When Margo tells him, "Leave me alone or I'll kill you," he praises her "spunk." When Margo first throws her purse at him, hears it hit, then quickly strikes in the same area with the box cutter, Diogenes again compliments her. "My, my, another good trick. You are far more formidable than I had supposed. And now you *have* cut me." His feelings at this point are mixed. On the one hand, he is genuinely surprised at Margo's ability to resist becoming his victim, and he genuinely admires her for it. On the other hand, he is angry that she has managed to hurt him, and this rouses him to hurt her physically in return.

From Margo's viewpoint, the authors tell us, "the man seized her wrist and—with one terrible twist that cracked her bones—sent the box cutter flying." When Margo struggles, Diogenes "twisted again," but Margo manages to punch him "with her free hand." This causes him to pull "her up against him in a brusque, horrid movement that almost caused her to faint from the pain to her broken wrist." To Margo, "his hand was like a steel manacle around her arm," and Diogenes reiterates the reason for her pain: "'You *cut* me,' he whispered." That Diogenes is able to connect with Margo easily in the dark, while she must follow the quiet sound of his voice and guess implies that he is using night vision goggles of some kind. That the authors do not specifically mention this contributes further to the build-up of Diogenes as an incredibly powerful nemesis for his elder brother.

Yet, though he shoves her in doing it, Diogenes then releases Margo. He offers her mercy, while telling her even more about himself. "Although I am a cruel man," he says, "I will not let you suffer." I believe Diogenes is at least partially sincere in this, granting what he thinks will be a quick death to someone who has proved a worthy opponent. It is also possible that he simply decides to finish her off without further ado because he fears drawing things out could lead to his getting caught. I think, however, that though he would never admit it even to himself, Diogenes has a certain subconscious reluctance to kill women. This is part of the reason Margo survives, in addition to her own innate toughness and Pendergast's whisking her off to his favorite hospital. Some subtle lack of precision in aiming the knife, a minute hesitation of thrust—and Margo lives. Diogenes' Pendergast upbringing as a Southern gentleman is so ingrained that he finds it difficult to completely overcome. It also contributes to his decision to offer Margo a swift end.

This chapter describing Diogenes' attack on Margo has a few

other notes of interest. One is that when he breaks her wrist and draws her close, Margo notes that "his hot breath, smelling faintly of damp earth, washed over her" (*Dance of Death,* p. 201). Geosmin is what makes damp soil smell the way it does; it is also found in beets, carrots, catfish, and surface water sources such as ponds. It is anyone's guess how Diogenes acquires this particular scent in his breath; it is even possible that on top of his other psychopathology he has a problem with pica. I was so intrigued by this aspect of his physicality, however, that I messaged Douglas Preston on Facebook about it. I asked him what he and Mr. Child were trying to say by having Diogenes' breath smell like damp earth. He replied: "Death." I then asked him whether that had been poetic license on their part, or whether this was something Diogenes' had deliberately tried to cultivate? Mr. Preston admitted: "It was perhaps a bit of poetic license," but called my speculations about geosmin and pica "interesting."

The second noteworthy thing is that from Margo's viewpoint the motion leading up to Diogenes' knife stroke are described thus: "There was another swift movement, like the rush of a giant bat above her" (*Dance of Death,* p. 202). This could just be a function of Diogenes' superior height, coupled with the fact that Margo has just been thrown to her knees. In any case it gives the sense of Diogenes as a long-limbed, gangly person. Perhaps the tatters of his greatcoat assist in causing Margo to mentally liken him to a bat, but in doing so she evokes the thought of another powerful fictional male predator: Dracula.

The last thing Margo hears as she loses consciousness is another of Diogenes' chuckles—an "astringent" one, no less

(*Dance of Death,* p. 202). True, he could be mocking his victim as the blood flows from her, forming a gradually cooling pool around her. Or it could be that Diogenes has managed to retrieve the box cutter, and decided to completely obscure the DNA sample Margo won from him by saturating it with a vial of his brother's blood.

The reader learns only a few things about Diogenes in the following chapter, in which Captain Hayward arrives to assess Margo's crime scene and interview witnesses. To begin, the knife he used to stab Margo has an ivory handle. One presumes it can either be traced to his brother, or that Diogenes purchased or purloined it from someone or some company whose conservation consciousness leaves something to be desired. It could not have been an item he personally valued, or he would not have left it in his victim. In fact, his leaving it in Margo is further evidence of the subconscious weakness in favor of women I mentioned earlier. One of the crime scene officers tells Captain Hayward: "It went with the victim to the hospital. You know, you can't pull it out--" (*Dance of Death,* p. 205). If Diogenes truly wanted to ensure Margo's death, he would have withdrawn the knife. If he had needed it to lead back to his brother or to even send Aloysius a message, he could have left it beside her.

Another important revelation is that if, indeed, Diogenes decided to obscure his own DNA on the box cutter by covering it in a larger sample from Aloysius, he must have complicated things even further by wiping it all off. Though Captain Hayward orders it tested, there is no blood visible on it when she finds it. No doubt she is meant to find it, too— Diogenes is, in fact, counting on her investigative thoroughness. If the box cutter did not cause "a large dent in the new wooden floor molding" (*Dance of Death*, p. 209) when Diogenes first struck it from Margo's hand, he made sure it did after he retrieved it. He also made sure he placed "a drop of blood about the size of a dime" between Margo and the box cutter. Whether or not this drop of his brother's blood covers a more minute spot of his own, or whether he only left a bit of his own on the box cutter, is a matter for speculation.

After the attack on Margo, Diogenes sends Pendergast an actual tarot card (as opposed to just citing one), along with a note. The card is the Tower, and Pendergast observes it is "from *El Gran Tarot Esoterico* variant of the deck. The card is said to indicate destruction, a time of sudden change" (*Dance of Death*, p. 217). According to the website *Learning the Tarot, El Gran Tarot Esoterico* employs "bright, primary colors"--an interesting choice for the colorblind Diogenes.

In the note to his brother, again headed with the salutation "*Ave, Frater,*" he congratulates himself on lying about Smithback while going after Margo. He does inform Aloysius that she "put up a most spirited struggle" (*Dance of Death*, p. 217). Of course, one can only wonder if Diogenes has truly abandoned Smithback. He compliments Aloysius on his "cleverness" in hiding the reporter, adding, "I haven't yet found him." Why would he still be looking, if not to preserve at least the option of harming him? Then again, perhaps Diogenes only wishes Aloysius to *think* he is still looking for Smithback. He actually declares his next target to be Vincent D'Agosta, but he considerately outlines his brother's dilemma for him. "Am I telling the truth? Am I lying again?" (*Dance of Death,* p. 217).

In addition to showing D'Agosta the missive in which he is named, Pendergast reveals the pattern behind Diogenes' attack on Margo. He speaks of "the murder of a spinster aunt of mine" (and thus of Diogenes'). Apparently this relative "was stabbed in the back with a pearl-handled letter opener by a disgruntled servant" (*Dance of Death,* p. 218). Despite his probable ambiguity about killing women, it is likely that Diogenes used a knife instead of a letter opener to be surer of his kill. Why he did not trouble to find a pearl-handled knife, however, is difficult to determine.

Pendergast also assures D'Agosta that Captain Hayward is in no danger from his brother, indirectly confirming for readers that Diogenes is depending on her expert police work to help frame him. He does not mention this aspect of things to D'Agosta yet. He does offer an opinion about Diogenes, saying, "nor would he ever operate with a proxy" (*Dance of Death,* p. 218). Aloysius, at least, would not believe the possibility that someone else pursued him and Smithback in the black Mercedes.

Diogenes, meanwhile, has larger seafood to sizzle than either D'Agosta or Smithback. Despite the fact that Pendergast has just assured D'Agosta that "Diogenes can know nothing of my—my *interest* in her" (*Dance of Death,* p. 218), his younger brother has managed to persuade Lady Viola Maskelene to board a plane for New York City. The letter Diogenes writes to her in the guise of Aloysius is so knowledgeable and intimate that almost irregardless of how much his elder brother might have babbled in delirium after his rescue, it argues for Diogenes having actually witnessed the couple's meeting on Capraia. How else would he have known: "Something happened between us"--i.e., that Aloysius's attraction to Viola was mutual? (*Dance of Death*, p. 227). This, despite Pendergast's words to D'Agosta just pages before about how isolated the island is, and how any stranger (especially one as tall as Diogenes!) "would be instantly noted" (*Dance of Death*, p. 218). Again, Diogenes' managing to accomplish such a seemingly impossible feat is part of Preston and Child's build-up of him as a virtually invincible nemesis for Special Agent Pendergast. He has exactly the amount of information he needs to fool Viola, including the knowledge of the brevity of her encounter with his brother, and all of the things about his family history Aloysius could not possibly have had time to tell her.

Compared to observing his brother on the island of Capraia without being discovered, Diogenes' ability to write a letter that sounds just like Aloysius is all too easy. To Viola, "the old-fashioned, somewhat awkward wording was so like Pendergast that she could almost hear his voice" (*Dance of Death*, p. 228). Not only does Diogenes know his brother well (better than Aloysius knows him, because he remembers The Event and his brother at this point does not), but he shares the Pendergast upbringing and genetics that has imprinted each man's use of language. Readers probably need not marvel at Diogenes' accurate guess that Viola would not be put off by such a letter, however. He is taking a shot; if Viola does not accept his phony proposition, he has other ways to get back at his brother. Viola *is* the grand prize, though, and Diogenes has nothing to lose by trying. Of course, a little later readers learn that Diogenes has indeed done his homework where Lady Maskelene is concerned.

Of course, while imitating Aloysius, Diogenes still allows himself touches of his own unique humor, referring to himself as "my dear brother, Diogenes" (*Dance of Death*, p. 228), and asking that Viola sign her return telegram "Anna Livia Plurabelle" (*Dance of Death*, p. 229). Anna Livia Plurabelle is a character in James Joyce's *Finnegan's Wake;* according to the *Encyclopedia Brittanica*'s website, www.brittanica.com, she "symbolizes the eternal and universal female."

It is interesting to note that while describing himself for Viola so that she will recognize Aloysius's brother at the airport, Diogenes attributes his two different-colored eyes to "a childhood accident" (*Dance of Death*, p. 228) rather than the familial cover story of scarlet fever. This is evidence that Diogenes believes Aloysius knows the truth of The Event, and believes his older brother views it callously as an "accident."

That Diogenes claims (in the guise of Aloysius) that he (Diogenes) will not recognize Viola does not weigh heavily against the possibility that he spied on her meeting with his brother on Capraia. Even if he accomplished this solely through the use of listening devices, Diogenes has researched Viola and has surely seen photos of her. Giving the information away, however, would only serve to make Viola suspicious. Also, Diogenes knows that airport security is far less likely to remember seeing a woman approach a man in this kind of situation than vice-versa.

Meanwhile, readers learn only one new thing about Diogenes

when Pendergast decides to consult a forensic profiler, namely Eli Glinn of Effective Engineering Solutions. Pendergast tells Glinn that Diogenes tested out to an IQ of 210 while still a child. This, of course, is higher than 99% of the world's population. Pendergast reiterates his beliefs about his brother to Glinn, including the myth of scarlet fever and his impression that "he was strange before the fever" (*Dance of Death,* p. 236). He also reasserts his belief that his burning of Diogenes' journals was the act that made Diogenes hate him badly enough to devote his life to revenge upon him. He does expound more emphatically, however, on the effect the death of their parents had upon Diogenes, telling Glinn: "Diogenes saw it all, heard their cries for help. That drove him over the edge." It is interesting to note that Aloysius, who seems to put nothing past his younger brother, never seems to entertain for an instant the possibility that Diogenes himself could have intentionally started the fire or intentionally murdered their parents. If Aloysius does not suspect this, I believe we are safe in dismissing the possibility also. I think, too, that there is some truth in Aloysius's feeling that their parents' deaths made Diogenes worse. His mother was probably the reason he tried to confine his atrocities to his journal pages; with the one person he actually loved (or that he admitted loving to himself) gone, there was no longer any need for self-control. Although, of course, he needed to remove himself from the watchful eyes of his elder brother before embarking in earnest upon his career of evil.

What is most interesting in this chapter, however, is that for the first time, someone disputes Pendergast's assumptions about Diogenes. Glinn asserts that Pendergast's burning of

Diogenes' journals "happened far too late to produce such a deep, pathological, obsessive hatred. Nor," Glinn continues, "can a mere bout with scarlet fever create hatred out of thin air. No, Mr. Pendergast: this hatred stems from *something else* that happened between you and your brother at a much earlier age" (*Dance of Death,* p. 239). Of course, Glinn is precisely correct, but we will address that in its proper context later.

In the following chapter (Forty), readers learn that Captain Hayward has now linked all four murders (she is as yet unaware that Margo Green has survived). She, too, has ordered a forensic profile, which "confirmed that the homicides were psychologically consistent and could have been committed by the same perp." Not only that, but "they were dealing with a serial killer. A meticulous, intelligent, methodical, cool, and utterly insane serial killer" (*Dance of Death,* p. 242). Though that last line definitely describes Diogenes, Hayward is also informed that the blood samples, tested three times, "matched one of the Bureau's top agents" (*Dance of Death,* p. 243). Of course, by "Bureau," the man who presents Hayward with the report means Federal Bureau of Investigation. Though he tells Hayward the reason for triple verification of the DNA match was "a major problem because of confidentiality issues" and that the results are "explosive stuff" (*Dance of Death,* p. 243), I cannot help wondering if the smaller portion of Diogenes' blood in at least one of the samples caused complications with the matching. In any case, Diogenes has succeeded in framing his brother as a serial killer—a serial killer of his own friends, no less.

Next the focus returns to Pendergast, whom Eli Glinn has persuaded to go along with a psychological interview designed to yield missing information about what really triggered Diogenes' extreme hatred for him. Glinn's perspective on the question is refreshing; while immediately respecting Aloysius' intellect, he reflects that Diogenes "appeared to be even more intelligent, and yet utterly malevolent." He also mentally makes the observation that Diogenes "had devoted his life to the object of his hatred" and that this is "not unlike a man under the spell of obsessive love" (*Dance of Death,* p. 245), Glinn is the first character to point out the strong link between hatred and love, and surely Diogenes did once love his brother deeply to have turned upon him so fiercely, even though Aloysius does not yet recall this.

Though Pendergast obviously has gaps in his memories when it comes to Diogenes, and his impressions of and feelings about him are colored by these gaps, he is still a useful source of information about his younger brother. Thus the memory exercise he undertakes with Glinn's staff psychiatrist Dr. Krasner is worth examining for our purposes. When Pendergast begins this, the first thing we learn about Diogenes is that he was ten years old in 1972, giving him a birth year no later than 1962. This, of course, is from the period when Preston and Child were still putting dates in the Pendergast novels, instead of blurring time as much as possible to keep A. X. L Pendergast perpetually in his forties. Of course, Diogenes benefits from this anti-aging treatment as well, always being two to three years younger than Aloysius.

Dr. Krasner has asked Aloysius to imagine himself in a

favorite place. He chooses Aunt Cornelia's upstate New York mansion Ravenscroft, though he does not populate this imaginary refuge with his family members, including Diogenes, until Dr. Krasner insists he do so. Pendergast describes his then-ten-year-old brother thus: "Tall for his age, pale, with very short hair, eyes of two different colors. He is very thin and his lips are overly red" (*Dance of Death,* p. 249). A quick survey of internet health pages suggest a few medical causes for "overly red" lips, including allergies and high blood pressure; Kawasaki disease is not likely, because it would have had much more severe effects that Diogenes would have difficulty overcoming. The allergies and the blood pressure problems are possible, though the latter is not likely in a ten-year-old. More than likely, it is just the authors giving him yet another distinctive feature to differentiate him from Aloysius, but it could also be that the redness is relative to his paleness. I like to think that he just has a very rich capillary system, and thus a good blood supply, in his lips.

When Dr. Krasner asks Aloysius to look into Diogenes' eyes, and asks if Diogenes is looking back at him, Pendergast replies that he "has turned his head away. He does not like to be stared at." When Krasner demands he "keep staring at him," Aloysius eventually admits, "I have averted my eyes" (*Dance of Death,* p. 249). Why does he have trouble looking his brother in the eye, even in an imaginary exercise? Although it is not difficult to imagine Diogenes winning a staring contest, even with his formidable brother, it is also possible that Aloysius is subconsciously ashamed of what he did to Diogenes in The Event, even though he does not yet consciously remember it. This could be why he has difficulty meeting his brother's eyes. Even after Krasner reminds Pendergast that he is control of the imagination exercise, and asks him again to keep staring, he declares: "I don't choose to" (*Dance of Death*, p. 250).

As Pendergast and Dr. Krasner continue with this exercise, the Special Agent acknowledges the ease of getting his younger brother to agree to meet Krasner in Ravenscroft's summerhouse: "He will come to see the doctor. He is curious that way." This suggests that Diogenes at ten is interested in anyone who can increase his knowledge—perhaps even especially interested in someone who can increase his *self-* knowledge. Quite possibly, he seeks a greater understanding of what has happened to him in The Event, and how better to cope with it. Perhaps, even then, with his mother still living, Diogenes is still seeking a way not to become completely evil.

Through Aloysius, of course, Dr. Krasner asks for Diogenes' earliest memory of his brother. Though I doubt Pendergast's answer is exactly correct, I do believe he is not far wrong when he specifies Diogenes being six months old at the time. He himself has told D'Agosta that his own memories go back to before his first birthday; naturally he assumes his brother's are similarly early. Interestingly, Pendergast's fine motor skills are apparently not as precocious as his powers of recollection, because although Diogenes supposedly remembers the two-to-three-year-old Aloysius "drawing a picture," it is merely "scribbles" (*Dance of Death*, pp. 250-51).

When Krasner asks for Diogenes' opinion of his elder

brother, he—in Pendergast's mind—replies as a ten-year-old. "He thinks of me as the next Jackson Pollock" (*Dance of Death*, p. 251). Jackson Pollock was an abstract artist best known for his paintings composed of seemingly random drips and streaks of paint. Of course, the sarcasm of this reply, comparing a child's scribbles to abstract art, partially belongs to Aloysius, but we can take him as believing he shares this quality with Diogenes, even from childhood. To add more layers to this, Mr. Pollock was married to a woman named Lee Krasner. One can view this merely as Preston and Child being clever about choosing a name for the character of Glinn's staff psychiatrist, or also as Aloysius being clever by bringing up an artist married to a woman with the same last name as his partner in the psychological exercise, or Aloysius believing his brother would bring this particular artist up for the same reason. In any case, Diogenes (and undoubtedly Aloysius as well) knows far more about culture than the average ten-year-old.

Next, Krasner asks what Diogenes sees when he looks at Aloysius. Pendergast replies: "He said the word *nothing*." When asked for clarification, Diogenes-through-Aloysius quotes a line from a Wallace Stevens poem, "The Snow Man": "I see nothing that is not there and the nothing that is." Pendergast adds that "even at ten, Diogenes was partial to Stevens" (*Dance of Death*, p. 251). When Krasner asks if this means he thinks Aloysius is "a nonentity," according to Pendergast Diogenes laughs and "says the words are yours, not his" (*Dance of Death*, p. 251). It is interesting that Diogenes (even in Pendergast's mind) backs away from the direct insult here. In part, I believe this is because ten-year-

lxviii

old Diogenes still has some respect for adults—or at least for adults who have had the years of higher education necessary to become a psychiatrist. He is not quite committed to having the doctor see that he would insult his brother this severely. The retreat is certainly not for his brother's sake. Perhaps, too, he believes the doctor would report such a cutting dismissal to his mother. Part of this backing away, however, shows us the beginnings of Diogenes' extreme enjoyment of setting up his victims (in this case, the doctor) to deliver the "killing blow" themselves—such as when he causes Charles Duchamp to leap from his own window, and later tries to tip Constance Greene over the emotional edge to suicide.

Of course, Diogenes does not extend his respect for the doctor to all adults. After answering Krasner's query about what school he attends—St. Ignatius Loyola—he answers the question of how he likes school (through Aloysius, of course) thusly: "As much as you would like being shut up in a room with twenty-five mental defectives and a middle-aged hysteric" (*Dance of Death,* p. 251). I think in this instance Pendergast is extremely accurate in choosing Diogenes' words for him. We cannot know for sure, but it is probable that the teacher Diogenes is calling "a middle-aged hysteric" is a nun. Even at the age of ten, Diogenes may well feel that anyone who would give up a normal life of marriage and family in the service of deep religious faith would merit the label of "hysteric." Though Diogenes probably already realizes he himself is not destined for a future that includes starting his own family, he might well find it impossible to respect someone who would give this up for what he would view as fanciful reasons. We can only speculate about what

Diogenes knows about sex at this age, but both he and Aloysius are both very curious boys and voracious readers. Diogenes may well be aware at this point of theories concerning links between mental health and sexual repression, and this knowledge may also have influenced his choice of the word "hysteric," with its Greek root.

As for labeling his normal peers "mental defectives," children continue to baffle Diogenes well into adulthood. Later in *Dance of Death* he will refer to a gemologist's children as "dimpled lunatics." Not only is he already far superior to his fellow students intellectually, and must have little patience with what he would view as their backwardness and stupidity, but their innocent playfulness must be incomprehensible to him. Their normal playground games and activities must appear sheer lunacy.

Hence, though I believe Aloysius' attitude towards Diogenes colors his interpretation, it is still instructive to examine the answer he gives for his ten-year-old younger brother when Krasner asks about Diogenes' favorite school subject. Aloysius begins, "experimental biology," then after a meaningful pause adds, "on the playground" (*Dance of Death*, p. 251). This gives the impression that Diogenes tortures his "mental defectives." I think Aloysius, at least, intends Krasner to imagine Diogenes committing sadistic acts of violence upon the actual persons of his peers. This is possible in milder forms that could be hidden from the "middle-aged hysteric" and which he could frighten his victims into not revealing. More likely, I believe, is that he forced them to watch vivisections of animals he came across or brought to the playground for this purpose. Perhaps

Incitatus served in this way before Diogenes returned his corpse to Aloysius' room. Unfortunately, it is probable that even the most hunting-hardened boys in his class begged Diogenes to put the creatures out of their misery. So, while he most likely did not inflict physical injuries upon his peers, he would have contented himself with the psychological trauma he caused instead.

Dr. Krasner only manages to get in one of the next three questions he has for Diogenes before Pendergast confesses he is losing patience with the entire exercise. Krasner asks what Diogenes' favorite food is, and Pendergast replies for him: "Wormwood and gall" (*Dance of Death,* p. 252). This particular answer is interesting on a few different levels. One is its origin in the Old Testament, the book of Deuteronomy in particular. The verse, Deuteronomy 29:18, reads thus in the King James' Version: "Lest there should be among you man, or woman, or family, or tribe, whose heart turneth away this day from the LORD our God, to go *and* serve the gods of these nations; lest there should be among you a root that beareth gall and wormwood." The passage concerns idolatry, and likens wormwood and gall, bywords for bitterness, to the impulse toward idolatry. Verses that follow this one promise all manner of horrible curses will rain down upon the person who "beareth" this impulse; while Diogenes may not necessarily bear it, he claims it for his favorite food. Instead of cursing the most basic disobedience to God, Diogenes would seemingly reward it. This probably fits in well with his basic feelings about being in Catholic school. In other words, he feeds on the things that bring misery to others.

On another level, the wormwood response is amusing because

Diogenes as an adult is fond of absinthe, and insists upon the kind that still includes wormwood as an allegedly mild-altering ingredient. At this point in the story, Aloysius does not know of Diogenes' predilection—unless he started drinking it at a very early age, which in a family with European sensibilities like the Pendergasts, is entirely possible.

Then Krasner puts Pendergast through another exercise in which he is to imagine shooting Diogenes and having his brother dead in front of him. Of course, the authors have set this up very skillfully, because in fact a gunshot wound is what actually caused Diogenes' physical damage during The Event. Though Aloysius did not pull the trigger himself, Diogenes obviously blames him for what happened. The first part of the exercise, however, involves giving Diogenes the chance to shoot Aloysius. The elder Pendergast brother explains that Diogenes does not pull the trigger because "it's too soon." Aloysius does believe Diogenes intends to kill him, but wants "to play with me for a while." More specifically, "to pull off my wings and watch what happens." Pendergast concludes: "I am his ultimate insect" (*Dance of Death,* p. 253).

When Dr. Krasner asks what Diogenes whispers to him as he lays dying from Pendergast's gunshot, the answer is a quotation in Latin, which turns out to be the mad Emperor Nero's last words: "O, what an artist dies with me!" At this point, I am not sure that Pendergast is not just playing with Krasner, yet he still retains a certain resonance with Diogenes' sense of humor. Perhaps Pendergast believes his brother is mad enough to speak "facetiously" on his deathbed

(*Dance of Death,* p. 254). If not by the end of *Dance of Death,* however, then definitely by the end of the last novel in the trilogy, the reader realizes that Diogenes is indeed an artist—or at least views himself this way. He is a macabre performance artist of terror and mayhem.

The rest of the chapter consists of Pendergast reiterating his denials. That Diogenes hates him simply because of who he, Aloysius, is. That Diogenes "was born that way, empty and cruel" (*Dance of Death,* p. 254). We learn nothing more about Diogenes himself, merely Pendergast's attitude towards him at this point in the series.

In Chapter Forty-Three, Viola Maskelene arrives at Kennedy airport, and readers are treated to a fairly detailed description of Diogenes. Interestingly, he has chosen to garb himself for this occasion in a "gray flannel suit," evoking the 1950s novel and film, *The Man in the Gray Flannel Suit.* Like Diogenes, the titular character suffers from PTSD, but his is from having fought in World War II. The novel and film also speak to the futility of middle-class society's pursuit of status; I suppose Diogenes identifies with the futility of going along with *any* of society's values, though he has far too much wealth and breeding to have much in common with the middle class.

After Viola notices "a tall man in a gray flannel suit standing at the fringe" of the group of people waiting for arriving passengers, "she recognized him instantly, so uncanny was the resemblance to his brother, with his high smooth forehead, aquiline nose, and aristocratic bearing." She goes on to note the differences, though, between Diogenes and Aloysius; Diogenes "was taller and less wiry, a little more heavily built perhaps; but his face was sharper, the cheekbones and bony ridges around the eyes more pronounced, all of which, taken together, gave his face a curiously asymmetrical feeling. His hair was ginger-colored and he sported a thick, neatly-trimmed beard. But the most startling difference was in his eyes: one was a rich, hazel green, the other a glaucous blue" (*Dance of Death,* p. 260).

When she smiles and waves at him, he smiles back and moves toward her "with a languid step." Diogenes "grasped her hand in both of his, hands cool and soft" (*Dance of Death,* p. 261). The moment he speaks, however, Viola notices the same things that Margo did. "His voice had much of his brother's buttery southern tones, yet although his manner of speech was almost as languorous as his walk, his words were very precisely enunciated, as if bitten off at the ends" (*Dance of Death,* p. 261). Again, the authors are emphasizing the damage to Diogenes' prefrontal cortex—and the diligence with which he has fought to overcome it. No matter how harshly we must condemn his lack of morality as a serial killer, it is difficult not to admire his persistence and sheer force of will. Of course, one may ask why none of the other characters observe any hint of this with Dr. Menzies or any of Diogenes' other alter egos. Is this a deliberate omission on the part of Preston and Child, akin to their never mentioning that Dr. Menzies could once have been a star on the college basketball court? Or is it that when Diogenes creates a voice for one of his personas he is able to let his words flow more naturally, much like the way country singer Mel Tillis has a difficulty with stuttering when he talks that disappears entirely when he sings?

When Diogenes offers Viola his arm like the gentlemanly Pendergast she expects him to be, she notes: "It was surprisingly strong, the muscles as hard as steel cables, very different from the soft, languid impression his movements gave" (*Dance of Death,* p. 261). Obviously, Diogenes works out. As much as he depends upon his brilliant mind to keep him from suffering the consequences of his life of crime and subterfuge, he also depends on his body. If a victim manages to escape him, Diogenes' chances of being apprehended go up drastically. So, being in excellent physical condition and being stronger than the vast majority of his chosen prey helps keep him safe to follow both his whims and his grand scheme of revenge against the brother he feels made him this way. Diogenes' peak physical condition also argues against a preference for female victims. His size and his gender alone would make him able to overpower most women; devoting significant amounts of time to working out would seem a waste if he primarily hunted females. Unless, of course, one takes into account purposes of seduction—but this will be addressed later in this analysis.

It is right after encountering Diogenes' strong arm and contrasting its hardness with the fluidity of his movements that Viola chooses to comment: "There'd be no mistaking you for anyone but Aloysius's brother." His reply is ironic: "I'll take that as a compliment" (*Dance of Death,* p. 261). For him, there is a conscious decision behind the common conversational phrase, a decision made because he needs to keep Viola deceived about the true nature of his relationship with his brother a little while longer.

Before, and for a short time after he gets Viola into his car—

he appears to have swapped his black Mercedes for a black Lincoln—Diogenes engages his brother's would-be girlfriend in seemingly normal polite conversation. Even these normal beginnings are worthy of examination, however. When Viola complains of the cold weather outside the airport, and remarks how temperate Capraia was when she left, Diogenes speaks of his envy that she lives there year-round. We later learn he has a home in Italy himself, but this is an early hint. Of course he cannot live there year-round when he is busy being Menzies. When she tells him that she usually spends a great deal of time in Egypt as well, Diogenes says he has been there, too. There is no reason to doubt his word on this matter, especially as the circumstances are revealed. Apparently, he was "a junior member of the von Hertsgaard expedition." Viola recognizes the name immediately: "Not the one that went into Somalia looking for the diamond mines of Queen Hatshepsut? The one where Hertsgaard was found decapitated?" (*Dance of Death,* p. 262). After Diogenes admits this is the very expedition, Viola goes on to ask if there is any truth to the rumors that "Hertsgaard may have found the Hatshepsut mines just before he was murdered." Readers cannot help but assume Diogenes is behind that decapitation; this is also the first hint we get of his fondness for diamonds. Even when this motive is confirmed for us later in the book, we cannot be sure if von Hertsgaard's murder was a necessary part of keeping the mines undiscovered by anyone but Diogenes, or if he took a particular enjoyment in it.

The only lie Diogenes tells about his time in Egypt is when he replies to Viola's question: "I sincerely doubt it." After a quick dismissal of "rumors," he changes the focus from the diamond mines to Hatshepsut herself, and is able to impress Viola with the recitation of a rather sexy Egyptian inscription about how Hatshepsut was allegedly conceived. I think Diogenes uses the inscription to move Viola's mind even further from the diamond mines, but it is also a passage he enjoys for its own sake. He does seem to favor sensuality in the arts. I believe the reference is also the beginning of a small test he has constructed for Viola, to help confirm that his efforts to lure her to a place where he can use her to torture his brother have been worth it. The test is as follows: Diogenes quotes the sensual Egyptian inscription, Viola does not blush. This means that her blushing responses to his subsequent allusions to her burgeoning relationship with Aloysius are particular to her feelings for his brother, and she is not just a person who blushes at any mention of sensuality.

By making these allusions to their relationship, such as, "It seems you two are made for each other" (*Dance of Death*, p. 263), Diogenes is trying to get Viola in touch with her feelings about Aloysius. The more in touch with these feelings Viola is, the more fun Diogenes will have sowing his seeds of doubt and fear in her. Playing with Viola is not strictly necessary to using her against his brother, but as long as she is in such a vulnerable position, Diogenes' warped sense of humor will not allow him to resist the opportunity.

Before throwing the first of many salvos at Viola's peace of mind, Diogenes has some fun describing the case his brother must finish up before she can see him. He tells her it "involves a serial killer, a truly insane individual, who for various obscure reasons has conceived a deep hatred for

Aloysius. He's been killing people and taunting my brother with his inability to catch him." I think Diogenes also somewhat enjoys taking credit for saving his brother from Count Fosco, and is gratified by the unwitting irony of Viola's response: "I'm so glad he has a brother like you" (*Dance of Death*, p. 263). But then he settles down to work, telling Viola, "I was so worried about him after that dreadful accident with his wife in Tanzania." The authors tell us that "Viola found herself wanting very much to ask what had happened" (*Dance of Death,* p. 263). In a modern world saturated with murder mysteries in books and on film and television, she cannot avoid the thought that an "accident" that kills a wife is sometimes caused by the husband.

After informing Viola that he believes Aloysius "is already in love with you," Diogenes begins to tell her how difficult his brother is to read. He is attempting to increase her growing realization that she does not really know Pendergast well at all yet. Though his words have a purpose in manipulating Viola's feelings, Diogenes is probably truthful when he says, "I could never tell what he was thinking, even when he was a boy." He has no idea that Aloysius has no recollection of The Event. He even thinks Aloysius lured him into the situation on purpose, and that at the age it happened to him, Diogenes had been unable to read what he believes in hindsight to have been his older brother's malicious intent.

Diogenes then turns the conversation towards the Pendergast family's more bizarre members. He begins with Great-Aunt Cornelia. His adding that she "lives not far from here, at the Mount Mercy Hospital for the Criminally Insane," leads me to speculate that he, too, may have been visiting his only living ancestor, just as Aloysius has. How he may have kept his older brother from learning of these visits is an interesting question, but the ability is surely not beyond the scope of the villain Preston and Child have endowed with such remarkable intellect.

When Viola appears taken aback by this bit of information, Diogenes eases off somewhat with the disclaimer: "Every family has its black sheep, I suppose" (*Dance of Death,* p. 264). Though he admits "some families more than others," he turns the focus back upon Viola to temporarily reassure her before building back up to completely undermining her. He asks her: "Any interesting criminals in your ancestry?" While Viola denies the criminal aspect, she tells Diogenes of her mad violinist ancestor. He uses the compliment of "no dull accountants or traveling salesmen in your lineage, eh?" as the launching place for the story of how a traveling salesman played a huge role in building the present-day Pendergast fortune. In addition to serving its psychological purpose with Viola, Diogenes' tale of his and Aloysius's Great-Great-Grandfather Hezekiah provides readers with heretofore unknown information about the Pendergast family. Following the story of his ancestor's lucrative and deadly Compound Elixir and Glandular Restorative, which contained "cocaine, acetanilid, and some rather nasty alkaloid botanicals," Diogenes poses an important question to Viola: "Do you think there is such a thing as a criminal gene?" (*Dance of Death,* p. 265). Despite her reply in the negative, Diogenes *wants* Viola to at least fear Aloysius may be prone to the effects of hereditary criminality. Yet it is a question he himself must surely ponder—is his own fate a result of The

Event, which he blames on his brother, or would he have eventually succumbed to the family's genetic curse? And is Aloysius, who shares the same ancestry, really that much further from madness than Diogenes is himself? To a small degree, Viola's brisk denial of such a possibility must be a small balm to his feelings.

Diogenes uses his question, however, as a reason to tell her about their Great-Uncle Antoine, with whom readers are already familiar. He then digresses slightly into a discourse on the history of crime in England versus that in the United States, in which he manages to insult Lady Maskelene's upper class origins, while simultaneously informing her that "in every generation, the Pendergast family seems to have produced a killer." Apparently in Antoine's generation it produced two, because Diogenes moves on to tell Viola about Comstock Pendergast, Antoine's brother. "He killed his business partner and the man's poor family, and then committed suicide." He neglects to tell her, however, how Comstock's sins have carried on unto the present Pendergast generation—if anyone can be said to be the true author of The Event, it would be Comstock. Diogenes knows this, even if he places more importance on his brother's role.

Viola expresses disbelief at Diogene's claim that Comstock cut his own throat, so he tells her: "Oh, yes. Twice. The first time he didn't quite get it deep enough, you see. I guess he didn't relish the thought of bleeding slowly to death." Diogenes then becomes somewhat confessional. "Myself, I wouldn't mind dying a slow death by exsanguination—I hear it's rather like going to sleep. I would have plenty of time to admire the blood, which has such an exquisite color." Except, of course, he would not actually be able to see the color, but Viola cannot be sure of this.

Similar to what he discussed with Margo Green, Diogenes asks Viola if she likes "the color of blood" (*Dance of Death*, p. 266). I cannot help wondering if one of them had responded enthusiastically, he would have dropped his plan to use her for revenge on Aloysius and tried to romance her instead. Viola, however, is quite creeped out by now, and when she finds out he plans to drive two more hours before reaching their destination, she asks him to turn the car back around so she can stay in the city. Diogenes seemingly obliges by taking the next exit, but quickly puts her under with chloroform.

Chapter Forty-Four tells readers little about Diogenes except to reiterate how much Pendergast fears his ability to murder all of his friends and acquaintances. Chapter Forty-Five, however, is worth a closer look, even though it primarily consists of a psychological profile that Captain Hayward has ordered based on the three murders and Margo's attempted murder. In large part the profiler makes the assumptions that Diogenes wishes him to make in order to point towards Aloysius, but he is probably unable to completely erase himself from the picture. Obviously there are aspects of the profile applicable to both Pendergast brothers, such as: "He is a person of considerable financial means," and "He is very adept at disguises" (*Dance of Death*, p. 277). Ironically, the part about having "suffered a crippling emotional trauma involving a close family member" while still "a young boy" also proves true for both men. Its place in the profile probably comes from Diogenes himself unintentionally rather than as something he did deliberately to point to his brother. In Diogenes' mind, The Event did not traumatize Aloysius at all, so why would he construct crimes to reflect a profile in which it had? It is also difficult to distinguish parts of the profile Diogenes intended to lead to his brother from those the profiler simply guessed incorrectly. Is Diogenes clever enough to have pointed the profiler towards his brother's lesser (but still extremely impressive) IQ "in the 180 to 200 range," or is the profiler merely underestimating Diogenes? One can also imagine that both brothers fit the description of having "difficulty forming relationships with the opposite sex" (*Dance of Death,* p. 277), but readers do not really know Aloysius that well at this point in the series, nor can we conceive of Diogenes *wanting* anything that most normal people would think of as a "relationship" (barring an affirmative answer to the "color of blood" question). Did the profiler guess incorrectly about "a cold, controlling mother," because Diogenes has positive feelings about his, or did he do something to point the profiler towards the way his mother may well have treated Aloysius based on the way she perceived his role in The Event? In any case, Diogenes was masterful in constructing his crimes in such a way that the profiler concludes: "The target subject may manifest symptoms of a rare form of multiple personality disorder, a variant of Munchausen syndrome by proxy, in which the subject acts out two separate, diametrically opposite roles: that of killer and of investigator" (*Dance of Death,* p. 279). The profile goes into further detail and possible scenarios, but in essence Diogenes has succeeded in preventing almost everyone from believing Pendergast if he tries to tell them about his long-presumed-dead younger brother. It is only the combination of D'Agosta's strong loyalty with the random chance of his actually having seen Diogenes on Fosco's hillside that saves Pendergast from losing one of his staunchest allies.

In chapter Forty-Six, we learn about the conditions in which Diogenes is keeping Viola. Despite his fatal intentions towards her—and we do learn they are indeed fatal in this chapter—he keeps her in a comfortable, elegant, albeit escape-proof environment. The bed has a frilled canopy; the room is wallpapered and contains "some old Victorian furniture" (*Dance of Death,* p. 282). It has a window, though it has bars on it. She has been provided with an adjoining bathroom and toiletry items. Diogenes has also given her an actual drinking glass, despite the fact she could conceivably break it and use it as a weapon. Diogenes is obviously confident in his ability to either keep her from using it on him or subdue her even if she does. He also seems certain that she will not use it on herself, to rob him of the satisfaction of killing her in imitation of the death of Great-Uncle Comstock. Though he probably does mean for her to use the glass in exactly the manner in which she does—to attempt to dig through plaster only to find that the walls of her prison are actually made of steel—he may also believe in the niceties of glassware rather than paper, plastic, or styrofoam.

When Diogenes checks in on his captive, we learn yet more about Viola's environment, and more about him. Firstly, he is in disguise, and Viola recognizes only his voice. Later, in *Book of the Dead,* she does not recognize Menzies, so it is not this particular alter-ego Diogenes is using. He is probably putting his latest message to his brother in motion, the one containing a lock of Viola's hair, and cannot afford to have someone recognize Menzies in connection with it.

His conversation with Viola is informative. He confirms that once he heard her name from Pendergast during his recovery from near-death at the hands of Fosco, he did thorough research on her. He also assures her that he has no personal feelings about her at all, that all is being done strictly because of his brother's feelings for her. He states that he has come primarily to tell her "two things you *don't* know—and should" *(Dance of Death,* p. 285). He tells her what she has already guessed through exploration—that her erstwhile prison is escape-proof. Diogenes goes on to add, however, that "There are books in the bookcase," and "some hard candies in the bottom drawer of the bureau for you to suck on." The most important thing he tells her, however, is that he intends to kill her at dawn.

It fascinates me that Diogenes will not let her spend what is supposedly her last day on earth without books to read, but that all he mentions in the way of food is hard candy. Books are obviously important to him, and he would apparently have felt uncivilized if he didn't provide his prisoner with them. But what of the traditional condemned person's last meal? Of course, it may be that Diogenes did bring Viola more conventional things to eat during her imprisonment, but the authors failed to mention this. It could be that he wants to keep her in a weakened state for better control, but it could also be that he wants to avoid certain messier aspects of killing a person suddenly, specifically keeping any evacuation of the bowels to a minimum.

Even after Diogenes tells Viola of his plans to kill her, she mocks his accent and his formality. He allows himself a frown at this "before neutrality returned" (*Dance of Death,* p. 286). As she continues to insult him, he only says, "My, my. We certainly have a sharp tongue this morning." Though he does not care for Viola's behavior, he does not lose his temper with her. He seems to have a surprising degree of self-control, or else he really has little care for what his fellow humans think about him (except as it suits his purposes, such as when he is acting as Hugo Menzies). Of course, Diogenes is just as capable of dishing it out as he is of taking it. He tells Viola she is "as chattery as a monkey and almost as smart" (*Dance of Death,* pp. 286-287). He finally stops her stream of invective, however, by telling her *how* he intends to kill her. "Specifically, I will cut your throat. Twice. In honor of our Uncle Comstock" (*Dance of Death,* p. 287).

When Viola asks why, he congratulates her on "finally" asking "a sensible question." Diogenes launches into a lengthy philosophical answer, which *is* self-revelatory to a degree. What he does not share with her, however, is why he has chosen to use her to mimic Comstock's death in particular. I believe he wishes to kill the person his brother holds most dear in the world in a manner that Diogenes knows will be evocative of Comstock Pendergast—the architect of the machine of The Event. Not knowing that Aloysius does not recall The Event, nor his own mostly unwitting role in it, Diogenes nevertheless wants to give him an especially painful reminder of these things.

Diogenes' words to Viola are instructive, however. He calls himself an "existentialist," which, of course, would mean he believes in existentialism, which is defined in the Merriam-Webster online dictionary thus: "a chiefly 20th century philosophical movement embracing diverse doctrines but centering on analysis of individual existence in an unfathomable universe and the plight of the individual who must assume ultimate responsibility for acts of free will without any certain knowledge of what is right or wrong or good or bad." Diogenes defines it much more colorfully. "I carve my own meaning out of the suppurating carcass of this rotting universe," he tells Viola. "Through no fault of your own, you have become. part of that meaning. But I do not feel sorry for you. The world is abrim with pain and suffering. I simply choose to direct the festivities instead of offering myself up as another witless victim." Diogenes is not entirely truthful when he adds, "I take no pleasure in the suffering of others—except one." He does enjoy most of his victims' pain and fear. The "one" to whom he refers, though, is Aloysius, and in relative terms, any sadistic play he has with an actual murder victim produces only minor gratification in comparison with causing his brother to suffer. This declaration does make me think that in general (aside from victims chosen for their value to Aloysius) Diogenes chooses victims that he strongly dislikes, or that he feels deserve it for some reason, even if it is a reason understandable only to himself. I also think that in general, they tend *not* to be female. Interestingly, he admits to his captive: "I live for my brother, Viola; he gives me strength, he gives me purpose, he gives me life. He is my salvation." Which means that Diogenes is consciously aware of the degree of emotional complexity involved in his feelings toward Aloysius.

At one point, Viola tells him that both he and his "brother can go to hell." This allows Diogenes to reveal that he believes this life "*is* hell." He goes on to add: "Except that you are about to gain your release." This is another way he rationalizes his own behavior. Life is horrible anyway; if *he* wasn't making a particular person suffer, someone or something else would be. Any time he kills someone, he feels he is actually putting him or her out of misery; if he pauses to inflict a little more intense misery on his victim, it is a small price to pay in that person's gaining his release from "hell."

As Diogenes no doubt predicted, Viola eventually rushes him with a shard of the water glass she has broken in the course of exploring and trying to escape her environment. "In the blur of an instant she found herself pinned to the floor" (*Dance of Death*, p. 287). Diogenes finds it very easy to physically control her. He "now lay on top of her, his face inches from hers, his breath, sweetly smelling of cloves, in her face." This last detail is curious. Margo smelled damp earth. I wonder if Diogenes has been smoking clove cigarettes, or chewing clove gum? If the latter, has he planned his next action all along? He tells her, "Good-bye, my lively little monkey," then "kissed her tenderly on the lips." Note that he does not kiss her harshly, or aggressively, or hungrily—but "tenderly." I think Diogenes feels a certain gratitude toward her for cooperating relatively easily with his plans for vengeance upon his brother. On the one hand, there is no question that Diogenes is forcing an unwanted attention on her; on the other, it is a surprisingly gentle gesture that seems to ironically indicate that he would be too much a Southern gentleman to do anything of a more sexual nature to her without her consent. He is a sadistic killer, and will later prove a seducer, but he is no rapist.

Of course, he manages to release her and exit the room before she can either escape or hurt him. Again, the authors make (to my mind) the Dracula comparison: "And then, in one swift batlike movement, he rose and was gone, the door slamming behind him."

In Chapter Forty-Seven, readers learn a few more things about Diogenes from Pendergast's perspective. Aloysius has finally figured out the familiarity of the handwriting in Diogenes' notes to him. "That was my handwriting," he tells D'Agosta, "but altered just enough so it would appear—to a handwriting expert, anyway—that I was trying to disguise it" (*Dance of Death,* p. 291). Not only has Diogenes added another perfect nail to the coffin of his brother's frame-up job, but he has managed to have another message delivered to him in his most secret bolt hole. With this last missive, he encloses a lock of Viola's hair, probably collected while the chloroform was in effect. This time he has chosen "tobacco-colored ink" to inform Aloysius of his intentions. Though he does not mention Viola by name, he does mention Capraia in relationship to the dark lock of hair, and while he does not baldly say he will kill her, he tells Aloysius he may keep the hair "as a memento of her passing." Then Diogenes taunts him with the possibility: "I could be lying about everything. This lock could belong to someone else. Search your heart for the truth." He ends his letter with the Latin phrase, "*ave atque vale*" (*Dance of Death,* p. 295), which means, "hail and farewell," implying that this is the last time he intends to contact Aloysius.

Pendergast adds one more detail about his brother in explaining to D'Agosta how Diogenes could possibly have discovered Viola and her importance to him. After saying he "was raving" while under his younger brother's care, and that he could well have mentioned Viola during that time, he adds: "Nothing escapes Diogenes—nothing" (*Dance of Death,* p. 297).

By contrast, not much is added about Diogenes in Chapter Forty-Eight except for the possibility, which is later confirmed, that if he is not actually expecting Aloysius to follow his trail with Viola, he is at least anticipating the possibility of it. The airport security digital files reveal that Diogenes "nodded formally at the camera, raised his hand just a little, and tipped a wave. His lips moved as if in speech" (*Dance of Death,* p. 303). One curious note in this chapter, however, is a discrepancy in the description of his attire. The security camera has recorded Diogenes "dressed in a dark overcoat," when Viola had observed his gray flannel suit upon her arrival. Perhaps he had taken it off and draped it over his arm by the time Viola reached him.

In Chapter Fifty, readers finally see a return to Diogenes' alter-ego, Dr. Hugo Menzies. He is there to congratulate Nora Kelly on her respectful handling of the Tano Indian delegation, which she managed to turn into good publicity for the museum. Menzies is also there, of course, as head of the anthropology department, to help preside over the opening night gala for the Sacred Images exhibit. Since Diogenes did not appear to Viola as Menzies, we can only assume that he brought the accoutrements of this disguise with him into the city, applied them in some secret location before heading to the Musuem, and presumably had his tuxedo hanging already in his office, waiting for him.

In any case, he appears in front of Nora with a glass of champagne following her ordeal with the Tanos and the Museum's director. As he congratulates her on transforming a potential "publicity disaster" into a public relations coup, "he practically chortled with pleasure, his eyes sparkling. Nora had never seen him so animated" (*Dance of Death*, p. 317). While part of this bonhomie is Diogenes consciously trying to steer any suspicion from the crime he plans to commit later that evening from falling on Menzies—not only as the man who is just too genial and wonderful to have possibly done such a thing, but as a man whom Nora distinctly remembers being present at the gala—it is an excitement and vitality he does not have to feign at this point. He is about to steal a diamond collection he has long coveted, plus he believes he is about to put the finishing touches on the revenge upon his brother that he has plotted for decades.

As Menzies, he stays close to Nora throughout the evening, ostensibly to help her get through her duties as assistant curator of the exhibit to circulate with the guests at the gala. When he deems this duty done to the point at which seemingly no one in authority could object to either of them leaving, he dismisses her with, "now you may beat a discreet retreat home." He is sure to tell her, however: "I, unfortunately, have some work to do upstairs in my office," so that she can help him maintain this fiction later if asked (*Dance of Death*, p. 319).

The next chapter only serves to give us the set-up of the

Museum security system that Diogenes plans to victimize, and the knowledge that it is being switched over to a new one, which is why he has chosen this particular date. I am sure, given Menzies' influence in the anthropology department, that he chose the time for the Museum gala to coincide with the security system change in the Astor Hall of Diamonds. In Chapter Fifty-Two, however, readers finally see Menzies' own unveiling. Up to this moment, most first-time readers have probably perceived him as a benevolent character.

The authors follow Dr. Menzies' progress from the gala to his ultimate destination. Interestingly, as "he strolled meditatively down the long, polished corridor" that contains the anthropology curators' offices, they note that "Menzies smiled, already feeling a nostalgia for the old pile and its quaint traditions" (*Dance of Death*, p. 324). This apparent attitude is in marked contrast to Diogenes' later inner monologue about the years he has spent as Menzies in *Book of the Dead.* It is possible the two extremes in sentiment simply represent the difference between Diogenes in a good mood and Diogenes in a bad mood. I suspect in this former instance, however, he is still trying to appear as Menzies would for the benefit of any security cameras. There is also probably a distinction between Diogenes' feelings about the Museum building and the collections it houses, and his feelings about the institution's personnel, who receive the brunt of his later inner tirade. He appears to actually bear positive feelings for the former. As Diogenes travels through the Hall of Northwest Coast Indians, the authors write: "It was one of the oldest halls in the museum, a true gem of late-nineteenth-century museology, and it smelled of old cedar and smoke. Transformation masks, totem poles, slate bowls gleamed in the dark recesses. Menzies paused to inhale the air with delight" (*Dance of Death,* p. 324).

The sharper reader, who recalls Diogenes' conversation with Viola about Hatshepsut's diamond mine, may become suspicious about Menzies' true identity when he arrives at the Astor Hall of Diamonds. Others may just wonder why he appears to have security access to an area of the Museum that has nothing to do with his own field of study—unless his subspecialty is "Ostentatious Jewelry and its Cultural Implications Through the Ages." There is nothing suspicious per se about Menzies removing his contact lenses before submitting to the retinal scanner; especially at his alleged age, we might assume he wears them to enhance his vision. Although we did see him using reading glasses the first time we encountered him, at the meeting to address Margo's editorial, he might still need contacts. By this time, however, his digital stopwatch, along with the fact that he knows the security cameras are not currently operational, have tipped us off that Menzies' intentions are not entirely aboveboard. When Menzies gains access to the Astor Hall, however, he begins dismantling himself. Not only is he wearing a wig, but he divests himself of several inserts placed inside his mouth to alter the shape of his face. More readers, by this point, are guessing that he could indeed be Pendergast's evil brother, especially recalling Viola seeing him in disguise that morning. (We do not learn it cannot have been his Menzies disguise until the next volume in the trilogy.) Next, Diogenes removes the various pieces of equipment he has assembled to pull off this robbery from Menzies' canvas bag. The mylar, the dental mirrors, the weights, the calculations of timing—all are further proof of Diogenes' genius. In case we still have not figured out who Menzies really is, the authors end the chapter with the thief gloating over the prize diamond of the collection: "He could see his own eyes reflected and multiplied by the diamond's facets, creating a surreal kaleidoscope of eyes and more eyes, hundreds of them, staring every which way inside the gem. He moved the gem back and forth, from eye to eye, enjoying the spectacle. "And the strangest thing of all was that the eyes were of different colors: one hazel, the other a milky, whitish blue" (*Dance of Death,* p. 328).

Chapter Fifty-Three is a brief revisiting of the engineers involved in switching over the security system in the Astor Hall that night, basically confirming that Diogenes' plan has worked (except, of course, for one detail that will soon become important to the novel's climax). Chapter Fifty-Four returns us to Pendergast and D'Agosta, who are attempting to track Diogenes. We learn that Diogenes once more is actually hoping his brother is successful in following his trail; he has left Aloysius a message on another security camera, this one at a convenience store/gas station en route to his Long Island hideout. He holds up a paper bearing instructions in all capital letters, but his "TOMORROW, CALL AT 466 AND ASK FOR VIOLA" is a reference to the address of the New York City Morgue. He intends for this to be his "LAST COMMUNICATION" to his brother.

When Pendergast hears the news about the diamond robbery, however, he knows immediately that Diogenes is the culprit. He leaps to the conclusion that: "All these brutal killings, all these mocking notes and messages . . . nothing more than a smoke screen. A cruel, cold-blooded, sadistic smoke screen" (*Dance of Death*, p. 338). I personally believe that this is too harsh an assessment on Pendergast's part. True, Diogenes could fairly be called all of those things—brutal, cruel, cold-blooded, and sadistic. But his campaign of vengeance against Aloysius has been far more than a mere smoke screen to cover a diamond heist. That Diogenes had the opportunity to pull off such a brilliant and satisfying robbery, and use his brother's torment to distract him from being able to do anything to prevent this robbery is more like serendipity than a smoke screen. That it can appear to *be* a smoke screen is just another sharp jab of vengeance itself. Diogenes obviously does like diamonds, but the robbery of the Astor Hall is completely secondary to, and only a small part of, making Aloysius suffer. Aloysius can only think the way he does about the relationship of the murders and intended murders to the diamond theft because he does not yet remember The Event and has no true comprehension of Diogenes' desire for revenge. Diogenes, however, has already confessed to Viola how much his brother motivates him.

Chapter Fifty-Five, however, is the reader's first actual glimpse into Diogenes' own viewpoint. The first thing we learn is his colorblindness. "The world was black and white and it had no depth: it was flat, like a nightmare confection of Edwin A. Abbott" (*Dance of Death*, p. 340). He has obviously developed coping mechanisms for this disability; he manages to drive and also to shoot without much depth perception. Edwin A. Abbott is a Victorian author who published the satirical novella *Flatland* about a two-dimensional world. The quotation that follows in Diogenes' mind, *"Fie, fie how franticly I square my talk,"* comes originally from Shakespeare's *Titus Andronicus,* but is also quoted on the frontispiece of *Flatland.* These quotations, which the authors strew here and there throughout Diogenes' inner thoughts, give readers some insight into the voices that constantly run through his head. Incidentally, his head is described in this chapter as "large"; given his overall height, this is probably to be expected.

In this chapter Diogenes is driving, but the authors do not reveal whether it is the black Mercedes, the Lincoln, or another vehicle entirely. He knows when traffic lights turn green or red based on their position. Preston and Child describe the landscape he travels through, listing potato fields and houses, but concluding: "All gray, exquisite gray." I doubt Diogenes truly finds the gray exquisite; it is mental sarcasm on his part. The authors further state that "He felt neither triumph nor vindication, only a curious kind of emptiness: the sort that came with the achievement of a great thing, the completion of a long-planned work." After this odd revelation comes an even stranger one. It seems Diogenes is not completely colorblind after all. "Color did not enter his world, except fleetingly, when he least expected it, coming in from the corner of his eye like a Zen koan" (*Dance of Death,* p. 341). The Merriam-Webster online dictionary defines *koan* thus: "A paradox to be meditated upon that is used to train Zen Buddhist monks to abandon ultimate dependence on reason and to force them into gaining sudden intuitive enlightenment." A sudden unexpected glimpse of color, to Diogenes, is like that sought-after burst of enlightenment;

still, it is interesting that Diogenes goes to Zen for a simile. As already noted with the peculiar knots used to hang Duchamp, I believe Diogenes has dabbled (or more than dabbled) in every one of his brother's areas of expertise and interest, and Zen Buddhism is no exception. Yet it is the sound of the word *koan* that sets off another voice in his head, with an altered spelling of one of the stranger quotations from poetry: "*Ko ko rico, ko ko rico...*" This comes from T.S. Eliot's "The Waste Land," the poem Professor Hamilton was attempting to teach as Diogenes' poison took effect.

After overcoming this distraction, Diogenes' thoughts continue to give us information. "There was a final repository of color in his world, and it was there, in the leather satchel beside him." This is a small inconsistency; previously the satchel has been described as canvas. In any case, the statement implies a circumstance which will be confirmed later—that Diogenes can see color when he looks into colored diamonds.

The next meaningful thing we are told, after he recognizes that "a shifting of the monochromatic landscape around him" means that morning is coming, is: "Diogenes had little use for sunlight, just as he had little use for warmth or love or friendship or any of the countless things that nourished the rest of humanity" (*Dance of Death,* p. 341). The authors obviously mean human warmth rather than sheer temperature. Diogenes, like his brother, is a New Orleans native, and just a few paragraphs prior we have seen him cranking up the heat in his car against the New York winter. Yet, note the words here are "little use," and not *no use.* Readers will learn shortly that Diogenes does remember love. It is even arguable that he retains some small, strange love for Aloysius; surely only a deep love could turn into such a burning hatred.

During his drive, Diogenes reflects back upon his execution of the robbery. "He went over every last action, motion, statement, taking pleasure in satisfying himself that he had made no errors." The inclusion of "statement" in this list is further proof that his conversation with Nora as Menzies was an intricate part of his plan. Apparently, however, Diogenes is capable of contemplating his future movements simultaneously as he checks those of his past: "At the same time, he thought of the days ahead, mentally ticking off the preparations he would have to make, the tasks he'd need to perform, the great journey he would make—and *aber natürlich,* the journey's end." The German phrase imbedded in the last sentence means "but of course"; I am surprised the authors did not opt for the French *mais bien sûr* given the Pendergast ancestry.

Diogenes realizes his superiority in possessing this ability, but expresses the idea in a unique way: "Unlike the other bags of meat and blood that made up his species, Diogenes mused, he could process several disparate trains of thought simultaneously in his head" (*Dance of Death*, p. 341). Though he loves blood, I still believe he has ambiguous feelings about the animal physicality of the human body; he is dismayed that humans are at base nothing more than "bags of meat and blood." Yet, while he feels superior, he does not exempt himself from sharing this baseness—by saying "other bags of meat and blood," he is admitting that he, too, is one.

Fast on the heels of this mixture of hubris and humility comes another startling detail about Diogenes: "The Event which had robbed Diogenes of color had also stolen his ability to sleep. Full oblivion was denied him" (*Dance of Death*, p. 341). This cannot be fatal familial insomnia, the prion-based disorder that usually has its onset in middle age and causes progressive neurological problems and eventual death, despite the Italian branch of the Pendergast lineage. The "waking dreams" described by the authors a few sentences later are enough actual sleep, especially REM sleep, to maintain Diogenes' physical health. Not to mention that this lack of "full oblivion" started in his childhood, and as the result of The Event rather than genetics. The images in these dreams come from his memories, and some are undoubtedly painful to him. At least one of the "conflagrations" mentioned must be the fire that destroyed his childhood home and killed his beloved mother, and his father. Another is probably Aloysius burning his journals. Yet "Diogenes never resisted" the images, not only because it "would be futile," but because some of them came from his favorite crimes and misdeeds. The phrase "racked bodies on splintered roods," of course, evokes his crucifixion of Incitatus. "A mason jar of fresh blood" could come from childhood, or might refer back to one of the strange news items Aloysius collected, hinting that Diogenes was indeed behind the exsanguination of the University of Paris chemist.

I must admit that the item, "a hair shirt fashioned from nerve ganglia," fascinates me. It is macabre, and awakens in the reader's mind questions about whether the donor of this anatomical curiosity was human or merely mammalian, and whether or not it still breathed while the sample was taken.

But might it also signify some level of guilt feelings on Diogenes' part? Hair shirts, after all, were worn by Christian monks in medieval times to mortify the flesh and do penance for sins. Then again, it might have been something he intended for Aloysius at some point during their adolescence, feeling his brother had much for which to repent. Or perhaps he made it more recently, thinking it a fitting gift for Great-Uncle Antoine, given his pioneering work with the caudal bundle. It is also worth noting that Diogenes mentally compares "the disconnected images from his past" to "a magic-lantern show" (*Dance of Death,* p. 342). Given the nature of The Event, this is completely fitting.

After a pause to reflect upon how finishing his decades-long project of fraternal revenge would change his life, Diogenes thinks back to the days and weeks of recovery after The Event. I do not wish to go into too much detail about The Event at this time. I prefer to focus on it more fully at the point in the series when Pendergast finally unblocks his memory of it. Nevertheless, there is pertinent information in Diogenes' recollection. The authors tell us that "after *it* happened—he had lost himself in the inner maze of his mind, wandering as far from reality and sanity as it was possible to go, while even a small part of him remained prosaic, quotidian, able to interact with the outside world, whose true nature now—thanks to the Event—stood revealed to him." Preston and Child are saying that Diogenes for a time took refuge in insanity, but was able to do so while remaining seemingly normal to his parents and others. They are also saying that whatever The Event was, it forever changed his view of the world in which he lived.

After a time, however, Diogenes lost his ability to take shelter along the rambling paths of insanity. Preston and Child tell us: "So he came back, but he was like a diver who had gone too deep, run out of air, and rushed to the surface only to be racked by the bends." They also tell us: "That was the worst moment of all." Apparently, it was at this same moment that Diogenes realized he could reclaim a sense of purpose in planning and carrying out a fitting punishment for the person he blamed for The Event: his brother, Aloysius.

As Diogenes reflects upon this, he allows readers access to the nature of the world that The Event left him with: "It was a world of pain and evil and cruelty, walked on by vile creatures of piss and excrement and bile" (*Dance of Death,* p. 342). Whatever this Event has been, it has robbed Diogenes of any belief in humanity possessing anything of a higher nature, anything immortal such as a soul to outlive the physical and all too corruptible body. It has reduced all people in his eyes, even himself, to their basest elements and grossest functions. The one person who might have, over time, helped him overcome this bleak and horrible perspective only reinforced it by perishing in a fire.

The plot to exact revenge upon his brother, "toward which he had bent all his intellect, made such a world *just* bearable," the authors tell us. Whenever that world threatened to overcome Diogenes, he took refuge in "certain temporary pastimes" (*Dance of Death,* pp. 342-343), probably animal torture and journal-writing, until he felt ready to carry on with his complex plans. Preston and Child go on to state: "The emotion that sustained him some might call hatred, but for him it was the mead that nourished him." Note that they, nor

Diogenes himself, are not counting themselves among that "some."

After this reflection, readers learn that Dr. Menzies is *not* Diogenes' only alter-ego: "He found he could live not merely a double life or a triple life, but in fact could assume the very personalities and lives of half a dozen invented people, in several different countries, as the needs of his work of art required." Further, "some of the personalities he had assumed years, even decades before" (*Dance of Death*, p. 343). Presumably Diogenes started one or two not long after he faked his death in Canterbury.

As Diogenes realizes morning is growing closer, he gloats a little, feeling certain that his brother has not been enjoying a good night's sleep—either from agonizing over what will be done to Viola, or from trying to prevent it. "Nor would Aloysius sleep well again: ever" (*Dance of Death*, p. 343). Note that Diogenes intends his brother to suffer one of the consequences The Event has had for himself—sleep disturbances.

Then the authors choose to confirm what they have already hinted at: "For only through the intense, brilliant refracted light issued by a deeply colored diamond could Diogenes escape, if only for a moment, his black-and-white prison. Only then could he recapture that faintest and most sought-after of his memories—the essence of color" (*Dance of Death*, p. 343). The use of the word "prison" correlates once more with Diogenes' great plan. He feels Aloysius has condemned him to the metaphorical prison of colorblindness; the fruition of his vengeance will see his older brother at least threatened with (if not in fact incarcerated) actual imprisonment. As might be expected, the color Diogenes most longs to see is red, but he is waiting until he returns to his Long Island lair to examine his primary prize, Lucifer's Heart.

After he has looked into the red diamond at his leisure, he intends to perform what he feels is the fitting end to his vengeance—killing Viola. When it comes to the experience of torturing her, it is either her personality and spirit, or her value in the eyes of Aloysius—or possibly the combination—that make her "a *grand cru* wine that merited being taken up from the cellar, brought to room temperature, uncorked, and allowed to breathe—before being enjoyed, one exquisite sip after another, until nothing was left" (*Dance of Death,* p. 344). The reasons "she had to suffer," however, stem solely from her relationship with Aloysius. "Not for her sake, but for the marks it would leave on her body." Diogenes believes that "no one would be better able to interpret those marks than Aloysius." This tells us that he judges his elder brother's knowledge of forensics to be if not superior to his own, then at least superior to any other expert's that the City of New York would have to offer. More importantly, however, the marks "would induce a suffering in ... [Aloysius] equal to, if not exceeding, the pain they caused the body's owner" (*Dance of Death*, p. 344). Yet, though he seems adamant that "she had to suffer," Diogenes has already prepared the instruments and tools he intends to use on her, and they are "honed, and stropped to their sharpest edges." If he truly wanted to maximize Viola's suffering, would he not rather leave them dull? Would not Aloysius recognize that the marks on Viola's body had come from intentionally unsharpened weapons? Again, Diogenes is showing a little weakness when it comes to physically harming women.

Though Diogenes already has it in mind to evoke Great-Uncle Comstock's gruesome suicide with Viola's murder, he cannot resist adding his own elements of art to his contemplation of the act. The Carvaggio painting *Judith and Holofernes* comes into his thoughts. "That had always been his favorite painting of Caravaggio's. He'd stood in front of it for hours, at the Galleria Nazionale d'Arte Antica in Rome, rapt in admiration" (*Dance of Death,* p. 344). Many painters over the ages have taken the subject of Judith and Holofernes, from the apocryphal *Book of Judith,* included in the Catholic Bible but not the Protestant. The *Book of Judith* tells the story of a Hebrew widow who abandons her mourning clothes and uses all of her beauty to seduce an attacking general named Holofernes who intends to destroy her people. She gets him drunk and beheads him. Interestingly, in one of the book's verses, it describes her as removing his head with two strokes of a sword—much as Diogenes intends to do to Viola in memory of Comstock Pendergast. Certainly, having gone to Catholic school, Diogenes is aware of this detail from the Apocrypha, and perhaps this commonality helps bring the Carvaggio painting to his mind. He even considers showing Viola a reproduction of the painting "before he got to work. Judith and Holofernes. With the roles reversed, of course, and the addition of a pewter bleeding bowl so that none of the precious nectar would be lost..." (*Dance of Death,* p. 344). In this instance, of course, Diogenes is pondering increasing Viola's suffering by increasing her level of anticipatory fear.

This is not something he can share with Aloysius unless he includes photographs, or better yet, video with sound.

That speculation is moot, because the perspective soon switches to Viola as she hears Diogenes arrive back at the house on Long Island. "He had made it a point to arrive just at dawn. In time for the execution." With Viola, readers listen to the sounds Diogenes makes, moving through the house. We know, though she does not, that he is preparing to look at Lucifer's Heart before killing her. "Then came a strange and terrible sound: a low, agonized keening, almost like the warning moan of a cat. It rose and fell in singsong fashion before suddenly ascending in volume to become a shriek of pure, undistilled, absolute anguish. It was inhuman, it was the shriek of the living dead, it was the most horrifying sound she had ever heard—and it came *from him*" (*Dance of Death,* p. 346).

Readers learn nothing about Diogenes in the next few chapters except for a hint in Chapter Fifty-Seven, when the Museum's director tells a press conference that "Lucifer's Heart *was not among the diamonds stolen*" (*Dance of Death,* p. 357). Coupling this with the horrible sounds Viola heard coming from him, and knowing that Diogenes certainly believed he had stolen Lucifer's Heart, the intelligent reader can quickly deduce that Diogenes has discovered whatever he has stolen is *not* the diamond he has long coveted. Further, he is extremely upset by this. As Pendergast puts it in Chapter Fifty-Eight, "Diogenes finally made a mistake" (*Dance of Death,* p. 361). All we learn in Chapter Sixty with regard to Diogenes is that Pendergast is hoping to be able to trade the real diamond for Viola's life.

Chapter Sixty-Two does not necessarily tell readers anything about Diogenes either, unless when diamond expert George Kaplan is contemplating the history of Lucifer's Heart, the authors are hinting that Pendergast's younger brother already has stones related to it. One cannot be certain one way or the other; though Kaplan reflects that the rough stone from which Lucifer's Heart was cut "had been found by an alluvial digger in the Congo in the early 1930s" (*Dance of Death,* p. 382), Preston and Child are vague about exactly when it was cut into its famous form by Arens. Whenever this happened, around the same time the diamond cutter "sold the dozen or so much smaller stones cut from the same rough for what was rumored to be an astonishing sum, but, strangely enough, none of the stones had ever resurfaced on the market." The authors go on to state that "Kaplan assumed they had been made into a single, spectacular piece of jewelry, which remained with the original owner, who wished to keep her identity secret" (*Dance of Death,* p. 384). Depending on the date all of this happened, however, it is possible that Diogenes acquired the stones himself, either separately or in the form of the one piece of jewelry Kaplan postulates. If he does possess them, it is probable he stole them as well, although with his resources it is within the realm of possibility that he actually bought all or some of them.

It is not until Chapter Sixty-Four that we hear from Diogenes again. First, however, Pendergast accurately predicts his actions. As Pendergast and D'Agosta listen to the news reports of Pendergast's own theft of the actual Lucifer's Heart from the insurance company holding it, D'Agosta asks how he can be sure that "Diogenes will hear the news?"

Pendergast replies: "He'll hear it. For once, he's at a loss. He didn't get the diamond. He'll be in agony, on edge—listening, waiting, thinking. And once he learns what's happened, there will be only one course of action available to him" (*Dance of Death,* p. 399). In continued conversation with D'Agosta, Pendergast expresses his certainty that his brother will know he is the one who has the diamond. I suppose this is logical; though both Pendergasts appear to believe that Diogenes is the one with the superior intellect, Diogenes would conclude that Aloysius would be the only other person able to pull off such a daring heist. Not to mention he would know Aloysius possesses an extremely urgent motive to attempt such a thing. Yet even so, there is evidence of an odd, brotherly bond in this level of confidence, especially when Aloysius has so recently admitted that Diogenes has fooled him so often during the course of this case.

True to Pendergast's expectations, Diogenes calls. Of course he has no trouble obtaining Aloysius's cell number; that is the proverbial piece of cake for a genius like himself. Diogenes speaks first, offering his habitual Latin salutation. Aloysius has trouble getting any words out, and Diogenes interprets this as "disapproving silence," demanding: "Is that any way to greet a long-lost brother?" (*Dance of Death,* p. 399). When Pendergast manages to answer, "I am here," Diogenes does not seem particularly satisfied with this response, either. "You're *there!*" he echoes, voice dripping with sarcasm. "And how honored I am to be graced with your presence. It almost makes up for the vile experience of being forced to call you" (*Dance of Death,* pp. 399-400). Despite everything he has done to Aloysius, and intended to do to him, Diogenes still feels like the injured party. This is an indication of how deeply and adversely The Event has affected him, and of how badly he feels Aloysius betrayed him in it.

Diogenes leaves off mocking his brother long enough to ascertain that Aloysius has indeed stolen Lucifer's Heart. Then he asks him why. When Aloysius counters "You know why," Diogenes' response is odd. "There was a silence at the other end of the phone," the authors tell us, "then a slow exhalation of breath." Then Diogenes says, "Brother, brother, brother..." (*Dance of Death,* p. 400). The lack of description surrounding this remark is interesting. The authors do not give us an adverb—he does not say it wearily, or softly, he does not sigh the words. The "slow exhalation of breath" beforehand, after a silence, makes me wonder what words he has bitten off, what he has thought better of expressing. I suspect he is struggling with envy over the fact that Aloysius has managed to score the prize he has missed. Yet I also suspect the repeated word claiming kinship holds an element of pity. In caring for Viola, his brother is showing a vulnerability to which Diogenes believes himself immune. He also assumes (correctly, given Aloysius's response) that it will irk Pendergast to be reminded that they are close kindred. Indeed, Aloysius protests, "I am no brother of yours."

Diogenes, however, will not let Aloysius deny him that easily. "Ah, but that's where you're wrong. We *are* brothers, whether we like it or not. And that relationship defines who we are. You know that, don't you, Aloysius?" This is as at once an astute observation on Diogenes' part (the pair really do have a great deal in common) and an attempt to get Aloysius to acknowledge their relationship. On the one hand,

Diogenes is trying to get his brother to admit his responsibility for The Event. On the other, he is beginning to take a stab at getting Aloysius to eventually believe the case that Captain Hayward is making against him—that he has a multiple personality disorder, and that Diogenes is merely a facet of himself, of which he remains unconscious. I do not think Diogenes actually believes there is much actual chance of this happening. I am not even sure he wishes it to happen, because he might well prefer Aloysius remain fully cognizant of what has been done to him. Then again, to make his brother mentally ill, when he feels Aloysius caused his own mental illness through The Event, would surely hold some appeal for Diogenes. In any case, Diogenes is probably experimenting with the possibility, and continues to scatter the seeds of it during his next exchange with Pendergast.

Pendergast responds to Diogenes' somewhat rhetorical question about kinship with insult: "I know that you're a sick man desperately in need of help." Diogenes does not deny it: "True: I am sick. No one recovers from the disease of being born." He turns it back on Pendergast, however: "But when you get down to it, we're all sick, *you* more than most. Yes, we *are* brothers—in sickness as well as evil" (*Dance of Death,* p. 400). Again, he is being accusatory about The Event. Pendergast must be sick and evil to have done what he did to his own little brother. They are now alike because Pendergast *made* Diogenes sick and evil, too, by putting him through The Event. Yet, of course, Diogenes is also hinting that Pendergast might just have done the crimes he has set him up for, and be hallucinating the entire phone call. He probably realizes, even before D'Agosta's later outburst, that

Pendergast has his friend from the NYPD accompanying him; if Diogenes decides he truly wants to make his brother believe the frame-up, he can always kill the witness later.

Pendergast continues to be sparing with his words, so Diogenes volunteers to "lead the discussion." He congratulates his brother with "a big fat bravo for pulling off in one afternoon, what I took years to plan—and ultimately failed to accomplish" (*Dance of Death,* p. 400). He even claps slowly—softly, but audible over the phone. No doubt Diogenes is actually nettled at Aloysius's succeeding where he did not, but he acknowledges the achievement. His use of language is interesting here. Viola has just recently upbraided him for sounding pompous, yet compared with his brother, Diogenes (at least in this segment) is more apt to blend the elegant with the colloquial in his speech. The "bravo" is what one would expect from a Pendergast, but it is difficult to imagine Aloysius calling it "fat." Also, Diogenes uses the more criminally appropriate phrase "pull off," where his brother probably would have opted for "achieve." At this point in the series, Diogenes is more flexible in his speech patterns, although Aloysius does loosen up later after more years of both emotional turmoil and association with Vincent D'Agosta.

Diogenes correctly guesses that his brother wishes to trade Lucifer's Heart for Viola. When Pendergast insists on knowing whether or not Viola is still alive, Diogenes "let[s] the silence draw out" before admitting that she is. Pendergast's threat to "hunt you to the ends of the earth" if Diogenes harms Viola produces a fascinating response— Diogenes changes the subject to Constance. "But while we're on the subject of women, let's talk a little bit about this young thing you've kept cloistered in the mansion of our late lamented ancestor. If indeed she is 'young,' which I'm beginning to doubt. I find myself most curious about her. Her *in particular,* in fact. I sense that what one sees on the surface is what one sees of an iceberg: the merest fraction. There are hidden facets to her, mirrors within mirrors. And at a fundamental level, I sense that something in her is *broken*" (*Dance of Death,* pp. 400-401). In this single paragraph, Preston and Child have set up a crucial aspect of the third book in the Diogenes Trilogy before the second book has concluded.

On one level, Diogenes is testing Aloysius to see if his older brother even cares about Constance. And Pendergast rises to his baiting, threatening him once more. Of course, Diogenes is also playing with his brother, delaying any real action on returning Viola by distracting him with the seeming red herring of Constance. On yet another level, Diogenes is cutting his losses. Though of course he would like to double-cross his brother and both wind up with the diamond *and* kill Viola, he is willing to give her up to get the real Lucifer's Heart. But he realizes there might be another woman he can use to harm his brother, and he wants to be sure she matters to him.

I believe, however, there is also genuine interest and curiosity on Diogenes' part. Yes, one of the points of interest is that he believes Constance is *"broken"* and that he can exploit this. Diogenes, too, is broken "at a fundamental level." Is it not possible that he might seek a kindred spirit? That he uses the term "facets" in describing Constance in the wake of a diamond heist and in the midst of trying to obtain the prize he most sought for is telling. I think it indicates he is actually attracted to her. It will be important to keep these words of Diogenes in mind when discussing his letter to Constance in *The Book of the Dead*.

When Pendergast threatens Diogenes if he goes anywhere near Constance, his younger brother cuts him off. "Do what? Kill me? Then my blood would be on your hands—more than it already is." Diogenes goes on to add that the blood of the four people he himself has murdered (at this point he still believes Margo to be dead, too) is on Aloysius's hands as well, that Aloysius is responsible for all of it. "You know it," says Diogenes. "You made me what I am" (*Dance of Death*, p. 401). This is a strong indication that Diogenes, at least, believes he would have had as good a chance at overcoming the hereditary Pendergast tendency towards madness as any other family member had he not been subjected to The Event. I do not think Diogenes is trying to make his brother feel guilty over something that time would have proven to be a moot point. Diogenes has no idea that Aloysius has suppressed not only any valid memory of The Event, but especially his own role in it. From anything Diogenes has ever seen or heard from Aloyius, he can only conclude that his older brother has done him a grievous injury and never even deigned to acknowledge it. It is this acknowledgment that Diogenes craves, and yet, because Aloysius never gave it to him in the past, he has no real reason to believe he will *ever* have it from him.

Still, Diogenes cannot resist trying to obtain it, or at least cannot resist complaining to Aloysius about how he wronged him. When Pendergast, still heavily in denial, states, "I made you nothing," Diogenes counters: "Well said! *Well said!*" This is ironic when we recall Pendergast's conversation with Dr. Krasner, in which he imagines Diogenes calling him a nonentity. But can Diogenes truly believe he is nothing? As we have noted, he has some feelings of superiority towards people of more average intelligence. Yet it is easy to imagine him wondering what he might have become had The Event never happened. It is not so much that The Event robbed him of ability, but that it robbed him of motive. Why become a brilliant surgeon, for instance, trying to preserve the lives of people who are only bags of blood and guts destined for death and decay anyway? "A dry, almost dessicated laugh came over the speaker," the authors tell us. To me, there is something pitiful in it.

Understandably more concerned with Viola than with whatever Diogenes is getting at, Pendergast dismisses it with, "Let's get to it." Diogenes, however, either is not ready to let go of his grievance or is not ready to soothe his brother's suspense about Viola—or, most likely, feels a blend of the two motivations. Diogenes protests Pendergast's attempt to change the subject, asking, "Don't you want to talk about how *utterly* and *completely* responsible you are for all this? Ask any family shrink," Diogenes concludes, "they'll tell you how important it is that we talk it out. *Frater*" (*Dance of Death,* p. 401). Again, Diogenes is mingling the use of the colloquial slang "shrink" with calling Aloysius by the Latin word for "brother." He is truly insistent upon Pendergast acknowledging his role in The Event, but it is also possible that this line of conversation could reinforce the possibility of

Aloysius eventually accepting Diogenes' frame-up job as reality. Pendergast certainly *would* be responsible, if he had re-created a dead brother as an alternate personality, and killed in his guise. Of course, returning Viola safely to Pendergast would ruin any chance of convincing him of this, because she would be able to attest to Diogenes' existence.

It is any reader's guess where this discussion might have gone if D'Agosta hadn't lost all patience at this moment and threatened to "take a sledgehammer to the diamond and mail you the dust." Though Diogenes is concerned when he hears "a resounding crash" over the phone, and bids D'Agosta be careful in a voice that is "suddenly high and panicked," he remains somewhat defiant. He continues to speak when D'Agosta has told him to "shut the hell up," and even comes up quickly with a witty insult to his brother's sidekick: "Stupidity is an elemental force, and I respect it" (*Dance of Death,* p. 401). If Diogenes does not actually respect D'Agosta, he does at least pay him the ultimate compliment by stealing his idea about the sledgehammer later in the trilogy.

Nevertheless, from this point Diogenes settles down to the business of the exchange. He comes up with a plan that meets Pendergast's requirements and satisfies Pendergast that he cannot cheat him. What we learn from the plan—to meet at a railway turntable known as the Iron Clock—confirms that Diogenes probably has as vast a knowledge of underground Manhattan as his elder brother. In addition to an awareness of hidden passages to enter the house at 891 Riverside Drive, Diogenes can add a mental map of railroad tunnels. When he assures his elder brother that "nothing's going to go wrong," he adds: "I want my diamond, and you want your Viola da Gamba" (*Dance of Death,* pp. 402-403). In referring to her this way, Diogenes is being at once whimsical and vulgar in an oddly classy fashion. A viola da gamba is a musical instrument, larger than a violin, smaller than a cello. It literally means "leg viol" in Spanish, and the instrument is played by placing it between one's legs.

The next chapter, Sixty-Five, brings us back to Diogenes' mind. The shock of finding he had only stolen a copy of Lucifer's Heart, or the strain of actually speaking to his brother over the phone, or the cumulative effects of both have apparently taken a toll on him. He "stared at the cell phone … for a long time" after the conversation. Yet, the authors tell us that "the only indication of the strong emotion running through him was a faint twitching of his left little finger." They also note that "a mottled patch of gray had appeared on his left cheek" and that his milky blue eye was probably "looking deader than usual." These are possibly indications of vascular and nerve damage caused by The Event; normally, presumably after much practice and a great force of will, Diogenes can control the twitching, at least. Preston and Child also give us an interesting factoid about Diogenes in this paragraph when they note that he only looks in mirrors "when applying a disguise" (*Dance of Death*, p. 404). Are the authors hinting at a lack of vanity about his appearance, or is it a dislike of looking at his sightless eye?

Next, Diogenes fills a syringe from a small vial, and at first readers may think he is about to cope with the situation by using an intravenous drug. After consideration, he increases the amount he has drawn out, but when he caps the needle and puts the syringe "in his suit pocket," we realize it is for Viola. He obviously wants to err on the side of caution in keeping her sedated en route to the exchange. It is interesting to note that Diogenes is using the old-fashioned "glass and steel" needle and syringe, rather than the disposable safety kind, even though the latter were already prevalent when the book was written. He does have a separate plastic needle cap, presumably so he does not accidentally sedate or poison himself, but Diogenes obviously has no pangs of conscience over the possibility of transferring blood-borne pathogens such as HIV between his victims. Then again, he may well be utterly meticulous in sterilizing his needles and syringes between uses.

Having readied Viola's prescription, Diogenes decides to consult his tarot cards, which are conveniently "sitting on the edge of the table." Preston and Child tell us that he prefers the Albano-Waite deck, which is revealing. The web site *Aeclectic Tarot* notes that this deck "is loudly coloured, sometimes garishly so." I feel his partiality for the Albano-Waite, then, is another example of Diogenes trying to keep others from knowing of his colorblindness. It is interesting, too, that this is the personal deck he keeps for himself, rather than the one he used to send messages to Aloysius. He could have annoyed his brother with their very garishness, but instead, he keeps them for himself. He likes that they are brightly colored, even though he cannot see the colors himself.

After shuffling, Diogenes lays out a simple three-card spread and turns over the first one. It is the High Priestess, and when it shows in an upright position, "it can show a personal desire for guidance and knowledge, particularly if you need to make a major decision," according to Liz Dean in *The Art of Tarot: A Complete Guide to Using Tarot Cards and Their Meanings.* Fitting, as far as Diogenes is concerned. He next turns over the Five of Cups, also in an upright position. This supposedly heralds "unhappiness in a relationship," and Dean advises someone who turns over this card to "focus on what remains, rather than dwell on what you have lost." This does not please Diogenes; he "drew in his breath sharply" and "hesitated a moment" before turning over the next card. This proves to be the Ace of Swords, in an upside-down position. In this reversed position, "a sense of frustration and loss may surround this card," Dean writes, because it "can predict delays to your schemes."

Apparently, the entire reading rattles Diogenes. His hand shakes as he raises the last card and tears it apart, "and scatter(s) the pieces" (*Dance of Death,* p. 405). From this point, he seeks refuge in the diamonds he *has* succeeded in stealing. "Now his restless gaze moved to the black velvet cloth, laid out and rolled up at the edges, on which lay 488 diamonds, almost all of them deeply colored," the authors tell us. "As he stared at the diamonds, his agitation began to ease." Diogenes chooses a huge, blue, 33-carat diamond, whimsically named the "Queen of Narnia" by Preston and Child in homage to C. S. Lewis, to begin his second augury.

When Diogenes looks into the Queen of Narnia, "it was like kicking open a door just a crack and catching a glimpse of a magic world beyond, a world of color and life, a *real* world— so different from this false, flat world of gray mundanity." The effect on him is so calming that "his mind loosened in its prison and began to ramble down long-forgotten alleys of memory" (*Dance of Death,* p. 405). The first memory the authors show us is of Diogenes'--and Aloysius's—mother, who wore a lot of diamonds, and with whom Diogenes has come to associate the precious gems he values so much. To Diogenes, even "her voice was like a diamond, pure and cool, and she was singing a song to him in French." Amazingly, Diogenes remembers this, although he was only two years old. Two years old and already deeply sensitive to music, for he "nevertheless was crying, not from sorrow, but from the aching beauty of his mother's voice" (*Dance of Death,* p. 406). The voice in Diogenes' head that interrupts this memory is quoting the D. H. Lawrence poem, "Piano." Although we cannot conclude absolutely that he shares its sentiment of *"the heart of me weeps to belong,"* why else would Preston and Child choose this quotation if they did not wish to imply this? Why would these be the words that invade Diogenes' mind if they do not resonate with his emotions?

If that memory is not enough to inspire some empathy for Diogenes, his mind shifts to another after being interrupted by the D. H. Lawrence quotation. It is this memory, of the Pendergasts' ancestral home in New Orleans as seen through the eyes of the child Diogenes, that more than anything else convinces me that he started out life as a relatively normal human being. Of course, he was born a Pendergast, and he was both genetically endowed with genius and well educated—but he was not born mad, or born destined to become a killer. In this memory of his home, he walks "down long corridors and past mysterious rooms." Though some of the rooms had "been shut up for ages," if Diogenes opened them he "would always find something exciting, something wondrous and strange." The list of possibilities the authors provide for us includes "dark paintings of women in white and men with dead eyes," as well as "panpipes made of bone, a monkey's paw edged in silver, a brass Spanish stirrup, a snarling jaguar head, [or] the wrapped foot of an Egyptian mummy." Diogenes' attitude towards these exotic objects is that of any bright child fortunate enough to grow up in such rich surroundings. There is no hint of unhealthy obsession with any of them; indeed, his memory includes the possibility of finding some of them frightening. He recalls "there was always his mother to flee to, with her warmth and her soft voice and her diamonds" (*Dance of Death,* p. 406).

In remembering the diamonds, Diogenes has the thought: "The diamonds were here, they were alive, they never changed, never faded, never died. They would remain, beautiful and immutable, for all time." He then notes the contrast: "How different from the fickle vicissitudes of the flesh" (*Dance of Death,* p. 406). Diogenes' mother is dead, but her diamonds—and others like them—remain. In his desire for diamonds, Diogenes is admitting his longing for comfort and constancy, for something he can count on— something he never really had for long in any of his family members.

Diogenes was sane as a young child, but he definitely is *not* sane at the time *Dance of Death* takes place. I am fairly certain that his belief "there were special vibrations from a diamond that reached the deepest levels of his spirit" and that "the gemstones spoke to him, they whispered to him, they gave him strength and wisdom," is a product of the brain damage he suffered in The Event. Though otherwise normal people can have synesthesia—the experience of two disparate senses mingled together so that, for instance, colors seem to have shapes, or sounds can be smelled—this effect might well be enhanced with damage to the pre-frontal cortex like that Diogenes suffered. In any case, he chose to consult the Queen of Narnia after his tarot cards displeased him because "each gemstone had a different voice, and he had picked this stone for its particular wisdom." Not only does Diogenes expect the diamond to talk to him, but he is willing to coax it to do so, "murmuring to the gemstone, beseeching it to speak" (*Dance of Death*, p. 406). According to Preston and Child, the Queen of Narnia obliges Diogenes: "a whispery answer came back like an echo of an echo, half heard in a waking dream" (*Dance of Death*, p. 407). Whatever it says, it satisfies Diogenes, and the perspective, mid-chapter, switches to Viola.

She perceives his knock on the door of her prison to be "polite," and the words that follow it most closely are indeed those of a gentleman. Diogenes tells her he "should like to come in," and though he is mindful of his own safety and cautious, about the possibility of attack or escape, he includes the word "please" in his request that she move to the side of the room furthest from the door. Yet, presumably, in all of his preoccupation, the gentleman has neglected to feed his prisoner. From the way Preston and Child have phrased Viola's viewpoint of this impending encounter, it appears that she has not seen or spoken with Diogenes since he told her of his intent to kill her at dawn. That dawn has passed, and "already, night was coming on." To be fair, it is likely that

Diogenes' emotional roller coaster has prevented him from eating anything, either.

When Diogenes opens the door to reveal himself in her doorway, Viola notices right away that "he looked different." She observes he is "slightly disheveled." Apparently even the Queen of Narnia has not soothed him sufficiently, for his face is still "mottled." Further, Diogenes' cravat is "askew," and "his ginger hair a little ruffled" (*Dance of Death,* p. 407). As to when, exactly, he was tugging at his cravat and unconsciously pushing his fingers through his hair, my money is on it having been while on the phone with his brother.

Yet, though he has decided to return Viola to Pendergast, he is determined to wound her first, and wound her in a way that will leave no physical trace his brother could use as an excuse to renege on their bargain. I believe Diogenes' highest hope in this exchange of words with Viola is to sow the seeds of eventual suicide. Even enough self-doubt to ruin her relationship with Aloysius would please him, although Diogenes' plans are still in place to render the point moot by framing his brother for crimes that will bring a sentence of life in prison at the very least, with execution a high probability.

Diogenes either begins the process with a disarming compliment, or has it surprised out of him by Viola's fortitude. He admits that he is "beginning to see what [Aloysius] found so fascinating" about her. He calls her "beautiful and intelligent," and "spirited." It is his perception that she has "no fear," however, that amazes him. Yet he cannot resist one last attempt to scare her, before getting down to the more subtle psychology. Diogenes tells her: "You *should* be afraid."

When Viola retorts that he is "mad," Diogenes gives readers further insight into his philosophy, saying that if that is the case it makes him "like God." His reasoning is that if God exists, "He is Himself mad." Only a mad God, Diogenes believes, would have let something like The Event happen to a child as young as he was at the time. Only a mad God would have created a man like Comstock Pendergast in his own image, to build torture boxes for human beings—and thus perpetuate the madness.

Diogenes quickly returns, however, to trying to induce a proper state of fear in Viola. He asks her whether she is "brave or stupid," or does she "merely lack the imagination to picture your own death?" (*Dance of Death,* p. 407). He goes on to assure her: "*I* can imagine it, *have* imagined it, so very clearly. When I look at you, I see a bag filled with blood, bones, viscera, and meat, held in by the most fragile and vulnerable covering, so easily punctured, so facilely ripped or torn. I have to admit, I was looking forward to it" (*Dance of Death,* pp. 407-408). Indeed, Diogenes *had* been looking forward to it, yet at the same time, he must be thinking only a mad God would put souls into such vulnerable and corruptible vehicles. He is satisfied, however, when he looks more intently at her after this last speech. He can see that he has "finally" created the "note of fear" he sought.

This time, when Viola asks what he wants, he reveals with a magician-like gesture that he has a diamond in his hand. He simply states its name: "Ultima Thule." Diogenes eventually tells us this is "Latin for the 'Uttermost Thule,' the land of perpetual ice." As he informs her that it reminds him of her, he tosses it to her. "A little *going away* gift," he says. Apparently he is trying to maintain her state of unease, because the authors note that the emphasis he puts on "going away" gives Viola "an ugly feeling."

She insists she does not want any kind of gift from Diogenes, yet for the moment, she still holds onto the diamond. Diognes replies: "Oh, but it's *so* apt," and goes on to discuss diamond grading. The gem he has given to her has 22 carats. It is flawless and its color grade is D. "D is given to a diamond utterly without color," Diogenes tells Viola. "It is considered by those with no imagination to be a desirable trait." He then reveals to her how deeply he has researched her, by telling her about her life—right down to a list of her romantic relationships that ranges from "an Oxford professor to a Hollywood actor to a famous pianist—even an Italian soccer player" (*Dance of Death,* p. 408). Diogenes exclaims, "How others must envy you!" before closing in for the psychological kill. "None of your relationships have worked out," he observes. He posits that she has blamed it on the men involved, but asks her: "When will it occur to you, Viola, that the fault lies in yourself?"

Diogenes uses Ultima Thule as a simile to drive his insults home. Like the diamond, Viola is to his mind "flawless, brilliant, perfect, and utterly without color." He elaborates: "All your sad attempts to appear exciting, unconventional, are just that—sad attempts." To Diogenes, a colorless diamond like Ultima Thule has no real value; it "is in reality dead common. Like you," he tells Viola. He adds that she is "unloved and unloving," and calls her "so desperate for love that you fly halfway around the world in response to a letter from a man you met only once!"

Preston and Child tell us that Diogenes does damage with his calculated attack. To Viola, "his words felt like one physical blow after another, each one finding its mark. This time she had no answer." Diogenes is not finished, however. After another invocation of "Ultima Thule, the land of perpetual ice," he concludes "There's no love within you, and there'll be no love for you. Barrenness is your fate." For Diogenes, this is not just a prediction based on what he has learned about Viola. It is also something he has worked to make true, by framing Viola's most recent romantic interest as a serial killer.

He has finally pushed her past self-doubt and back into anger, and she throws Ultima Thule back at him. Though Diogenes hopes his insinuations will return in full force when she is alone and his brother is awaiting execution, in the present moment he takes umbrage at her calling the diamond a "bit of glass." He tells her what he did the night before, whipping out a newspaper clipping about the robbery from the *New York Times.* There is something oddly straightforward and disarming in the way Diogenes tells Viola: "It is a crime I've been planning for many years. I created a new identity to pull it off. And you helped me do it. That's why I wanted to give you that stone" (*Dance of Death,* p. 409). Of course, he may be trying to make her feel guilt for her inadvertent role in the heist. In another way, though, he is being fair. Not only is he going to let her live (unless she dwells too much on his words about her lack of real worth), but he is giving her a valuable gemstone to help make up for everything he has put her through. He is admitting a certain gratitude towards her. Although, too, Diogenes is honest when he says he wanted her to have "a little keepsake, a memento, since we shall part, never to see each other in this world again" (*Dance of Death,* p. 410), partially because he knows such a "memento" would only hold negative associations for Viola. At this point, he believes the part about never seeing her again. He believes he will have his red diamond and his perfect revenge on Aloysius, and he plans on disappearing and leading the rest of his life as he pleases. I suppose it could be said that even given the way *Dance of Death* ends, Diogenes is still half-right; even if Viola technically does see him again, she does not know it is Diogenes at whom she is looking and with whom she is interacting.

When Diogenes finally moves to drug Viola, he calls her "Ice Princess" before he injects her. Though she attempts once more to escape, trying to run past him to the doorway, she finds "somehow he had anticipated it, whirling and leaping toward her with the speed of a cat." Like Pendergast, Diogenes too is cat-like. Again, Preston and Child emphasize his strength, as Viola feels "a shockingly powerful arm, tight as a steel cable, whip around her neck" (*Dance of Death,* p. 410). Diogenes is able, of course, to jab her with the syringe he has in his pocket, and she quickly loses consciousness.

Diogenes' next and final appearance in *Dance of Death* is technically not an "appearance" at all. Pendergast and D'Agosta do not actually see him, they just hear his voice. Diogenes has staged the exchange of Viola for Lucifer's Heart in such a way that he can see all of the other participants from an area where he remains hidden. An underground railway turntable with twelve tunnels is the setting, and no one can be certain in which tunnel he has chosen to lurk. When he speaks, his voice echoes so that he cannot be located by sound, either. I am sure he deliberately chose such conditions, to make his voice more frightening, to make himself seem more mysterious. Yet, even before Pendergast tricks him, Diogenes winds up revealing a great deal about himself.

He greets Aloysius with his traditional Latin: *"Ave, frater!"* (*Dance of Death,* p. 419). Diogenes asks his brother to move more fully into the dim light that helps distinguish the center turntable area from the surrounding tunnels, but he cannot resist taunting him while he seemingly has the upper hand. "Let's have a look at that pretty face of yours," he says. Soon enough, however, Diogenes begins betraying his actual state of neediness. When he asks if Pendergast has brought Lucifer's Heart, the authors tell us: "The tone was leering, almost a snarl; yet there was a curious hunger in it." Once Aloysius holds up the red diamond, Diogenes emits "a sharp intake of breath, like the crack of a whip" (*Dance of Death,* p. 420).

After brushing off Pendergast's first demand to bring out Viola, Diogenes instructs him to place the diamond in a small box he has placed in a hole at the center of the turntable. Pendergast does so, but then aims his pistol at it, reiterating his request to see Viola. Though this startles Diogenes, he maintains control of the situation for the time being, insisting his expert be allowed to examine the stone to verify its authenticity. When Pendergast declares the stone "is real,"

Diogenes counters: "I trusted you once, long ago. Remember? Look where it got me." This observation by Diogenes is followed by "a strange sigh, almost like a moan" (*Dance of Death,* p. 420). Diogenes is not only trying yet again to get Pendergast to acknowledge The Event, he is still suffering from it emotionally. I am not suggesting that Diogenes is justified in the things he has done in the pursuit of revenge, just that his pain is real. True, it is his own fault that both D'Agosta and Aloysius are too focused on Viola's safety to try to comprehend his accusations, but nevertheless, they remain oblivious (at least for the moment) of the point Diogenes is attempting to make.

Diogenes has abducted the same diamond expert that Pendergast and D'Agosta did in order to check the authenticity of the stone his brother has brought. He threatens Mr. Kaplan, but ultimately keeps his word to let him return to his "dimpled lunatics" (*Dance of Death,* p. 421). It seems to me, aside from the deceit inherent in assuming a disguised alter-ego, and aside from Viola's unplanned reprieve after he has told her he would kill her, the only person Diogenes actually lies to is Aloysius. It may well be that he feels more justified in deceiving his brother, because he feels his brother deceived him during the course of The Event. (Constance, in *Book of the Dead,* is a more complicated case, to be discussed in its time.)

Diogenes is—rightfully—so suspicious of his brother's intent to deceive him that he warns him back and even shoots at him when Aloysius tries to assist Viola in making her way across the railway turntable to him. He does not want Aloysius any closer to him than necessary. One of the reasons, aside from having had to satisfy his brother there was no possibility of Diogenes tricking him, that he has *not* prepared any unpleasant surprises for his *frater* is that he feels he has to expend too much thought and effort making sure Aloysius does not have anything up *his* sleeve. Yet he still maintains his sharp wit. When Pendergast protests his having drugged Viola, Diogenes' reply is at once indignant, dismissive, and ironic: "Pooh. Nothing more than a few milligrams of Versed to keep her quiet. Don't be concerned—she's *intact*" (*Dance of Death,* p. 423). On the one hand, he is being truthful. Unless we count the gentle kiss, Diogenes has not sexually assaulted her (or cut off any body parts, if we are talking about the more literal meaning of *intact*). On the other hand, given what he has so recently said to Viola about her various lovers, *intact* also conveys a great deal of sarcasm.

After D'Agosta has departed the scene, conveying Viola and Mr. Kaplan to safety, Pendergast returns to the field of Diogenes' vision. When Diogenes demands to know "what are you still doing here?" the authors describe his voice as "suddenly panicked." It is, of course, the innate fear of his brother double-crossing him, but it could also be fear of the train Diogenes still believes is coming killing Aloysius. Yes, Pendergast's death would put him beyond the reach of Diogenes' beautifully planned vengeance, but I believe there is also, at the core, real fear at the prospect of losing his only living relative, his only living link to the memories of his past—to his true identity. This, of course, is why Diogenes misses with the shots he fires at Pendergast, and Pendergast has already figured this out. Diogenes manages to use the threat of the train against his brother, even though he fears it—and the damage to Aloysius—himself.

Of course, Diogenes also fears any threat to the diamond. He sees quickly enough that his brother intends to take it back, and, until Aloysius reveals there is no train, fears the loss of it during the chaos a train wreck would bring. When Aloysius actually *does* pick up Lucifer's Heart again, Diogenes' anguish again echoes his feelings of betrayal in The Event: "Put that back—it's mine! You liar! You *lied* to me!" (*Dance of Death,* p. 426). Pendergast brushes this away with a technicality. When Diogenes threatens to really kill him this time, he does hesitate, just as Aloysius predicts. It is possible, however, that Diogenes' rage and hurt might have eventually overcome all else if the authorities had not shown up at this point.

Diogenes' thoughts, feelings, and utterances at this point are still all colored by the impending loss of Lucifer's Heart at the hands of his brother. Once he recognizes Pendergast's plan to allow his own capture, however, he is also upset at the prospect of his brother's immediate arrest. "You called the *police*? You fool, they'll get you, not me!" and "Idiot, you're what—using yourself as bait? Sacrificing *yourself?*" His distress makes me wonder if perhaps his revenge did not actually include his brother's imprisonment and possible execution. Perhaps Diogenes believed all along that his brother would evade the authorities, and his actual revenge would be forcing his brother into a similarly fugitive existence to his own. His last words to his brother before the NYPD bursts through one of the tunnels are: "You can't do this, you're utterly mad!" Preston and Child tell us that "the disembodied voice fell in another choking moan, so penetrating and inhuman that it sounded feral." Feral or no, Diogenes manages a supreme act of will and self-preservation in managing to stop the sound "abruptly, leaving only an echo" (*Dance of Death,* p. 427) before the police become aware there is anyone but Pendergast left at the scene of the transaction. Before Aloysius is taken away, he is able to glimpse what he believes is the only trace of Diogenes, looking into one of the tunnels : "Two small points of light were barely visible.... As he watched, the lights faded out a moment, then returned—as eyes would do when blinked. Then they dimmed, turned away, and vanished" (*Dance of Death,* p. 428).

There are a few last mentions of Diogenes in this volume. The first is an amusing testament to how well he has crafted the persona of Menzies; when Nora expresses her concern to her husband over the news that her department chair was recorded near the Astor Hall the night of the robbery and has seemingly disappeared, Smithback jokes that perhaps Menzies is Diogenes. Nora replies: "That's not even funny," and her husband apologizes for his "poor taste." Though Smithback makes the astute observation that "it's not over …. Not by a long shot," in announcing his intention to go after Diogenes, Nora makes the even more astute one that Smithback is "no match for him!"

Right before Viola takes leave of Pendergast in the lockup at Bellvue, we learn that Captain Hayward now actually believes in Diogenes' existence as a person separate from Pendergast. Not only has Viola helped convince her, but Margo Green has awakened and made statements to this effect as well. Before Pendergast is transferred to Federal prison to await trial, it is for fear of Diogenes that he tells Viola not to wait for him. When Viola recounts that his brother "said terrible things" to her, Pendergast states: "Diogenes makes it a game to find out a person's deepest fears. Then he strikes a deadly, well-aimed blow. He's driven people to suicide that way" (*Dance of Death*, p. 446). This not only sets up the scenario with Constance to come in the next volume, it confirms that Diogenes has actually caused a suicide before, and that he probably *was* hoping he could leave seeds of this sort in Viola's mind while technically returning her to his brother unharmed. Possibly, Pendergast is referring to his roommate at the English boarding school; possibly he knows something about Charles Duchamp that leads him to believe this had something to do with Diogenes' method in that death. Or perhaps Pendergast simply has knowledge of yet another instance. Aside from the fact that Diogenes always seems to enjoy his own wit in whatever he does, however, I would not say he makes a game of it. He usually has a deeply serious intent when he sets out to end another life.

Similarly, in the Epilogue, D'Agosta has the thought that "Diogenes' failure and flight only made him more dangerous." He also "recalled Diogenes' curiosity about Constance, during the phone conversation in the vintage Jaguar, and he shivered," noting that "Diogenes was a meticulous planner." When Eli Glinn arrives at 891 Riverside to propose breaking Pendergast out of Harkmoor, he is bearing the preliminary psychological profile he has completed on Diogenes, and offers the conclusion that "there may not be a more dangerous man in the world."

Clearing the Palate

Approximately a week elapses between the end of *Dance of Death* and the beginning of *Book of the Dead.* In that week, Diogenes manages to formulate a whole new plan for further revenge against his brother. One might be tempted to ask why. While driving back to the Long Island house with all the diamonds in his satchel, Diogenes was clearly thinking about leaving after he finished killing Viola. True, he ends up with neither Viola's blood in a pewter bleeding bowl, nor Lucifer's Heart, but he has managed to frame his brother for his own heinous crimes. Granted, Diogenes is furious that Aloysius has cheated him out of the magnificent red diamond. He may well be even more furious that every hint, every verbal nudge he gave his older brother about The Event was either denied or ignored by Aloysius. In any case, he is too distressed at the thought of leaving things unfinished—plus, he was extremely gratified by his brother's vigorous reaction to his inquiry about Constance. Especially in light of having to return Viola physically unharmed, Diogenes finds it difficult to pass up such a wonderful opportunity to cause Aloysius even more pain. Further, in my opinion, he is legitimately intrigued by Constance and finds the thought of her enticing on its own.

Diogenes forms his plan of action concerning Constance separately from his other overarching scheme. He has asked himself the question, "how can I draw Aloysius's attention to what he actually did to me in such a way that it will be impossible for him to deny it any longer?" This need to get his brother to acknowledge The Event, however, also ties into yet another motivation for Diogenes to remain in the New York area. Despite all the time and effort he put into framing his brother as a serial killer and the slayer of a Federal agent, I do not believe Diogenes anticipated Aloysius actually being taken into custody. He wanted to ruin his brother's life, but I do not believe he wanted to end it. I believe at the very least Diogenes has to see if his brother is sentenced to death; if this were to happen, he would probably come up with some way to prevent it. His unease at the prospect of his brother actually dying, however, is certainly not going to prevent Diogenes from planning more deeds to make Aloysius simultaneously suffer more and be forced to admit what a terrible brother he has been since that horrible day, many years before.

One thing Diogenes does in the week between the two novels is destroy the collection of diamonds that he stole, smashing them to bits with a hammer and an anvil. We learn this detail about mid-way through *Book of the Dead,* when Smithback explores the house on Long Island. Whether or not Diogenes does this before he comes up with the major points of his new plan or afterward, we may never know. In either case, his behavior is remarkable. Diogenes is genuinely enraged as he pulverizes the diamond collection, yet he has taken the time to run out to a hardware store and buy an anvil, and probably the titanium hammer as well. Surely the Long Island house where he held Viola captive had not already been equipped with an anvil? On top of these considerations, Diogenes has managed to complete the reduction of all the diamonds to tiny shards, and collect these bits and take them with him before the police manage to find the house.

Diogenes probably had it already in mind to send the

diamond grit back to the Museum when he smashed its collection. Why else would he have carried its remains away with him? Not only might he have been growing increasingly annoyed with the people he had to deal with daily as Menzies, but the Museum itself has now incurred his wrath to a degree second only to his elder brother. Diogenes' first coherent thoughts (after he finished howling) upon learning that the large falsely-colored red diamond he has painstakingly stolen is not Lucifer's Heart must have formed a virulent diatribe against the bureaucratic bastards who would own such a priceless treasure yet display a mere copy without notifying the public.

Then, adding insult to injury, Pendergast takes away his last chance at obtaining the real Lucifer's Heart. After this, Diogenes must have been asking himself what he could possibly come up with that would both drive home to Aloysius what he had done to him when they were boys, that would simultaneously humiliate the Museum that had made a fool of him. Of course, any suffering he could add to his already imprisoned brother would be sugar on the beignet. Perhaps he could induce the mysterious Miss Greene to help him with that aspect of things?

At some point in his thought process, Diogenes must have recalled a tidbit of information he had come across while searching the Museum's archives in pursuit of his Great-Uncle Antoine. An entire Egyptian tomb that had once been on display, but closed down because of rumors of a curse, and long forgotten. The Egyptian element might even bring Viola Maskelene back within his grasp—after all, Aloysius had reneged on *his* end of the bargain, had he not? One more thing Diogenes does, then, in the week between the second and third books in his triology, is to establish a European bank account containing at least ten million euros in the name of Comte Thierry de Cahors. Ah, to have that kind of disposable income! In any case, the closest we can come to answering the question of how long it takes all the diverse elements of a grand scheme to gel together in the mind of a mad genius is: one week, or less.

###

Troisième Course

The first three chapters of *The Book of the Dead* gradually reveal to readers what Diogenes has done with the Museum's diamond collection. The main question to be examined about him here comes straight from the first chapter, and it is this: Did Diogenes deliberately put a hole in the package to also cause an anthrax scare at the Museum, or was this just an accident of delivery? Unless Preston and Child write further on this matter, there is no way to be certain, but a case can certainly be made for Diogenes having maximized the mischief. The same post-9/11 state of caution that made Museum personnel fear a deliberate unleashing of anthrax would make it unlikely that any self-respecting messenger service would have accepted a package in that condition. Thus, it is unlikely Diogenes made a hole in the box and paper wrapping it before giving it to a delivery service. If Diogenes actually used a messenger, rather than delivering it himself disguised as a messenger, the package would have had to have accidentally scraped open when pushed roughly through the window of Curly's pillbox guard post. The messenger could well have been Diogenes, however. He is not well-described; he merely says, "Here, pops!" as he shoves the package at Curly. When Curly tries to stop him, presumably to get him to deliver the package to "the mailroom receiving dock" instead, the authors tell us that "the messenger was already speeding away on his fat-tire mountain bike, black rucksack bulging with packages" (*Book of the Dead,* p. 2). If Diogenes is disguising himself as a messenger, he is surely intelligent enough to carry something

like this rucksack, and have it at least *look* as though he has
other parcels to deliver.

The only other interesting point in this section relating to
Diogenes is the description of the package itself. It is a box
rather than a padded envelope, because it is "about twelve
inches by eight by eight," and it is "wrapped in greasy brown
paper, and tied up with an excessive amount of old-fashioned
twine." I cannot help wondering where Diogenes got the
paper and why it is greasy; this could be another example of
Preston and Child giving us just enough information to let our
own imaginations give us the creeps. There is no return
address, and it is directed "in a childish hand: *For the rocks
and minerals curator, The Museum of Natural History*" (*Book
of the Dead,* p. 2). Diogenes is no longer trying to make his
handwriting look like his brother's; that he is trying to
disguise it at all makes me lean towards him deliberately
trying to make it look like anthrax; no one but Aloysius
would suspect anthrax addressed with elegant penmanship,
and Aloysius is now in prison and unable to appreciate the
package.

Actually, it is in Diogenes' best interest to cause an anthrax
scare, because in this way the contents of the package get
analyzed more quickly. Chapters Two and Three chronicle
the process of discovering that the "sand" in the box is
actually diamonds, and of figuring out which diamonds they
once were. Chapter Four reveals how this seemingly senseless
turn of events is leaked to the press, practically assuring that
Diogenes has exactly the environment he needs to set his
latest plans in motion.

Not surprisingly, then, Chapter Five brings us the return of Hugo Menzies. It is fascinating that he is one of the few people that the Museum's director, Collopy, calls to an emergency meeting on how to handle the public relations disaster that the news of the diamond collection's destruction has created. Menzies is the only department head there; the others are an attorney and the head of public relations for the Museum. Apparently, despite having been seen near the Diamond Hall on the security videos from the night of the robbery, Menzies has managed to make himself such a trusted figure—with a reputation for resourcefulness—that Collopy considers him an essential part of this meeting.

As Menzies, Diogenes is quick to speak. After allowing the lawyer and public relations head to scold Collopy for the mess he has made in trying to cover up what happened to the diamonds, he quickly takes control of the meeting with a simple, yet polite "May I?" It is as though Collopy has been praying someone would do it. Menzies' first point is that they must have "no more dissembling" to the media and the public. It is interesting that the authors tell us "his intense blue eyes" are "darting to the window." Diogenes is using the crowd of protesters that has gathered outside to help pressure Collopy and the others to adopt the plan he is about to propose, but he is probably somewhat uncomfortable. Any angry mob is going to have associations for him, and remind him of the one that set his ancestral home on fire. The "darting" is real, but it does not prevent Diogenes from taking advantage of the situation.

Menzies goes on to state: "We need to do something glorious. We need to make a fabulous announcement, something that will remind New York City and the world that, despite all this, we're still a great museum." The ideas he throws out include "a scientific expedition" or "some extraordinary research project." Diogenes is smart enough not to say the phrase that describes what he will eventually do: "a really cool exhibit." When asked by Collopy for more specifics, Menzies replies, "I haven't gotten that far" (*Book of the Dead*, p. 23). If he were to have a specific idea, ready to propose, it would seem too perfect, and perhaps a little too suspicious. Instead, Diogenes creates serendipity.

The timing is such that Diogenes must have arranged to have the bank wire sent the moment Collopy commanded Menzies' presence at the emergency meeting. The four gathered have already more or less admitted the viability of Menzies' basic idea, when Collopy's secretary interrupts the meeting by buzzing his intercom with the news of "a bank wire transfer donation of ten million euros." Collopy is eager to have the money, but complains about the donor, one Comte Thierry de Cahors, and his "bloody restricted funds." The catch is that Cahors wants the money to go specifically to opening up and restoring the tomb of Senef, still located within the Museum, but apparently long closed off and forgotten. Collopy orders his secretary to "fax this count whoever and see if you can't persuade him to make this an unrestricted donation" (*Book of the Dead*, p. 24). Menzies, however, calls the secretary back. "Please wait a few minutes before contacting the Count of Cahors." When his secretary looks to Collopy for the final say, he nods in agreement that she should, indeed, wait. It fascinates me that Diogenes, as Menzies, has gained so much trust and respect from the Museum's director.

Of course, Menzies just happens to remember all of the pertinent details about Senef's tomb, and the history behind its acquisition by the Museum. It is not long before he gets to: "Don't you see? This is precisely what we're looking for!" He elucidates: "We make a big announcement of the count's gift, set an opening date with a gala party and all the trappings, and make a media event out of it" (*Book of the Dead,* p. 25).

Before he manages to get Collopy to rubber-stamp his idea and accept the fake Comte's donation, Menzies makes an interesting statement. In explaining how Senef's tomb could have lain forgotten all these years, while still being within the walls of the Museum, he says: "This museum simply has too many artifacts, and not enough money or curators to tend them. That's why I've lobbied for years now to create a position for a museum historian. Who knows what other secrets sleep in the long-forgotten corners?" (*Book of the Dead,* p. 26). This is another detail that points in the direction of Diogenes having an intimate knowledge of the Museum's archives, and possibly having discovered his Great-Uncle Antoine's whereabouts through them before Pendergast and Nora did. There is also something wistful about it. Not only does it give the impression that Diogenes has been Menzies for so long that he has come to actually feel the way his alter-ego would be expected to about some of the collections, but the last sentence evokes his earlier memory in *Dance of Death,* of exploring the rooms of Rochenoire as a small child.

The Comte de Cahors may be a fake, but the money is real, and it is Diogenes' money. The authors thoughtfully tell us in the next chapter that when the novel takes place, presumably in the early 2000s, ten million euros is roughly equivalent to thirteen million dollars. The amount of money Diogenes is willing to spend to make his point to his brother and simultaneously wreak havoc on what might potentially be millions of people is truly impressive.

On the heels of getting the Museum to adopt his plan, Diogenes/Menzies goes to inform Nora that she is being drafted into helping him with it. Diogenes does not choose her out of any special sense of revenge for her association with Pendergast, even though she certainly has one. Although there may be a certain sense of keeping her near as a potential victim capable of causing further pain to Aloysius, as there was in *Dance of Death,* Diogenes does not seem to have anything planned for her beyond the fate anticipated for everyone who partakes of his sound and lights show. I think he chooses her for her anthropological, organizational, and people skills—and also because he senses that she likes and trusts Menzies. Having Nora as an integral part of his team is going to help shield him from suspicion in the weeks to come, until it will be far too late to stop him.

Ironically, the creaking of her laboratory door as Diogenes/Menzies opens it to look for her brings Margo's attack to Nora's mind. Yet she relaxes immediately when she recognizes Menzies. Nora notes that "He was still a little pale from his recent bout with gallstones, his cheerful eyes rimmed in red." We cannot be sure if what she is seeing is Diogenes still suffering the effects of losing the diamond he most coveted and being tricked by Aloysius—and possibly the stress of getting everything into place for his new plan— or if Diogenes has augmented his Menzies disguise to compliment the gallstone excuse he had given for his absence. The red-rimmed eyes could be from having to wear contacts so often!

Now that readers who have already digested *Dance of Death* know who Menzies really is, they might well find it sinister when he asks Nora if she is alone in her basement lab. Diogenes is only there for recruiting purposes, however, and Nora is safe for the moment. Their conversation, however, is worth noting for what Diogenes reveals. Nora asks him, "How are things up top?" and Diogenes/Menzies' first reply is: "The crowd outside is still growing." He follows this with "It's getting ugly. They're jeering and hectoring the arriving staff and blocking traffic on Museum Drive. And I fear this is just the beginning." He concludes with "God save us from the fury of the *vulgus mobile*" (*Book of the Dead,* p. 29). Of course Diogenes wants to make things sound as serious as possible to make Nora feel obligated to help. Yet at the same time, I think once more his previous traumatic experience in young adulthood makes this extremely easy for him.

After Nora apologizes for Bill's role in provoking the protests, Diogenes/Menzies assures her that her husband "did the museum a favor in exposing this ill-advised cover-up scheme before it could take hold." This may or may not be true, but Smithback definitely did Diogenes a favor by putting the Museum in a tight enough spot to make it almost certain to grasp his plan as a way out. Then Nora innocently remarks to Menzies: "I can't understand why someone would go to the trouble to steal the gems and then destroy them."

Menzies' response is loaded with Diogenes' wry humor.

"Who knows what goes on in the mind of a deranged individual?" He then goes on to reveal that "It evinces, at the very least, an implacable hatred of the museum." I think Diogenes gets at least some enjoyment from telling Nora parts of the truth. Perhaps it even serves as something of an escape valve for him, to be able to discuss things he has had to keep to himself. When Nora asks, "What had the museum ever done to him?" his response is: "Only one person can answer that question" (*Book of the Dead,* p. 29). I can only imagine him adding in his mind, *and you're looking at him.* The statement does tell me, however, that Diogenes definitely had a reason for what he did; it is not as though he is having second thoughts or wondering why he gave in to a fit of blinding range. If that had been the case, Menzies would have said to Nora that the culprit probably did not even know why himself.

Overall, however, Menzies does not take long to get down to his real purpose with Nora, asking her to be his right hand woman on the Tomb of Senef project. He uses a skilled combination of flattery and guilt mixed with a little temptation to persuade her; it is interesting to note that he does not resort to simply invoking rank, telling her that he is her boss and she must do as he says. If it came to that, he probably would, but Diogenes/Menzies is able to avoid it. When Nora protests, "But I put off my research for months to help mount the Sacred Images show!" Menzies' "ironic smile" admits the injustice of this. He then compliments her by saying, "I saw the work you did on Sacred Images. You're the only one in the department who can pull this off." He must sense her weakening when she asks how long she would have to put the exhibit together.

When Nora is incredulous at how rapidly they would have to work, Diogenes/Menzies changes back towards guilt as a motivation, telling her: "We face a real emergency. Finances have been in a sorry state for a long time." He follows these statements with a subtle reminder of her husband's role in the institution's difficulty: "And with this new spate of bad publicity, anything could happen" (*Book of the Dead,* p. 30). He then adds a sprinkle of enticement, telling her how much money the generous Comte has given the museum to make the exhibit happen. What researcher in any field does not wish to hear once in his or her career, "Money is no object"? Menzies' follow-up line, "We'll have the unanimous support of the museum," has to be a rare and tantalizing thing to Nora's ears as well.

Of course Nora's plea for Menzie to "give it to Ashton" is futile. Diogenes/Menzies obliges her with more flattery: "Ashton's no good at controversy. I saw how you handled yourself with those protesters at the Sacred Images opening. Nora, the museum is in a fight for its life. I need you. The *museum* needs you" (*Book of the Dead,* p. 30). He even has an answer to her final, valid objection that she is no expert on ancient Egypt, telling her they have already hired "a top Egyptologist" to help her.

Once he coaxes Nora into agreement, Diogenes/Menzies wastes no time before he starts eliciting ideas from her for Collopy's press conference. I think this is primarily a formality; Diogenes probably already has a reasonably clear idea of what he wishes to do with this project. He is just using this conversation as a means of getting Nora used to the fact that there will be a sound and light show in connection with the tomb exhibit. He steers her towards it, reminding her that "this is the twenty-first century and we're competing with television and video games" (*Book of the Dead,* p. 31). Eventually, she obliges Menzies by exclaiming: "If done right, with computerized lighting and so forth, it would give visitors an experience they'd never forget. Make history come alive inside the tomb itself." Diogenes reinforces and encourages her enthusiasm, assuring her: "Nora, someday you'll be director of this museum." He is an astute judge of people, because "she blushed. The idea did not displease her." Before leaving to prep Collopy for the press conference, Diogenes/Menzies admits: "I'd been thinking of some sort of sound-and-light show myself." He adds: "As for the computer effects, let me manage that side of things" (*Book of the Dead,* p. 32). Indeed.

Menzies next appears in Chapter Eight, to introduce Nora to her British Egyptologist helper, Adrian Wicherly, and, with the help of a senior member of the Museum's maintenance department, find the location of Senef's tomb within an abandoned area. There are three points for discussion in this chapter in terms of Diogenes' character. Firstly, he tells Nora and Wicherly that "as I understand it, nobody knows quite precisely where the Tomb of Senef is anymore" (*Book of the Dead,* p. 38). I cannot help wondering if this is true. Would Diogenes build a plan around a transplanted Egyptian tomb he had not yet seen for certain? It is possible that he has somehow already scouted it out, given his knowledge of underground New York as evidenced by his meeting with

Aloysius at the Iron Clock and his ability to enter 891 Riverside at will, coupled with the tomb's location near the Museum subway stop. Even if he has not, Diogenes is confident in his ability to change his strategies if need arises. He is a meticulous planner, but part of that is a recognition of the value of contingency options.

Readers are also treated to further evidence of Diogenes' shared upbringing with Aloysius, and of how closely he has followed his brother's career. During the search for the tomb, the party travels through "a long, once-elegant corridor lined with dingy frescoes. Nora squinted: they were paintings of a New Mexico landscape, with mountains, deserts, and a multistoried Indian ruin she recognized as Taos Pueblo" (*Book of the Dead,* pp. 39-40). Diogenes/Menzies immediately identifies the artist, just as Aloysius did in *Relic.* "Fremont Ellis." He goes on to explain: "This was once the Hall of the Southwest. Shut down since the forties." As Menzies, Diogenes has made it his business to be as familiar as possible with the Museum, but I also think Fremont Ellis was an artist favored by some Pendergast ancestor or another, perhaps even his and Aloysius's parents. In *Relic,* Aloysius declares that "anyone who knows Ellis would recognize these" (page 85), so I think Diogenes would recognize them even if he had not cultivated an encyclopedic knowledge of the Museum. Interestingly, in that novel, the head of Museum security tells Pendergast the area has been closed off since the 1920s rather than the 1940s. If I were a betting woman, I would place my money on Diogenes' dates.

When Wicherly points out "a rather nasty stain" on one of the paintings, saying "they're rather in need of curation,"

Diogenes/Menzies at first blames it on the Museum's lack of funds. When McCorkle, their guide from maintenance, pipes up that "It's not only money," however, Menzies provides the antidote to Nora and Wicherly's puzzlement. "I think what Seamus means is that the, ah, first Museum Beast killings happened in the vicinity of the Hall of the Southwest." Again, his automatic knowledge of this suggests that Diogenes has been following his brother's career avidly.

Chapter Eight ends with the foursome about to enter the tomb and explore it. Before they have even pinpointed the location of the plastered-over door, however, they hear the roar of a subway train arriving at the 81st Street station. Diogenes/Menzies immediately asserts: "We'll have to find some way to dampen that sound," adding that "It destroys the mood" (*Book of the Dead*, p. 43). Undoubtedly, it would also dampen the effects of the electronic torture he is planning.

Menzies reappears in Chapter Ten as his group continues the tour of Senef's tomb, but readers learn little more about Diogenes. He is primarily letting Wicherly talk, allowing him to explain the Egyptian mythology behind the tomb paintings and show off his ability to read hieroglyphics. Diogenes probably already has him in mind as an early victim, someone who will unwittingly help him fine-tune the larger-scale "pain factory" he plans to construct within the tomb. He flatters him to build trust, to make him comfortable and put him off guard. "Right on target," says Diogenes/Menzies, when Wicherly guesses the date of the tomb (*Book of the Dead,* p. 49). Yet, at the same time, he cannot resist antagonizing him somewhat, with parts of the tomb's story that he knows will displease the Englishman. After tracing the tomb's ownership from its

French discovery through its possession by a Scottish baron who sold it to an American benefactor of the Museum, he cheerfully tells Wicherly that the Scot "received a thousand pounds for it" (*Book of the Dead,* p. 54). Actually, this also tells readers something about Diogenes—that he can "smile" (albeit in another persona) over the pittance that once purchased the tomb he is paying approximately thirteen million dollars just to rent. Money is nothing to him compared with Aloysius's anguish and acknowledgment.

Diogenes/Menzies' only other concerns in this chapter are purely practical. At the point where the group crosses a narrow, rickety bridge that is supposed to carry visitors over a fifteen-foot deep well, which Menzies asserts "must have been cut into the Manhattan bedrock" during the tomb's original installation within the Museum. He notes: "We'll have to bring this up to code" (*Book of the Dead,* p. 53). Diogenes would not want a narrow bridge to slow the flow of foot traffic he needs to get victims through his "pain factory" at the proper rate of speed for maximum effect and efficiency. As they are about to leave the tomb, Nora assumes Menzies has been sharing her thoughts about "how dusty" it is and "how much work lay ahead," because he wore "a smile that was half eager, half rueful" (*Book of the Dead,* p. 55). More likely, the rueful stemmed from the necessity of dampening down the eagerness.

In Chapter Thirteen, Diogenes Pendergast meets Constance Greene. This is his first appearance in the novel without his Menzies disguise. He is, however, wearing "a severe black suit." The somber clothing probably helps him slip into the library without Constance seeing him, but Diogenes also wants to remind her of Aloysius, who customarily wears a black suit. Yet, at the same time, he does not employ the same enhancements he used at the Decker crime scene to make people think they had seen his brother—he allows himself his own ginger hair and beard, his own differently-colored eyes. Perhaps this is because he already has the end game in sight, and knows that elements of disguise such as wigs will not hold up under the physical intimacy. I also think, however, it means more to him if he can win Constance over with her knowing exactly who he is. It will certainly make her more ashamed when he eventually seduces her and abandons her.

Of course, despite the fact that "Constance had never seen this man before […] she knew immediately who he was" (*Book of the Dead*, p. 68). Naturally she is startled by someone suddenly appearing in the room when she thought herself completely alone in the house, but her instantaneous realization of his identity frightens her more. Constance drops her cup of tea, but Diogenes reveals his amazingly fast reflexes by catching it before any of the tea spills. He has also cleverly placed himself between Constance "and the room's only exit."

Diogenes can see the effects he is having upon Constance. His first move, so to speak, after catching the cup is to assure her he is not there to hurt her. At this point it is useful to reference a moment from later in the novel: When Pendergast is finally remembering The Event through use of a memory crossing, something his little brother says causes him to reflect "that Diogenes, who was only seven, hadn't yet learned that truth is the safest lie" (*Book of the Dead*, p. 290). Diogenes has certainly acquired this knowledge, however, by the time he introduces himself to Constance. "I mean you no harm," he says, and he does *not*—at least not physically, by his own hand. In this initial encounter, and in every other visit he has with her at 891 Riverside, the words Diogenes speaks to Constance are mostly true—and I would argue they are *more* true than the devastating ones he eventually leaves written on cream laid paper for her.

When Constance admits that she does indeed know who he is, Diogenes tells her: "I am gratified." This is more a commentary on his brother than on Constance. After all the time he has spent trying to get Aloysius to acknowledge what he has done to him, Diogenes almost expects never to have been mentioned to Constance. Even though the reader knows that Pendergast has indeed warned Constance about Diogenes, and even sent her into hiding in *Dance of Death*, Diogenes still cannot be sure that Aloysius is the reason Constance recognizes him. Great Uncle Antoine may have told her about his only living relatives, and he knew Diogenes was not really dead before Aloysius did. Diogenes can see that Constance is affected by the family resemblance, but if he strongly resembles Aloysius, he also strongly resembles Antoine. Antoine, after all, looked a great deal like Aloysius. Of course, "the buttery New Orleans tones" Constance finds "familiar" are probably also common to all the Pendergast men (at least those the reader has heard of at this point in the series).

Diogenes manages to reveal that he has appeared in the library with a purpose directly related to Constance. "Because it's time we spoke, you and I. It's the least courtesy you could pay me, after all" (*Book of the Dead*, p. 68). He barely manages to begin an explanation before Constance attacks him with a letter opener. In another display of his formidable reflexes Diogenes avoids her assault, despite the fact that "she had done nothing, said nothing, to warn the man of her strike" (*Book of the Dead*, p. 69). When, undaunted, Constance retracts her weapon from the chair in which it has lodged instead of Diogenes' chest, he "coolly dodged the stroke and with a flick of his arm seized her wrist." In the struggle, the pair end up on the floor, with Diogenes in the superior position, "pinning her body under his, the letter opener skidding across the rug."

In trying to soothe her, Diogenes says her name very softly in her ear, and adds, "*Du calme. Du calme.*" This is not only French for "calm down," but it is also a quotation from the novella *Heart of Darkness* by Joseph Conrad. The scenario in the novella is that a French-speaking doctor is examining the narrator before he embarks on his journey deep into Africa. The doctor seems to be under the impression that Europeans who go there are prone to become insane, and even asks almost the same question Diogenes asked Viola as he was driving her from the airport: "Ever any madness in your family?" The doctor approves of the narrator's slow, steady heart rate, and tells him that keeping calm is the key to maintaining one's sanity in the heart of the African jungles. "Avoid irritation more than exposure to the sun," he tells the narrator. As they part, the doctor adds the final admonition: "*Du calme, du calme.*" The reference is especially appropriate once Diogenes begins to talk about insanity to Constance later in their encounter.

Their positioning is intimate; as Constance struggles

cl

underneath him, Diogenes continues trying to sooth her. "Please understand, Constance, I'm not here to hurt you. I'm restraining you simply to prevent harm to myself." Eventually, after noticing that her own heart is "racing painfully," Constance "became aware of the beating of his own heart—much slower—against her breasts" (*Book of the Dead*, p. 69). The doctor from *Heart of Darkness* would approve of Diogenes' ability to stay calm!

Throughout their encounter up to this point, Constance has been hurling insults at Diogenes and assuring him she will never listen to a word he says. She has confronted him with everything he has done to Pendergast. When Diogenes asks her if she will "promise not to attack" him again if he releases her, she does not answer. Even so, Diogenes reads her correctly and knows he has tantalized her with his supposition that "you may learn that everything is not as it seems" (*Book of the Dead,* p. 70). He lets her go, but still makes sure that he is blocking her exit from the room. He is probably also on guard in case she should try to attack him again, but she cautiously obliges him when he asks her to sit.

Constance is not finished verbally insulting him, however. When Diogenes asks if they can "speak now, like civilized people," she scoffs at him and asks how a serial killer and a thief can call himself civilized. Diogenes replies: "Naturally, my brother has taken a certain line with you. After all, it's worked so well for him in the past. He's an extraordinarily persuasive and charismatic individual." At no point does Diogenes ever claim that he is *not* a serial killer and a thief. Plus, the things he is saying about Aloysius are true. When Constance claims Diogenes is insane, "or worse, you do these things as a *sane* man," he does dispute her. He asserts: "I am not insane—on the contrary, like you, I greatly fear insanity."

Proving one way or the other whether Diogenes is telling the truth in this line is difficult. Possibly, he believes he is not insane; he at least *thinks* he is telling the truth. One could also take the approach that he knows the things he does are wrong, and that therefore he would never meet a legal definition of insanity. Yet given the philosophical constructs that Diogenes has had since The Event—that people are no more than bags of meat and blood and guts; that if God exists, He is mad; that nothing in the world really has meaning—he really does *not* feel that he is doing anything wrong. Therefore, perhaps, Diogenes *might* meet a legal definition of insanity. Does he actually fear insanity, in any manner close to the way Constance does? Possibly, but unlikely. His memories of the time right after The Event, as found in *Dance of Death,* imply that Diogenes feels he has already experienced insanity, found it an inadequate shelter, and come back from it. It seems as if the only reason he might fear insanity is that it might distract him, might weaken his drive for revenge upon his brother. Of course, the violent urges he has had to deal with since The Event also make it difficult to maintain long-time personas such as Menzies that are crucial to his overarching scheme surrounding Aloysius. If he is caught in connection with any of his victims, the game is over, so in that sense, he may fear his own insanity. In any case, Diogenes leads Constance away from the question of whether he is even more reprehensible for the deeds he has committed as a theoretically sane man.

He does, however, make an understated admission: "It's true

that I am far from perfect and cannot yet expect your trust." Note that he chooses the word *expect*, rather than *deserve*. Again, Diogenes is sticking as close to the truth as his purposes with Constance will allow. After emphasizing once more that he has no intent to hurt her, he turns her subsequent insult into a veiled hint that he knows her secret. When he speaks of her eyes being "so wise and so old," and exclaims over "What strange and terrible things they must have seen!" (*Book of the Dead,* p. 70), he concludes that "childhood was a luxury you were denied. Just as I myself was denied it." This statement causes Constance to go "rigid" (*Book of the Dead,* p. 71), and Diogenes senses he has his opening. Again, he is telling the truth, at least as he sees it. Ironically, as Diogenes has more or less deduced from at least one previous encounter with his ancestor Antoine and from observing the house at 891 Riverside since Antoine's demise, Constance had an excruciatingly *long* childhood in the biological sense. The things that happened to her before Antoine Leng Pendergast took her into his home, however, both devastated and hardened her to the point at which she could accept the gifts of food, shelter, tutelage, and longevity from the man who had killed her sister. As for himself, of course, Diogenes feels The Event. took his childhood, his sleep, and his color vision, leaving nihilism, bloodlust, and consuming need for revenge in their places.

At last, Diogenes returns to the point he claims he has been trying to make from the beginning of their encounter—that his purpose in introducing himself to Constance is to tell her "the *real* truth [....] About the relationship between me and my brother." Some of the words he has spoken so softly that

Constance must actively listen to him to make them out, and this is another of Diogenes' strategies to win her over. She must look at him to help discern his words, and when she does, "in the soft light of the dying fire, Diogenes Pendergast's peculiar eyes looked vulnerable, almost lost. Gazing back at her, they brightened slightly" (*Book of the Dead,* p. 71). No doubt Diogenes is able to make himself look this way deliberately, the better to win Constance over. Yet when it comes to how Diogenes actually feels about what he believes his brother has maliciously done to him, I cannot avoid the thought that he may simply be purposely lowering his defenses and allowing Constance to see what he looks like in his moments of weakness. There *is* truth in what Constance sees. Diogenes *is* lost, although if confronted by a neutral party of no value to him, he would argue he is no more lost than the rest of the helpless meatbags wandering the planet.

If his purpose is to talk about his relationship with Aloysius, however, Diogenes keeps deliberately straying from the subject to sympathize with Constance. He can sense that she yearns for attention, and he definitely plans to give it to her. As much as I want to assert Diogenes is staying at least close to the truth, even I cannot believe him when he tells her that "gazing on you like this, I feel I would do anything in my power to lift from you that burden of pain and fear and carry it myself." As much as I believe Diogenes feels genuine attraction toward Constance (which he is nevertheless always ready and willing to sacrifice upon the altar of revenge against Aloysius), I cannot believe he feels genuinely protective of her after having just seen her for the first time. I *can* believe him, though, when he says "when I look at you, I see *myself*." I think if there is anyone Diogenes can identify with, it is Constance.

Diogenes' analysis of Constance is fairly accurate—at least in these beginning stages of their relationship. "I see a person who longs to fit in, to be merely human, and yet who is destined always to remain apart," he says. "I see a person who feels the world more deeply, more intensely, than she is willing to admit … even to herself." Later in the series readers learn that Constance chooses to continue taking Antoine's longevity serum even after he himself stops it; presumably Pendergast has stopped it, perhaps with her willing acquiescence after he shares Aunt Cornelia's reasoning with her. Therefore, I am not convinced that Constance longs to be "merely human." She may wish to fit in as Diogenes assumes, and merely by virtue of her origin in the late 1800s, she is, as he says, "destined always to remain apart." The deeper question here is whether these last lines are an accurate part of Diogenes seeing himself in Constance. Does he wish "to fit in, to be merely human"? Judging from his thoughts as he looked into the facets of the Queen of Narnia, I would say yes, at least some part of him does. He recognizes, too, that he is "destined always to remain apart." The one person Diogenes has known between the time of his parents' deaths to this moment, meeting Constance—who might have been capable of understanding him, of sharing the memories of what it was like to be raised a Pendergast—is the one he feels has betrayed him and (by not acknowledging The Event) rejected him. I think, that on some level, Diogenes recognizes that Constance is the only other person who might possibly understand him. After all, she has been raised as a

Pendergast as well, though not by name. I think the possibility of having feelings for her and yielding to these feelings remains a constant temptation to him, and only the long-standing, all-consuming need to make his brother suffer allows him to resist.

Again, Diogenes is accurate when he tells Constance: "I sense both pain and anger in you." He guesses that she feels abandoned, and confirms that she has been, "once again"— indirectly pointing a finger at his brother for circumstances he himself put in motion. Even if Diogenes is following the twisted logic that Aloysius did not *have* to give himself up to the police, it is not as though he would have had the luxury to stay at home with Constance if he had not. Though Diogenes would argue his brother could have taken her with him on the lam if he truly cared.

When Diogenes tells his own tale of abandonment, he includes some truth, but fudges some of the details and rearranges chronology. He may well feel as though the fire that destroyed his family home was his fault, and that he should have died instead of his parents. He did love his mother, and we have hints throughout the passages that record his inner thoughts that his life (aside from revenge) is not that valuable to him. Though most signs point to Great-Aunt Cornelia being the one to provoke the mob's ire, Diogenes probably realized his own actions and reputation had done nothing to make any of its members less hostile— thus making him, in his own mind, at least somewhat responsible. He follows this, after a comparison to Constance's guilt feelings over her sister Mary (and now she must know that Diogenes knows her secret!), by saying

"Later, I was abandoned by my brother." This is bad chronology if Diogenes is talking about The Event, which took place long before Rochenoire was destroyed and his parents murdered. Yet The Event is truly when he feels Aloysius abandoned him. Diogenes could be talking about his brother's initial unwillingness to give him family money before he came into his inheritance, or the lack of contact with Aloysius in the brief span of time between that inheritance and faking his own death. If so, he can hardly be taken as sincere—by readers, anyway. Constance, of course, is another story.

When Diogenes perceives that Constance does not believe Pendergast could have done such a thing, he counters with: "But the again, you know so little about my brother" (*Book of the Dead,* p. 71). Even Constance at this stage in the series cannot deny the truth of this statement. Any character thus far introduced could share that condition—with the possible exception of Diogenes himself.

Diogenes tells Constance he is going to leave, but he lingers to promise more details at a later visit, and to make a few more interesting comments. He says his "older brother […] took the love I offered and flung back scorn and hatred" (*Book of the Dead,* p. 72). From the interaction we see later in the novel as Pendergast remembers The Event, and even in the later Preston and Child short story "Extraction," there is nothing particularly evocative of "love offered." There is, however, a fair amount of typical elder-brotherly "scorn" on Aloysius's part. I do not doubt the love was there, before. Diogenes hurt and anger toward his brother is so strong that it can only have its root in love.

Diogenes also says that Aloysius "took pleasure in destroying everything I created—my journals of childish poetry, my translations of Virgil and Tacitus." Is this Diogenes' interpretation of the horrific journal Aloysius tells D'Agosta about burning, or is it truly an earlier effort that Aloysius tore up simply because it was not good? It is difficult to imagine the latter, considering Diogenes' precociousness. Given that Tacitus is the Roman historian who chronicled, among other things, Nero's time as emperor, and given that Diogenes' interpretation of these writings and the more violent scenes from *The Aeneid* would tend to be as lurid as his post-Event mind could make them, these probably are the writings Aloysius found too ghastly to read more than one page from before setting them ablaze. When Diogenes adds that Aloysius "tortured and killed my favorite pet in a way that, even today, I can barely bring myself to think about," the most likely explanation is that he is attributing his own atrocity upon Incitatus to Aloysius. There is a small space for reasonable doubt, but it is very small, indeed. Great Aunt Cornelia said that "nobody had to ask" who had crucified the rodent, but she never presented any evidence, did not speak of Diogenes' parents confronting him with the deed, etc. It is possible that someone else entirely did this—a disgruntled servant?—and each boy blamed the other. Perhaps Incitatus had belonged to both boys, though it is difficult to imagine the Pendergasts not having enough money to get a mouse for each of their sons. Perhaps Diogenes did what he did to Incitatus after Aloysius had done something to a different pet that *was* his?

In any case, Diogenes tells Constance that Aloysius has

"made it his mission in life to turn everyone against me, with lies and insinuations, to paint me as his evil twin." This, of course, is a gross exaggeration; for example, Diogenes has indeed committed the bizarre murders his brother told D'Agosta about, and has indeed stolen and destroyed what he could of the Museum's diamond collection. I feel Pendergast did exaggerate about Diogenes' journal when they were younger, however, and is still (albeit with understandable psychological reasons) stretching the truth having told D'Agosta and Glinn that his younger brother was evil from earliest memory. Once more, Diogenes fudges the chronology, though. He laments: "And when in the end none of this could break my spirit, he did something so awful … so, so *awful...*" Preston and Child state that "at this, his voice threatened to break." The impression is that Diogenes is hamming it up here, but it is also possible that his emotion is genuine. After he masters himself (or pretends to), he commands Constance: "Look at my dead eye." He concludes: "that was the *least* of what he did." Diogenes may be just using a good storyteller's technique of building to citing the most extreme wrong his brother committed against him as a climax, even though The Event took place before Incitatus or the journal-burning. Yet despite how much Diogenes misses the ability to see color, he is being truthful that the injury to his eye is "the *least* of" what happened to him as a result of The Event. He lost any belief in humanity, any belief that his brother cared for him, any sense of purpose other than revenge. He lost the amazing man he might have been had it never happened. Ironically, the eye injury itself was self-inflicted.

As Diogenes finally takes his leave of Constance, he says, "you'll find I've left you with something." He calls it "a gift of kinship, a recognition of the pain we share." Whatever the actual truth of the Incitatus incident, it is revealing that the little white mouse Diogenes leaves in Constance's pocket (a gesture both intimate and evocative of the Pendergast family tradition in magic) proves to be tame and fully trained. Did Diogenes hire someone, or buy a mouse that had already been taught tricks? Or did he spend the time to gentle the rodent himself, as patiently as his older brother once trained Incitatus?

Neither Diogenes nor Menzies appears in Chapter Fourteen, which chronicles Nora's pursuit of information about the Tomb of Senef. I cannot help wondering if some of what she finds has been planted by Diogenes—or, conversely, if some of the things missing from the Museum's files have been removed by him. He may have manipulated the contents of the various folders pertaining to the exhibit to heighten both the Museum's employees' and the public's sense that the tomb is cursed. This, Diogenes would believe, would enhance the ultimate effects of the sound and light show he has planned. I think that the newspaper stories are legitimate—the Egyptian bey probably *was* upset about the Tomb being on display in New York, and probably *did* invoke stories of its being cursed. A child may have been badly injured falling into the well—although if Diogenes wanted to create fake newspaper clippings, I am sure he could do a capable job of it. Even easier for him to create would be the letters Nora finds, "a flurry … from various people, many of them clearly cranks, describing 'sensations' and 'presences' they had

experienced while in the tomb" (*Book of the Dead,* p. 80).
The exhibit truly did close down when "the pedestrian tunnel
connecting the IND line subway station to the museum" was
built, but the correspondence surrounding it, and the notes
scrawled by L. P. Strawbridge could have been forged by
Diogenes. In particular, the hysterical marginalia scribble
reading "Tell him anything. I want that tomb closed" (*Book of
the Dead,* p. 81), could be pure fabrication.

Similarly, the only thing that happens concerning Diogenes in
chapter fifteen is that Captain Hayward meets Smithback
while both are re-investigating the scene of Margo Green's
attack. Hayward reveals to Smithback her current thinking
about the case—the case that everyone on the force has been
encouraging her to forget because Agent Coffey has already
decided Pendergast is responsible for everything: "It seems
Diogenes Pendergast has vanished. Completely. The trail
stops dead at his hideout on Long Island, the place where he
held Lady Maskelene prisoner. Such an utter disappearance
just doesn't happen these days, except for one possible
circumstance: he slipped into an alter ego. A *long-established*
alter-ego" (*Book of the Dead,* p. 86). Even if Diogenes were
apprised of this, he probably would not be terribly concerned.
They have no idea who that alter-ego might be.

In Chapter Sixteen, the reader finds out just as much about
one of Diogenes' prospective victims as about the villain
himself. The unfortunate Jay Lipper will, in a later chapter,
become the first person Diogenes uses to calibrate the effects
of his special sound and light show, though his assistant,
Theodore DeMeo, can certainly be considered a casualty as
well. Does Diogenes have Lipper's fate already in mind when

he hires him on as a technological consultant for the project? Is he thinking to use whomever he hires in this capacity as a test case, because someone intelligent enough to program the superficial show will have to be rendered unable to work before Diogenes himself can slip in the coding that will switch the expected edutainment into his own reproduction of Comstock's phantasmagoria on a grand scale? This is probable. Yet surely Diogenes refined his ideas for his test case after watching Lipper's expressions and body language in regards to DeMeo during Menzies' progress check with Nora, Wicherly, and Ashton. DeMeo may be clueless about how much Lipper despises him, but Diogenes must have recognized it immediately. He would anticipate that what would happen to DeMeo would prove a measurement of how well his pain factory functioned.

Lipper's status as a computer programmer, however, along with the level of education that usually comes with it, makes him more interesting as a test victim to Diogenes. Though each human being is a unique individual (okay, maybe not in Diogenes' mind), in general terms one might expect more educated people to be better at controlling their impulses than those with less education. It is this impulse control that Diogenes is attempting to override with his lights, lasers, and hideous sound waves able to damage the prefrontal cortex.

We do learn some things about Diogenes in this chapter, though, and ironically it is through his victim's eyes. Listening to Lipper's narration of the presentation, the first point at which Diogenes/Menzies interrupts is to say that "the point where they break through the sealed door is critical" (*Book of the Dead,* p. 91). Among the other details he demands is "a piercing shaft of light like a bolt of lightning." No doubt he is planning to cover his first laser stroke with this, the beginning of the assault upon his victims' brains.

Interestingly, Lipper finds this insistence on Menzies' part an "irritation." The computer consultant thinks: "Menzies, while charming enough, had been intrusive and meddlesome about certain technical details." The authors go on to note: "Lipper was worried he might micromanage the installation as well." Before Lipper can get far into the rest of the show, DeMeo proudly announces he has found previously drilled holes in one of the walls. This prompts Diogenes/Menzies to ask, "What's on the far side?" DeMeo answers that it is "a storeroom" (*Book of the Dead,* p. 91). Though it is probable that Diogenes has already guessed this from a study of old Museum documents, he had probably also been unable to confirm it until then. As skilled, knowledgeable, and secretive as he is, he probably did not have actual access to the tomb until McCorkle unsealed the entrance for the scouting expedition in Chapter Eight.

Diogenes/Menzies interrupts Lipper again once he has finished explaining the part about the tomb robbers taking the scarab from the mummy's wrappings, and he does so "excitedly." He exclaims that this is "the climax" of the program. "That's where I want the peal of thunder, the strobes simulating flashes of lightning" (*Book of the Dead,* p. 92). I think it likely that Diogenes' genuine enthusiasm for his plan is showing through Menzies' veneer. I think, too, that Diogenes originally created Menzies knowing he would have to spend a large amount of time in this alter ego, and therefore he made him as much like himself as he could while still making him likeable and a dependable pillar of the Museum's anthropology department. Thus, by the time Senef's tomb is about to be re-opened, Diogenes could practically inhabit Menzies in his sleep—if Diogenes slept. Aside from the obvious age difference, Menzies is probably very close to what Diogenes might have been if The Event had never happened. If Menzies were real, he would be enthusiastic about his project coming together, in much the same way Diogenes is about the true project underlying it. For the moment, character and alter-ego are in perfect synch, but Diogenes is underneath everything trying to ensure that the point at which his secret, damaging program truly jumps the tracks from the expected is strategically placed at a moment of maximum effect.

When Nora asks Diogenes/Menzies if "this level of theatricality" is "really necessary" (*Book of the Dead,* p. 93), he feigns surprise to increase her level of doubt towards her own objections: "Why, Nora! This was your idea to begin with." This is not precisely true; Menzies has coaxed her along this path from the beginning, but he wants to remind her of her agreement/psychological investment in it. When she continues to object that she "was imagining something lower-key, not strobe lights and fog machines," Diogenes/Menzies good-naturedly steers her back into proper alignment with his plans: "As long as we're going this route, Nora, we should do it right," he tells her. "Trust me, we're creating an unforgettable educational experience." To the second-time reader, the truth and irony of his words are delicious. Diogenes *is* "creating an unforgettable educational experience," in that his subjects will never be the same afterward, and it will educate them in how quickly they can succumb to their baser impulses. He concludes: "It's a marvelous way to slip a little learning to the *vulgus mobile* without them ever realizing it." This is another interesting sentence; again, the use of the Latin phrase *vulgus mobile* underpins the innate similarity between Menzies and Diogenes. Diogenes would not say this unless he knew he had built an alter-ego with whom it was perfectly in character. As a museum curator, Menzies is expected to be—or at least excused for being—a little snobbish. Diogenes is also a good enough judge of character to know that no one will call Menzies on it, not even Nora. Also, the phrase gives us an additional insight to Diogenes' motivation. He is not only striking back at Aloysius by demonstrating what his older brother has done to him, but also somewhat at the mob who killed his parents and destroyed his home. To Diogenes, of course, this is truly "marvelous," so he is once more completely truthful in his words.

I wonder, though, if there is anything of Menzies' usual nature in what Lipper sees during the negotiation of the time frame for the exhibit's completion. When Lipper tells Diogenes that "a rule of thumb says the debugging takes twice as long as the original programming," he immediately protests: "Eight days?" Lipper, the authors note, feels "uneasy from the sudden darkening of Menzies' face." I cannot escape the conviction that Diogenes is shining through Menzies' usually jovial visage. Diogenes needs more time than Lipper's initial estimate in order to test his secret program. He bids the computer consultant down: "Can you finish the debugging in five?"

Again, Lipper finds himself disquieted by the mild-mannered anthropology head: "Something in Menzies' tone led Lipper to think it was more an order than a question" (*Book of the Dead*, p. 94). When he pledges to "try" to meet Menzies' demand, Diogenes/Menzies takes it as a given, and moves on to talking about the gala for the opening. Before returning to more-or-less intimidating Lipper, he makes a private joke; speaking of dividing the opening night guest list of approximately six hundred into two groups to tour the tomb, Diogenes states: "With two showings, we'll get guests through the exhibit within an hour. Finish off the entire crowd." (And more, if Diogenes has his way.) When he admonishes DeMeo and Lipper one more time about finishing the wiring and programming on his accelerated schedule, Lipper finds Menzies' blue eyes "disquieting" (*Book of the Dead*, p. 95).

The train Menzies has to catch at the end of Chapter Sixteen proves in Chapter Seventeen to make a stop at the Feversham Clinic, the hospital section of which contains the recuperating Margo Green. Diogenes has at last discovered, after learning that he did not succeed in killing her, where his brother has hidden her. Naturally, he enters Margo's hospital room as Menzies, offering pleasantries about her view of the Hudson River Valley and the painters that the location has inspired. I feel nearly certain that his older brother has mentioned the Hudson River Valley school of painting on some prior occasion; Diogenes/Menzies adds his opinion that the quality of light there is "second only to Venice" (*Book of the Dead*, p. 98). At this point, the evidence is mounting that Diogenes has spent a great deal of time in Italy.

Still speaking as Menzies, he mentions, "I had to charm my way past half the staff," causing Margo to reflect that "if anyone could charm his way in, Menzies could." She feels fortunate to have him over her at the Museum, and compares him favorably to the other curators; unlike them he is "affable, receptive to the ideas of others, supportive of his staff." Margo's opinion is further evidence that Diogenes has superior people skills when he wishes to use them; further, he can "charm" both in the manner of a dignified Museum department head—and in a deeper, more personal way as he does with Constance. Of course, Margo's belief that Menzies is "receptive to the ideas of others" is just greater proof of Diogenes' manipulative abilities—he can get what he wants from Menzies' colleagues while making them believe it was their own idea.

As Diogenes gradually begins to reveal himself, he undoubtedly counts himself fortunate that he has arrived in Margo's room while she is still receiving intravenous fluids. If she had not been, Diogenes probably would have administered the drug he uses on her by finding his own vein, but with a greater risk of being found out by medical personnel afterward. It is tempting to see Diogenes as slowly medicating Margo from the beginning of Menzies' visit, since she keeps noticing that she "grow[s] tired so easily." She even tells her boss at one point: "I'm still a little out of it." It is not until several conversational exchanges later, however, when Diogenes/Menzies "laid a comforting hand on hers," that she also notices him "slipping his other hand inside his jacket." It is only after he withdraws that hand from his jacket that whatever dangerous chemical he is using begins to enter

Margo's veins. He starts playing with her mind a while before that.

As Diogenes/Menzies seemingly consoles her over the loss of "so much blood," he purposely inserts a phrase he used during his attack on her in the darkness of the Sacred Images exhibit: "There's a reason they call it the living liquid." "Living liquid" does create a frisson in Margo. Diogenes, however, backs off immediately. When Margo asks Menzies to repeat himself, he quickly lies: "I said, have they given you any indication of when you can leave?" Margo takes him at his word, and allows herself to relax. Diogenes is deliberately trying to assist in that relaxation, again, even before administering the drug. "Menzies' voice was low and soothing, and Margo felt torpidity returning" (*Book of the Dead,* p. 99).

He chats with her a little longer before stating he feared she "might have been having nightmares." When Margo denies it, Diogenes/Menzies exclaims, seeming encouraging: "That's my girl! What spunk!" "What spunk!" is exactly the phrase Diogenes used in *Dance of Death* when Margo threatened to kill him if he did not leave her alone, and at this point Margo feels "that strange electric tingle again." She also notices that Menzies' "voice had changed—something about it was both foreign and disquietingly familiar." Diogenes is deliberately letting his own voice slip through at this moment. Something in Margo recognizes it, and she starts to sit up in her hospital bed, but Menzies, "with a gentle but firm pressure on her shoulder … guided her back down onto the pillow." He compliments her, saying, "Not everybody could put such a traumatic event behind them."

When Margo admits that she does not "seem to remember what happened very well," this is the point at which Diogenes/Menzies puts one of his hands on hers, and uses the other to take his syringe out of his jacket. He has told her that it is "just as well" that she does not remember. He is probably starting to inject the substance into her IV port as he says, "nobody would want such memories." Diogenes/Menzies then goes on to detail the sequence of his attack on her, including things Dr. Menzies could not possibly know, such as "the falling of boards." Though he also mentions "laughter in the blackness," he is still "talking in his low, soothing voice"--the voice Margo knows as Menzies' own. Then, however, Diogenes laughs. As himself. Margo notices that it is not Menzies' voice, but "another voice entirely: a hideous, dry chuckle" (*Book of the Dead,* p. 100).

By this point, Diogenes is "looking at her intently, as if gauging the effect of his words," so surely he has seen the "sudden, dreadful shock" that "burned through the gathering lethargy" that he himself had begun to induce. Yet Diogenes has carefully timed the use of the drug he has chosen for Margo, and he has allowed for complete self-revelation to his victim before she slips back into oblivion. He winks at her, and he sees her try to move away from him, to scream, but the drug is already taking effect. Diogenes knows she still has awareness, however, and he removes the hand he had placed upon hers so that she can see the other one with the syringe. "Even as she watched, he withdrew the syringe, palmed it, then replaced it in his suit jacket." Diogenes cannot resist gloating: "My dear Margo … did you really think you'd seen the last of me?" (*Book of the Dead,* p. 100).

Though the chapter ends with Margo struggling to breathe and losing consciousness (while Diogenes, back to using Menzies' voice, covers his tracks by summoning help), readers of the series know that Diogenes does not kill Margo this time, either. While there is certainly some truth to his thoughts much later in the novel that he had enjoyed "keeping her on the brink of expiration" and "teasing out her widowed mother's pain to the greatest possible extent" (*Book of the Dead,* p. 378), I still think Diogenes has something of a weakness where women are concerned. Yes, he intends to kill her on his way out of the country after the debacle at the Museum, but this is to some extent out of sheer fury that Aloysius has once again bested him. Before Diogenes is prevented from carrying out the full effects of his sound-and-light show, there is no real need to kill Margo. Assuming any news would reach his brother in Harkmoor at all, just knowing that Margo's steady recovery had suddenly turned into a coma would have told Aloysius that Diogenes had found her once more, despite the care he had taken in hiding her.

In Chapter Eighteen, all readers learn about Diogenes is that he has apparently been tinkering with the computer programming. When Lipper checks out the network, trying to discover how many bugs in the system he will have to fix, he does not find any, and the thought he has is telling: "It was as if someone had already worked out the kinks" (*Book of the Dead,* p. 102). Diogenes (possibly disguised as Menzies, but not necessarily) is lurking somewhere nearby to make the scratching noises Lipper attributes to a rat. He knows that these sounds will make Lipper fear a rodent chewing at the electrical cables, and go to investigate just as he has caused the computer program for the sound and lights show to load automatically. It is possible that a first-time reader might guess that Lipper in turn causes DeMeo's demise, but those who are re-reading know that Diogenes has made his first test of his ultimate project.

Chapter Nineteen tells us nothing about Diogenes except that he has already managed to win Constance's silence, if not her regard. She has obviously not alerted Wren, D'Agosta, or Proctor about his visit—or visits?--to Riverside Drive. D'Agosta's observation proves that Diogenes has achieved a certain level of intimacy with her, though he will not take her virginity until later in the novel. "Next, D'Agosta's gaze fell on Constance…. She was wearing a severe black dress with a row of tiny pearl buttons in the back, running from the base of her spine up to the nape of her neck. D'Agosta found himself wondering who had buttoned them up for her" (*Book of the Dead,* p. 109). The answer has to be Diogenes. If it were just one of the staff, the authors would not have bothered to mention it. By the end of the chapter we have learned that Constance has become quite invested in maintaining Diogenes' secrecy—and thus his visits—because she lies about how she came to have the little white mouse.

Chapter Twenty focuses on Pendergast in prison, but in Chapters Twenty-One and Twenty Two readers begin to see the kind of effects produced by Diogenes' sound-and-light show. The average first-time reader, however, may not deduce that the carnage described is directly linked to Diogenes' programming, even though (if they have been reading the trilogy in sequence) they know that Menzies is

Diogenes and they can assume that Diogenes is up to *something* nefarious.

It is difficult to know how much real resemblance there is between the brain damage Diogenes is inflicting with his lasers, strobes, and horrible noises, and that he himself suffered from the combination of Comstock's box and the self-inflicted gunshot wound. Firstly, as I and so many others keep having to remind ourselves, this is fiction, and Preston and Child are particularly adept at walking the high wire between solid research and poetic license. Secondly, are the differences in effects upon the various victims differences in exposure to the stimuli, fine-tuning of the stimuli (which may or may not have taken place between the exposures of Lipper and Wicherly, and/or Wicherly and the opening night crowd), or individual differences between the subjects themselves? I find myself wondering if Diogenes as a child experienced the leg-drag that Lipper and some of his other victims did— something later in the novel noted to be related to the swelling in the brain that results from the freshly inflicted laser damage—and then recovered from it after the swelling went down? Does Diogenes have to fight the urge to strew his victim's guts about, as Lipper did with DeMeo? Or is his fascination with blood a milder version of this impulse?

Chapter Twenty-Three tells us nothing about Diogenes, and Chapter Twenty-Four tells us very little, and only in a round-about fashion. In the latter, Nora is in the Museum's Secure Area, investigating the Tomb of Senef's history as an exhibit in the Museum. She reflects upon "how easy it had been to gain access," noting that "Menzies had been instrumental in helping her with the paperwork" (*Book of the Dead,* p. 135).

This tells us that Diogenes *wants* Nora to find out as much as possible about the Tomb's ominous history, to build the sinister atmosphere in which he plans to launch his large-scale version of Great-Uncle Comstock's box. It is tempting to think Diogenes may have fabricated many of the materials Nora looks at, including the documentation of the three murders during the 1930s, in which the victims turned out to be related to people instrumental in the Tomb's discovery and removal from Egypt. Their bodies were placed in the sarcophagus, just as DeMeo was. However, if Diogenes *had* made all of that up, the authors would have had Pendergast, Hayward, or Smithback discover this at the end of the novel. Too, even if he had come up with the details of how the 1930s victims were found, Diogenes could not have predicted that his very first test subject would duplicate the scenario. Thus, it is likely that these details Nora uncovers are real, though Diogenes had probably found them previously.

The longer I consider the question, the more I think that Diogenes definitely had Wicherly in mind for testing his sound-and-light show from the time he hired him. For one thing, Wicherly being out of commission would make the perfect excuse to bring in Viola Maskelene as the new Egyptologist. I think Diogenes intuitively knows that asking her onto the project in the first place, instead of Wicherly, would have drawn the wrong kind of attention to Menzies. Such an invitation would have also found Viola in a more cautious place, fresh from her kidnapping. As it is, even Diogenes must have had difficulty believing how easily he managed to lure Viola back within his reach.

Diogenes probably knew about Wicherly's reputation as a

ladies' man, and this helped in his hiring decision. He deliberately threw the Englishman together with Nora as often as possible, knowing her to be a happily committed newlywed and trusting in her character to frustrate Wicherly's impulses. Perhaps Diogenes had also looked at Wicherly's previous dating history and seen a distinct preference for redheads? It would probably be too great an assumption to make if I said Diogenes had specifically arranged to lock Nora and Wicherly in the special collections room together the day before he planned to run the latter through a private viewing of the sound-and-light show. It *is* possible, however, that Diogenes had listening devices in the room, and chose to begin Wicherly's test case when he knew the Egyptologist had been freshly frustrated and humiliated by Nora's rejection.

Chapters Twenty-Five through Twenty-Seven concern other characters in *Book of the Dead,* and do not really touch upon Diogenes at all—except, of course, that the other characters are dealing with the aftermaths of his plots, plans, and deeds. Chapter Twenty-Eight reinforces some things the reader already knows about Diogenes; Laura Hayward is trying to puzzle out his motive in kidnapping Viola, and within minutes of her embarking upon this train of thought, D'Agosta arrives in her office to explain it. He tells her of the relationship between Pendergast and Viola, and that Diogenes knows of it. D'Agosta also reveals to Hayward that Diogenes had been the one to rescue his older brother from Fosco—for his own nefarious purposes. He tells her of Glinn's profile of Diogenes, and how it predicts that "all of what he's done so far—the killings, the kidnapping, the diamond theft—has been leading up to something else. Something bigger, maybe *much* bigger" (*Book of the Dead,* p. 167). Because of her anger at D'Agosta, Hayward is not receptive to the information at the time; nevertheless, it stays with her, forming connections in the back of her mind.

Chapter Twenty-Nine, however, brings us back to Diogenes, undisguised except for his intentions, with Constance. He is reading Russian poetry to her, demonstrating command of yet another difficult language. More difficult than Latin, because to master it, he has to quickly interpret the Cyrillic characters before he can understand the meaning of the words. Diogenes' ease with this is further evidence of his genius; the description the authors give us in this scene is further evidence of his seductiveness. "He spoke softly, his voice as liquid as honey, the warm cadence of the Deep South strangely appropriate to the flow of the Russian" (*Book of the Dead,* p. 169).

The poet Diogenes has chosen to read to Constance is Anna Akhmatova, of whom he says: "No one else ever wrote about sorrow with the kind of astringent elegance she did." Of course, Diogenes is trying to manipulate Constance, to make her feel that he understands her, and after she protests that she herself is unable to read Russian, he adds: "It's a shame, because I sense hearing Akhmatova speak of her sorrow in her own tongue would help you bear your own." Yet, regardless of his nefarious purposes, would Diogenes even be familiar with this poetry, and be able to take this tack with Constance, if he had not sought his own comfort in this way?

When Constance tries to deny that she has any sorrow,

Diogenes offers himself—and attempts to push Constance into viewing him—as a confidant. He calls her "child," which perhaps seems ironic to the reader, but is at once a role to which she is accustomed, and an endearment which helps reassure her that Diogenes does not think of her as a one-hundred and thirty-some-year-old freak. He continues: "This is Diogenes. With others, you may put up a brave front. But with me, there's no reason to hide anything. I know you. We are so very alike" (*Book of the Dead,* p. 170). Of course, Diogenes is trying to put her into the mindset of the two of them against the world, but again, he would not be able to do this if there were not some underlying truth to his statement. He does know her. He has studied her carefully, imagined what her life has been like, and actually does have quite a few things in common with her, including the underlying madness which he winds up underestimating.

After reminding Constance of his version of childhood with Aloysius—which still stirs an urge to protest in her, but she now stifles this urge—Diogenes asks if she has had any communication with his brother. Though his aim with Constance is to cause her to doubt that Aloysius cares about her, he also wants to gauge his own safety. If, for instance, Pendergast has heard about Margo's turn for the worse, he might have people on the lookout for him at the Feversham Clinic. Constance reassures him by protesting that her guardian cannot possibly contact her because he is in prison, and further accuses, "you put him there." Diogenes, of course, is quick to chip away at her confidence in his brother: "Others in similar situations find ways to get word to those they care about."

Diogenes seemingly turns his tack towards encouraging Constance to liven up her life, but does so while continuing his attempt to build a sense of isolation within her. He tells her she is "trapped in this dark house, a prisoner," and calls Wren, Proctor, and D'Agosta her "jailers." He adds: "They don't love you" (Book of the Dead, p. 171). Though it fits with Diogenes' purpose to undermine Constance's belief that "Aloysius does," he is actually revealing to her the truth as he sees it when he asks her: "You think my brother is capable of love?" Diogenes may have seen the lengths Aloysius went to in winning Viola's safety, and who can say what he may have witnessed of his brother's marriage, having spied upon him all of those years? Yet he cannot believe that anyone capable of love could have purposely led his little brother into a deadly trap. Too, Aloysius was probably quite stoic in the face of his parents' deaths, adding to Diogenes' assumption that he did not feel the tragedy as he did. It is this very stoicism, however, that Diogenes counts on when he asks Constance if Aloysius "ever told you he loved you?" He knows his brother would not express such love even if he felt it. As Diogenes continues to urge Constance to explore the more sensual side of life, he also continues trying to undermine her faith in his elder brother. Interestingly, he chooses color as an example for both purposes, and even though he has drawn Constance's attention to his blind eye on a few occasions, he takes pains to conceal the fact that he is colorblind. "Live in color, not black and white," he exhorts. Perhaps from Diogenes this is honest advice, even including the passionate suicide he has envisioned for her. I think it may be legitimately difficult for him to see Constance, with all of her advantages of long life and normal vision, confining herself to a life he calls "dull. Even stultifying."

When Diogenes asks Constance what color the ceiling is in the library at 891 Riverside, he makes it appear to be a rhetorical question. Diogenes is attuned to the variations of gray; he must have been confident that it had been a different shade on his last visit to Antoine Pendergast, or he would not have followed it up with the question: "Was it always that color?" (*Book of the Dead,* p. 172). Though undoubtedly Diogenes' view of Aloysius is biased by his perception of The Event, he still knows his brother extremely well, and he has some justification in pursuing this line of questioning: "How long do you suppose it took him to pick the color?" When Constance concedes that it probably happened fairly quickly, adding: "Interior decorating is not his forté," Diogenes compares his brother to "an accountant selecting an itemization," and elaborates: "Such an important decision, made so flippantly." Pointing out that the library is the room in which Constance spends most of her time, Diogenes asks Constance: "Very revealing of his attitude toward you, don't you think?" It does seem inconsiderate that Pendergast did not consult her on the question, given that 891 Riverside has been her home for so many years.

Diogenes then proceeds to spin Constance a yarn about the way he chose the color scheme for his own library. Like much of what he tells her, it is a lie, but one based in truth. To me, there is something plaintive in the way he begins: "In my house—my *real* house, the one that is important to me—I have a library like this." Diogenes is acknowledging to

Constance that he has bolt holes all over the world, but there is one place he has found for himself and made into his home. Further, the library he has arranged there is "like" the one on 891 Riverside—which in turn is modeled upon the Pendergasts' ancestral home in New Orleans, Rochenoir, where Diogenes and Aloysius grew up. He tells her why he rejected certain colors for his library, and "settled on a light summery green" because "in shimmering candlelight, it gives the dreamy, languorous effect of being underwater." It is interesting that Diogenes "hesitated" before telling Constance one of the details that later helps her track him down, but I do not think he actually fears this, because he already believes she will die by her own hand. He hesitates deliberately, to build the sense that he is overcoming a natural reticence in order to trust her with a great confidence. Pretending, perhaps, to be embarrassed by his own fanciful notion: "I live near the sea. I can sit in that room all lights and candles extinguished, listening to the roar of the surf, and I become a pearl diver, within, and as one with, the lime-green waters of the Sargasso Sea" (*Book of the Dead*, p. 172).

Though surely innocent Constance is unaware of the use of "pearl diver" as a euphemism for someone who performs cunnilingus, perhaps Preston and Child are not. If the authors' double-entendre is intentional, it follows that Diogenes is deliberate as well. A reader might think he uses the expression for his own amusement, but perhaps the books he has left as gifts for Constance may enlighten her to the point of comprehension. With or without a sexual undertone to his words, Diogenes also makes a literary allusion. Though the Sargasso Sea is an actual geographic location, near the

Caribbean islands, *The Wide Sargasso Sea* is a novel by Jean Rhys that offers a new perspective and a prequel to Charlotte Brontë's *Jane Eyre*. Rhys's novel is told from the viewpoint of the first Mrs. Rochester—the viewpoint of a woman who goes mad and eventually kills herself after setting her home ablaze. It may not be precisely the modus operandi Diogenes has in mind for Constance, but he is probably mindful of the spirit of the work as he speaks.

In his account of choosing "a light summery green" for his library, Diogenes tells Constance that "the various pearl grays, my second choice, were also unacceptable: they lose their bluish gloss and are transformed into a dead, dusky white." The reader finds out later, when Pendergast arrives at his brother's home in pursuit of Constance, that Diogenes lied about this detail as well. Pendergast catches "a glimpse, beyond an open door, of an extraordinary library, rising two stories, done up in a surreal pearl gray" (*Book of the Dead,* p. 425). One wonders if Diogenes' "dead, dusky white" is Aloysius's "surreal"; or has the younger Pendergast brother chosen the *only* shade of pearl gray that creates the effect for him that the green would have for those with color vision? Then again, perhaps Aloysius is every bit the interior decoration expert Constance and Diogenes believe him to be, and he is not recognizing the actual color as he views his brother's house in the dark, with the aid of a flashlight. Whatever the truth is, it is staggering to realize how detailed Diogenes' memory of color is, and to recognize the amount of intellectual prowess and artistic sensibility he displays in his ability to analyze the effects of varying degrees of light upon something he has not been able to see for himself since he was seven years old.

After assuring Constance of the aesthetic superiority of his library to his elder brother's in the visual sense, Diogenes moves on to attack Aloysius's very books, though to some degree these must have been inherited from Great-Uncle Antoine. "Look at the volumes you're surrounded by. Bunyan. Milton. Bacon. Virgil. Sobersided moralists all" (*Book of the Dead,* p. 173). He reveals to the reader that he has been giving Constance books, and other presents; later in Constance's reflections we learn what they are. He wants her to assure him she has opened them; Diogenes claims "they will show you there are other universes out there—perfumed universes, full of wonder and delight, ready to be enjoyed. Monte Carlo, Venice, Paris, Vienna. Or if you prefer: Katmandu, Cairo, Machu Picchu."

Diogenes proceeds to read more poetry to Constance. This time he chooses an American poet, Theodore Roethke, and begins reading the poem "She," with its talk of kissing and singing mouth to mouth. Constance interrupts him, citing the lateness of the hour and adding: "I think you had better leave." This reveals that Diogenes has not only gotten to her on a subliminal romantic level that frightens her, but that she has become invested in his not being found out by Wren, Proctor, or D'Agosta. It is probable that these motives have been present since the beginning of the chapter, and have her sitting in her wing chair "as if at attention, or perhaps poised for flight" (*Book of the Dead,* p. 169). Partly, Constance is protecting Diogenes—she feels that she has agreed to give him sanctuary while he tells and shows her his side of the conflict with Aloysius. Also, however, she has now reached the point where the loss of his visits and attention would pain her. This is especially true while Aloysius is absent and she has begun to doubt that he cares for her in any real sense of the word.

In any case, in addition to agreeing that it is best he not be caught here by her "jailers," Diogenes knows it is better to leave Constance wanting more than to push her too quickly. So, in bidding her goodnight, "he stepped forward and—before she could react—inclined his head, took her hand, and raised it to his lips" (*Book of the Dead,* p. 174). His action is quite effective: "The gesture was executed with perfect formality and the best of breeding. Yet there was something in the way his lips lingered just out of contact with her fingers—something in the warm breath on her skin—that made Constance curl inwardly with unease..." It is odd, however, that this air-kiss of her hand stirs her so, after Diogenes has obviously helped her with those pearl buttons D'Agosta noticed earlier in the novel.

Constance's thoughts after Diogenes leaves her this time are informative about him as well, at least as far as what he is telling her and how he is able to manipulate her thoughts and opinions about him. He must realize the effect he is having on her, because he trusts her to conceal even the traces of his visits—one of the first things she does after he leaves is to remove "the half-finished glass of pastis…. Making her way into the back parts of the house, she entered the service kitchen, where she rinsed and dried the glass." Diogenes would not have left this evidence behind if he did not have faith that Constance would protect him.

In her mind, Constance goes over the main points Diogenes has made to her—that Aloysius did something absolutely horrible to him during their childhood together, and that "his brother had gone out of his way to poison others against him—herself in particular—by telling lies and insinuations, making him out to be evil incarnate" (*Book of the Dead*, p. 175). Diogenes has definitely made headway with this line of thought, because Constance is now asking herself: "*Could there be some truth to Diogenes' stories? Her head told her he was untrustworthy, a thief, perhaps a sadistic killer … but her heart told her differently.*" She notes that "he seemed so understanding, so vulnerable. So *kind.*" I cannot argue that he is kind, knowing his intent is to have her commit suicide over his eventual betrayal—and hence that his betrayal will also make her surrender to him a betrayal of Aloysius on her part. Constance is correct, however, in deeming him "vulnerable." The very real damage he has suffered at Aloysius's however unwitting hands has made Diogenes vulnerable, but he knows how to use that vulnerability to his own advantage. I think Diogenes also knows he has to play Constance as close to his actual feelings as possible in order to fool her most effectively, and thus he leaves himself vulnerable to actually feeling something for her that could possibly (though not likely) interfere with his plans to use her for further revenge upon his older brother.

Another interesting point Constance makes to herself in Diogenes' defense is that "he had even shown her evidence—documents, old photographs—that seemed to undercut many of the things Aloysius had told her about him" (*Book of the Dead*, p. 175). Though certainly some of the documents could be falsified, I would guess the photographs are genuine. Diogenes probably managed to save some of him as a small child, both eyes still hazel, gazing up adoringly into his mother's face from the comfort of her lap; possibly even one of himself and Aloysius taken before The Event that showed them playing together and proved—as comes out later in the series—that they were not always enemies. Also, Diogenes very cleverly does not try to paint himself as completely innocent: "he hadn't denied everything; he had also accepted a share of blame, admitted being a less-than-perfect brother— a deeply flawed human being" (*Book of the Dead*, pp. 175-176).

If Diogenes is appealing to Constance's logic, however, he is applying himself much more forcefully to her physical senses. He leaves her the volumes of poetry he has been reading to her, and as previously noted, these are additions to the books he has already given her on other visits. Not only is the writing within the books meant to stimulate her dormant sensuality, but the books themselves. When she "picked up the top volume," she observes that "it was exquisitely bound in silk, with gilt edging and hand-marbled endpapers. She turned it over in her hands, feeling the delicious suppleness of the material" (*Book of the Dead,* p. 174). Diogenes has also gifted her with Parisian bath oils in "small glass bottles" wrapped in "a beautifully papered gift box," which she decides to use after he leaves. "The heady scent of lavender and patchouli perfumed the air" (*Book of the Dead,* p. 175).

Perhaps most revealing of the effectiveness of Diogenes' strategy thus far with Constance is that before she descends into this luxurious bath, she "walked over to the full-length mirror and regarded her nude form for a long moment, sliding her hands over her sides, along her smooth belly." She has to be wondering what Diogenes would think of her body, if he would find it attractive, desirable, knowing what he does of her. As Constance bathes, Preston and Child tell us that "she wondered if Diogenes was telling the truth when he said he understood her—because, at some deep level she had yet to plumb, she believed him: she felt a connection. Most important, she was beginning to understand him as well" (*Book of the Dead,* p. 176). Despite how it eventually plays out between the two of them, I still think Constance's "deep level" is correct—she and Diogenes *do* understand each other, at least in the rudimentary way of all kindred spirits. This does not prevent Diogenes from placing his brother's pain above passion; it also does not prevent him from underestimating both Constance's ability to take his true measure and her will to live.

Finally, at the end of the chapter, the titles Diogenes has given Constance to read are laid before us: "The *Satyricon* of Petronius; Huysmans's *Àu rebours*; Oscar Wilde's letters to Lord Alfred Douglas; the love poetry of Sappho; Boccaccio's *Decameron.*" In including the Wilde and Sappho works, Diogenes proves himself as equality-minded as his older brother, who has spoken up for the humanity of gays and bisexuals on a few occasions in the series. He also pays Constance the compliment of assuming she will not be repulsed by such viewpoints. Diogenes may be bisexual himself to some degree, in that sex probably has a great deal to do with power for him, and in his lust for power, the gender of its object might not particularly matter to him. In any case, the reading material has the hoped-for effect upon Constance; in her thoughts, "decadence, opulence, and passionate love clung to these pages like musk" (*Book of the Dead,* p. 176).

Chapter Thirty does not concern Diogenes, but in Chapter Thirty-One Bill Smithback explores the house on Long Island in which Viola was held. Smithback discovers some things that readers already know, such as how impenetrable the house is, and some things that we did not. The anvil and titanium hammer have already been discussed, but while the other contents of the dwelling may be less sensational, they still hold interest. For the Long Island house to have steel walls and bulletproof glass, Diogenes would have to have had it built himself, or bought it himself and made renovations and reinforcements. So it is not a question of this being a rental, and some of the objects having come with the house. Though some of the furnishings may have been selected by Diogenes with an eye towards making it appear a typical Long Island beach house, nevertheless he chose them.

Curiously, while still on the outside looking in, Smithback sees "a tidy, old-fashioned kitchen, devoid of the usual utensils" (*Book of the Dead,* p. 186). Later, from the inside, Smithback finds the kitchen "spotless," and reasons: "The police would not have cleaned the house: he figured this was the way Diogenes habitually kept it" (*Book of the Dead,* p. 187). Not that Diogenes would be incapable of cleaning a kitchen, but given the lack of "usual utensils" visible from the side door windows, perhaps this is indicative of his eating most of his meals away from the house? Possibly many of them consumed as Menzies in the Museum's cafeteria? This might also help to explain his offering Viola nothing but hard candy during her captivity. Still, most of what Smithback views in the house points to a habitually neat and tidy Diogenes—except when he is in the grip of overpowering negative emotion. Even if Diogenes' wait to obtain the anvil helped cool him off somewhat, he is still infuriated as he smashes the diamonds to bits. Smithback discovers that the library containing the anvil and hammer "was unaccountably disordered. Books lay on the floor, some open, with gaps on the shelves. The rug was rumpled and turned up at one end, and a table lamp lay broken on the floor" (*Book of the Dead*, p. 188). Of course, hurry is another factor; Diogenes knew it was only a matter of time before the police came to his hideout. Though this was not the library he truly cared about, he had apparently stocked it with volumes he valued enough to carry away with him, hence the above-mentioned "gaps." The books he later gives to Constance may be among these, or perhaps there were others he wanted to keep for himself. Apparently, Diogenes felt he needed some of the books in his Long Island library more than he needed the coats that helped Smithback figure out that he had an alter-ego at the Museum. Either he had more items from Menzies' wardrobe stashed at other locations, or he replaced them very quickly.

Smithback adds another accomplishment to the reader's portrait of Diogenes. The grand piano he discovers in the living room of the Long Island house "was beautifully in tune," leading him to conclude: "Diogenes played the piano." The music Smithback finds open on the piano stand is Schubert's Impromptus, opus 90. He finds other pieces on the stand underneath the Schubert, including Debussy's "Clair de

Lune," and a grouping of Chopin's nocturnes, and these selections cause him to conclude that Diogenes is "a relatively accomplished pianist at that, but probably not at the concert level" (*Book of the Dead*, p. 188). I will accept that the late Mr. Smithback (and by extension, Preston and Child) has a greater knowledge of classical piano than my own. Yet I cannot help wondering whether the piano bench is one of those with a lid opening upon a storage space for sheet music, and music books Smithback never bothered to look for rested there. Perhaps the intrepid reporter was right, and Diogenes has no hope of playing the works of Alkan. Even if he cannot play "Les Quatre Àges," however, Diogenes still might have a few pages of other pieces from his favorite composer that he either has mastered, or is still learning.

Two items in the Long Island house I find particularly curious; Smithback finds on the upstairs landing that "a small, stuffed capuchin monkey crouched on a table, next to a glass dome under which stood a fake tree festooned with butterflies" (*Book of the Dead*, p. 188). Unless the authors later choose to enlighten us, we will never be sure whether Diogenes performed the act of taxidermy himself on a monkey on whom he "experimented" himself, or if there is a more innocuous explanation. I like to think the monkey came from Great-Uncle Antoine's collections, and that Diogenes took it from 891 Riverside after his death as a memento of his long-lived relative. Though the glass dome is evocative of Antoine's curiosities as well, the "fake" tree seems too cheap and common to have been chosen by a Pendergast. Even if the butterflies are *not* fake—again, we have no way of knowing—one would think Diogenes would have used an appropriately sized genuine tree branch with twigs to display them. If the butterflies *are* fake, the object being in the Long Island house is even more unfathomable, especially considering he has also decorated this temporary bolt hole with Chippendale furniture. Perhaps the glass dome, fake tree, and butterflies have some nefarious purpose upon which we can only speculate.

In Chapter Thirty-Two we learn more about what has happened to the first victim of Diogenes' sound-and-light show. Captain Laura Hayward has come to the psychiatric ward at Bellvue with the intention of interviewing Jay Lipper, but he is in such horrible condition that she is unable to elicit any response from him. Though the doctor in attendance explains the results of Lipper's EEG and MRI to Hayward, noting that the former "showed significant focal temporal abnormalities" and the latter "revealed a series of small lesions to the frontal cortex" (*Book of the Dead,* p. 192), it is difficult to determine how much of the apparent damage is the result of Diogenes' intentions. Lipper is also heavily sedated, because when his parents came to visit him, "he said he was going to kill them both and … rip out their guts" (*Book of the Dead,* p. 194). Prior to this, however, Lipper manages one moment of clarity, telling these same parents, "This isn't me." By the time Hayward sees him, though, she cannot be sure he even recognizes his name. The authors describe his condition thus: "He sat in a wheelchair, restrained. He was making slow circles with his head, and his lips were moving, but no sound came out.

"His face was shocking. It was as if it had caved in, the skin gray and slack and hanging in leathery folds, the eyes jittery and unfocused, the tongue hanging out, as long and pink and wet as that of an overheated retriever" (*Book of the Dead,* pp. 193-194). All of these details lead me to suspect that Diogenes is probably aiming to inflict worse than Great Uncle Comstock's box did to him, but this may be incorrect. By the time he tests the sound-and-light show on Wicherly, he seems to have refined it so the effects are not quite so severe—but is this due to a refinement in the procedure, or a basic difference in the subjects? It is also possible that the effects upon the seven-year-old Diogenes were far worse initially than they appear to be now that he has been an adult for many years. He could have had similarly bizarre effects like Lipper's while his brain swelled in response to the self-inflicted gun shot wound, but more than likely he would have been unconscious and hovering between life and death at that point. If Diogenes had suffered more significant brain damage than meets the eye presently, he could have been more quickly to recover than his sound-and-light victims, because a child's brain tissues are more capable of healing, the brain function areas more capable of adapting to replace other damaged segments.

It makes sense, however—at least in speaking of Diogenes—that he would want to cause more damage than he received. Not only would it be more pain and suffering that he could cause Aloysius, but it would please his sense of Pendergast family pride to best his Great-Uncle Comstock at his own game.

Chapter Thirty-Three returns the focus to Aloysius in prison and the mechinations of Spencer Coffey; Chapter Thirty-Four gives readers the thoughts of Diogenes' next victim on the way to his fate. This serves the purpose of giving us a baseline against which to measure Wicherly's actions after being exposed to the sound-and-light show; it also demonstrates how Diogenes is using the setting of an ancient Egyptian tomb to enhance the effects produced by the lasers and mind-altering sonics. Also, we learn that Diogenes, as Menzies, has commanded Wicherly perform a specific task in the tomb at three o'clock in the morning. Of course, this time has the advantage of the Museum being empty of potential witnesses, but it is also an hour of the night at which most human beings would be at their most easily frightened and vulnerable.

As the chapter opens, Wicherly is fixated on Nora and her rejection of him: "He flushed at the thought of the way she had led him on and then humiliated him; he had heard that American women liked to burst one's bollocks, and now he'd had a taste of it, good and proper. The woman was as common as muck" (*Book of the Dead,* p. 202). He soon changes focus, however, to the tomb and how creepy it is at this time of night—although he does pause to make the observation: "A backup tech to succeed poor Lipper had already reported for duty, but so far had proved superfluous. The grand opening was only five days away, and although the tomb's collections were only partially installed, the lighting, electronics, and the sound-and-light show were ready to go" (*Book of the Dead,* p. 203). Again, this is a sign of Diogenes' having already completed the computer programming and electronic work behind the scenes.

Walking through the tomb, Wicherly pays more attention to its inscribed curses than ever before. After the initial inscription that bids Ammut devour the heart of those who cross the tomb's threshold, he reflects that "in studying Egypt for so long, in learning to read hieroglyphics fluently, in immersing himself in their ancient beliefs, Wicherly had come to half believe them himself" (*Book of the Dead,* p. 204). He tries to shake it off, thinking: "Of course, they were all rubbish," but he cannot keep himself from adding, "but at one level he understood them so thoroughly they almost seemed real." This, perhaps, is another reason Diogenes chooses Wicherly as a test subject—his unconscious susceptibility to the atmosphere of the cursed tomb. Wicherly is especially affected by this tomb's rendering of Ammut. He notes its "squatting, grotesque form" and "its slavering crocodile jaws open and glistening, the scaly head morphing into a leopard's spotted body, which in turn segued into the hindquarters of a hippo." In his opinion, the "hindquarters were the most vile of all: a bloated, slimy, mishapen fundament spreading over the ground."

When he walks over the bridge spanning the well, Wicherly sees again the inscription from the Egyptian Book of the Dead. "The passage, it seemed to Wicherly, implied that those who invaded the place which was sealed—the tomb—would be deprived of their Ba-soul. In other words, those who defiled the tomb would be driven insane" (*Book of the Dead,* p. 205). Then the realization strikes him: "Isn't that just what had happened to that poor bugger Lipper?"

We never learn exactly what it is that Diogenes, as Menzies, has asked Wicherly to do in the tomb at three o'clock in the morning. We only know that it is the thought of this task that caused the Egyptologist to shrug off his prescient feelings of unease. "He had work to do. He had a special errand to run for Dr. Menzies" (*Book of the Dead,* p. 205).

In Chapter Thirty-Five, we see the aftermath of that errand. Basically, Wicherly attacks Nora, nearly strangles her, and is shot to death by a Museum guard. Though he is clearly violent, and displays some facial tics, his damage does not seem as severe as Lipper's. He is able to appear normal until faced with the object of his rage, Nora. He is still capable of intelligent speech, even sarcasm; he accuses Nora of "worrying that I might try to slip something unwelcome into your knickers?" (*Book of the Dead,* p. 207). Then again, readers never get to see him sedated by the same kinds of drugs used on Lipper. In a later chapter, however, Captain Hayward tells the Museum's director about Wicherly and Lipper's autopsies: "The bottom line is they both suffered identical, sudden brain damage to the ventromedial cortex of the brain" (*Book of the Dead,* p. 221).

The "identical" nature of the victims' injuries implies that Diogenes may not have calibrated his delivery mechanism between using it on Lipper and using it on Wicherly. He may simply have wanted to see how two different test subjects responded to the treatment. Once more it is somewhat relevant that both subjects chosen were male. Though Diogenes certainly knows that some of the people that will tour the Tomb of Senef during the opening gala will be female, and relishes the thought of his brother's lady love being among them, he shies away from singling out women for casual experimentation. At the very least, if one argues that Margo and her mother prove an exception to that last statement, Diogenes does not seem particularly fond of the idea of loosing crazed, animalistic women upon society. For this is exactly what he does with Lipper and Wicherly—after subjecting them to his sound-and-light show, he leaves them free to do as they wish, to create as much mayhem as possible. Diogenes displays a kind of fatalistic, gambling streak in his character by doing this. Lipper does not seem to be capable of telling anyone that he has viewed the Senef presentation in its altered entirety, but Wicherly *does* seem to have the ability. I do not believe Diogenes in either his own persona or that of Menzies would have taken the chance of bribing a guard to shoot Wicherly; he is fortunate that his second Senef victim is killed before he can talk about his experience. Then again, perhaps Diogenes is completely confident that the damage he causes will invariably lead to his subjects' committing heinous acts that immediately cause them to be killed, drugged, and/or institutionalized.

Diogenes' behavior as Hugo Menzies in Chapter Thirty-Five is also worth examining. In the more civilized hours of the morning that Wicherly was subjected to the sound-and-light show, Menzies appears at Nora's office, "his blue eyes worried, his brow furrowed with concern" (*Book of the Dead,* p. 206). Is this an act, or is Diogenes actually a little ill at ease over possibly having misplaced Wicherly? Menzies asks Nora: "You haven't seen Adrian, have you?" (*Book of the Dead,* p. 207).

Whether Diogenes has lost track of his latest victim or not, he is anxious to promote the belief that Menzies has no idea why the Museum's security system shows Wicherly in the Tomb of Senef between 3:00 and 3:30AM. When Nora protests that "it's very early, he probably isn't in yet," Diogenes/Menzies responds: "That's just the thing. He did come in at three this morning. Checked in through security and accessed the tomb, according to the electronic security logs." He goes on to tell Nora that Wicherly "left the tomb at three-thirty, locked it up tight. Strange thing is, he didn't leave the museum—he hasn't checked out." Menzies ends by admitting, "I can't find him anywhere." When Nora asks the logical question, "Do you know why he came in at three?" Diogenes/Menzies is quick to feign unknowing speculation: "He might have wanted to get a head start on the day; as you know, we have to start moving the final artifacts at nine."

What makes me believe that Diogenes *has* lost track of Wicherly at this point is that "Menzies seemed startled himself" when the brain-damaged Egyptologist appears in the doorway of Nora's office. Diogenes/Menzies "then smiled with relief." The smile and the relief are not just good covering improvisation on Diogenes' part. When he follows up by telling Wicherly, "I'd like to have a chat with you in my office about the artifact placements," he is probably already planning to kill him and claim to have been attacked. Better yet, Diogenes can easily provoke Wicherly into actually attacking him, and create enough noise to draw witnesses. Elderly Menzies' victory over his suddenly crazed younger subordinate would seem like a miracle, but as well-liked as the head of the Anthropology Department is, that miracle would be gratefully accepted without too much examination.

Diogenes does, however, allow Wicherly the private "word with Nora" he asks for, and even "shut[s] the door" to Nora's office "behind him" (*Book of the Dead,* p. 207). He quickly adjusts to the prospect of his victim attacking Nora rather than himself. Though he has no difficulty with leaving Nora alone with someone he knows is dangerous—and with whom he probably knows she already has tensions—to his credit, Diogenes/Menzies does arrive with help on time. Whether he does so because he cannot afford to lose Nora's crucial help with the tomb's opening, or because he prefers to save her for his own sound-and-light show is difficult to determine. It is possible that Dr. Menzies could have begun summoning Museum guards before any altercation started, but to do so would be to bet that Wicherly would indeed become aggressive by the time they arrived. Of course, Diogenes knows that even if Wicherly has done nothing to Nora by then, the arrival of armed guards would surely provoke him. Still, it is more likely Diogenes listened until Wicherly attacked the phone, when he "lunged forward and swept it from the desk to the floor, stomped on the cradle, yanked the wire out the back, and tossed it aside" (*Book of the Dead*, p. 209). Again, however, Diogenes may have had Nora's office bugged, allowing him to act sooner.

Yet Diogenes' behavior as Menzies at the end of Chapter Thirty-Five fascinates me most of all. Menzies is with the guards as they break into Nora's locked office, but the one guard's protest: "I had to do it, he came at me with a knife!" (*Book of the Dead*, p. 211) seems to preclude the possibility that Wicherly died because the department head excitedly screamed for them to shoot him. The first thing Nora realizes as she is coming to her senses after nearly being choked to death is that "suddenly Menzies was there, cradling her in his arms and calling for a doctor." From there, he "eased her down into the wing chair, whispering all the time: 'You're all right, my dear, everything's fine, the doctor's on his way.'" Diogenes/Menzies even tries to protect her from what has happened to her attacker and former colleague: "No, don't look over there... Close your eyes and all will be fine... Don't look, don't look" (*Book of the Dead,* p. 211). Perhaps such tender care is expected from Hugo Menzies, but Diogenes does not seem to have any difficulty giving it. He may be somewhat fond of Nora, and somewhat regretful of the fate he has planned for her; he may want to be as kind to her as possible in the time remaining. Surely he has more respect for her than he does most of the other anthropology department members. Or maybe Diogenes believes that Nora may be clever enough to figure everything out when she is in the tomb, being subjected to the sound-and-light show, and her feelings of shock and betrayal will be all the more intense for remembered kindnesses. In any case, the behavior is not completely alien to Diogenes—this instance is similar to how gently he kissed Viola, and we will see more of it later in the novel.

Chapter Thirty-Six marks the arrival of Captain Hayward upon the scene. This is the first time that she and Diogenes (or Dr. Menzies) are in the same room with each other. Diogenes/Menzies is still comforting Nora, though taking a respectful backseat to her husband by this point, merely reassuring her that the Museum can prepare for the upcoming opening of Senef's tomb without her for one day while she gets checked out at the emergency room. Hayward is questioning Nora about Wicherly's attack. Perhaps Diogenes does not expect Hayward to be quick enough in her deductions to ask whether Wicherly had been in the tomb when Nora tells her he had been at the Museum since three o' clock in the morning, but he decides the best defense is a good offense. As Menzies, he pipes up: "Yes, he did. The security log shows he entered the tomb just after three, spent half an hour in there, then left. Where he was between then and the attack, we don't know. I looked all over for him" (*Book of the Dead*, p. 213). Then again, knowledge that the crazed Wicherly had been in Senef's tomb before the attack was necessary to help build the atmosphere of an ancient curse that Diogenes counted on to sharpen the effectiveness of his "pain factory." This atmosphere was even more essential to ensuring him a huge number of victims.

Menzies is led away by another officer to have his statement taken. He is not in hearing range when Captain Hayward finally gets the medical examiner on her radio. Thus Diogenes does not know that she has asked him to look at Wicherly's brain for lesions "to the ventromedial frontal cortex" (*Book of the Dead*, p. 214). Neither is he privy to Hayward's conversation with Smithback about the probability of his having an alter-ego among the Museum's curators.

Chapter Thirty-Seven finds Diogenes seemingly in Menzies' element—in Collopy's office, persuading the Museum Director and the rest of his most trusted advisors to follow the course of action he desires. Though, as usual, the representatives of the legal department and public relations have already given their negative interpretation of recent events and extremely cautious and conservative recommendations, Collopy is "amazed at how cool, collected and composed Menzies looked" (*Book of the Dead*, p. 218). As Diogenes/Menzies begins to offer his disagreement, wrapped in sweetly polite compliments to his opponents, his "blue eyes, so full of calm self-assurance, impressed Collopy." Diogenes is extremely confident in his ability to manipulate everyone in the room, but Collopy in particular. The "self-assurance" he exudes as Menzies comes from a complete faith in his own superior intelligence. I believe some of Diogenes/Menzies' calm manner, however, stems from the recent satiation of his pathological hunger. He has just gotten to watch most of Adrian Wicherly's blood drain from his body, knowing he had caused it as surely as if he had pulled the trigger himself. Simultaneously, he enjoyed the chance to murmur soothing words to his attractive female colleague/prospective future victim. Diogenes is probably also experiencing the satisfaction of having an unpredictable situation—i.e., Wicherly's transformation—resolved with relative ease.

Briefly, Diogenes as Menzies makes the argument that not only were Lipper and Wicherly not official Museum employees, but further that there was no relationship between the two incidents. He notes that "during the same six-week period, New York City had sixty-one homicides, fifteen hundred assaults, and countless felonies and misdemeanors. Did the mayor shut down the city? No. What did he do instead? He announced the good news: the crime rate is down four percent from the previous year." Diogenes/Menzies goes on to tell the legal and public relations representatives to "by all means, issue a statement. But be sure to point out that this *is* New York City and that the museum is a vast place covering twenty-eight acres of Manhattan with two thousand employees and five million visitors a year, and that under these circumstances it's surprising that *more* random crimes don't happen" (*Book of the Dead,* p. 219).

Menzies also utters the lie that "the perpetrators have been caught," and points out that the mayor is planning on attending the gala and "might just use the auspicious occasion to announce his bid for re-election" (*Book of the Dead,* p. 220). When the issue of the curse rumors is raised, he gleefully responds: "The mummy's curse? It's marvelous. Now everyone will want to come." After he has managed to convince everyone to stay the gala's course, however, Captain Hayward arrives and asks to speak with Collopy privately. The authors tell us: "The door closed after Menzies—the last to leave—had said his goodbyes" (*Book of the Dead,* p. 221). Thus Diogenes is not present to hear Hayward's allegation that he has an alter-ego on the Museum staff.

The only thing we learn about Diogenes in Chapter Thirty-Eight is that, as Menzies, he has continued to visit Margo, and also phoned her mother to tell her all about what happened to her—of course, leaving out his own crucial role in it. Later we learn that the reason he speaks with Mrs. Green is to basically drink in her suffering over her daughter's condition. Margo's condition itself, however, is just one more revelation that Aloysius has not been exaggerating about his brother's genius. Diogenes has baffled his brother's favorite physicians. One of them explains to Margo's mother: "The bottom line is this: we simply don't have a diagnosis. We've performed every test we can think of and then some; we've consulted with the country's top coma and neurology specialists […] and we just don't have a handle on it yet. Margo is in a deep coma, and we don't know why" (*Book of the Dead,* p. 225).

In Chapter Thirty-Nine, Diogenes/Menzies is physically absent, but his influence is pervasive. Readers learn for the first time that Diogenes has plans to take his sound-and-light show to most of the world's English-speaking countries. "The local PBS station planned to cover the opening [of Senef's tomb] live, and they had energetically syndicated the show to ensure it would not only go out to most PBS affiliates across the nation, but also be carried by the BBC and the CBC" (*Book of the Dead,* pp. 227-228). Notably, this huge audience "was a public relations coup that Menzies himself had worked hard to arrange" (*Book of the Dead,* p. 228). One wonders how Diogenes, even if disguised as Menzies, has managed to make the acquaintance of an award-winning documentary director and persuade him to take on this project.

Diogenes' possible success rate in televising his destructive horror show is up for question. Even assuming that the damage from the lasers and sound waves would carry over the airwaves, surely those watching on television would shut off their sets or change the channel as the sensations became increasingly unpleasant. Granted, some audience members would watch longer than was strictly comfortable in an effort to find out exactly what was happening on the scene, much as news watchers linger in gory fascination over disaster footage. Even if Diogenes cannot hope to bring the full effects to his television audience, he will content himself with causing as much damage as he can. Perhaps subtle or not-so-subtle changes in the viewing victims' impulse control will make everything in the world a little worse; cruelty will beget cruelty, and it will eventually end in Great-Uncle Antoine's dream of humanity extinguishing itself in nuclear holocaust.

Readers also learn in this chapter that not only has Diogenes-as-Menzies brought Viola Maskelene in to replace Wicherly as the exhibit's Egyptologist, he has talked with her. Apparently he has done so without her suspecting a thing; Viola tells Nora: "Dr. Menzies has spoken so highly of you" (*Book of the Dead*, p. 230). It's possible that this speaking was done over the phone, and Viola would have more difficulty recognizing Diogenes strictly from a disguised voice. Still, she does not recognize him later during the opening night gala, either. If Viola found the sudden job offer from the very Museum Diogenes robbed while holding her hostage suspicious at all, she did not let that stop her from accepting it. When Nora realizes who she is, and mentions her having been "kidnapped by the jewel thief" (*Book of the Dead*, p. 234), Viola tells her that "all that was just another reason I was glad to take this job and return to New York." When Nora responds with puzzlement, Viola elaborates: "To me, it's sort of like falling off a horse—you've got to get right back on if you ever hope to ride again." On the one hand, Diogenes did manage to get under her skin. On the other, he did not frighten her enough to make her stay away from the geographical region of her victimization. True, other factors are relevant as well; when Nora brings up Viola's relationship with Aloysius, Lady Maskelene admits: "Agent Pendergast is the other reason I returned" (*Book of the Dead*, p. 234).

Chapter Forty briefly returns the focus to Aloysius Pendergast in prison, but Chapter Forty-One showcases Diogenes at his most charming and seductive. Though he has planned to take Constance's virginity all along, I do not believe it is just happy coincidence for him that he manages to succeed in this aim on the very eve of the opening gala for Senef's tomb. Rather, Diogenes' own sense of pleasure in pulling all the threads of his various plots neatly and tightly together has guided him in choosing that particular night. Yet as he turns his hand to attempting this crime against a woman's heart, he is also ironically at his most vulnerable. As mentioned before, Diogenes has learned that "the truth is the safest lie" by now, and he has to stick with the truth as much as possible to convince Constance both of his sincerity and their mutual affinity. For this momentous evening, Diogenes has chosen to wear "dark trousers and a silver-gray cashmere jacket" (*Book of the Dead,* p. 237). That he has abandoned the tactic of dressing like his elder brother reveals both his confidence that he has managed to change Constance's feelings towards him, and his own feelings about her seduction—he wants her to clearly choose him over his brother. True, this will enhance her feelings of worthlessness after he abandons her, knowing that she has betrayed Aloysius, but it is also a point of pride with Diogenes to be chosen for himself rather than the familial resemblance.

As the chapter opens, Diogenes is guiding Constance through the portrait gallery on the second floor of 891 Riverside. As he gives Constance information she has never had about the family that has had such huge effect upon her life, he gives the reader new information as well. The original family name is Prendregast, and dates back at least to the Norman conquest of England, though its scions apparently returned to France after the fighting. Diogenes cites one ancestor as "the largest landholder in Dijon during the late sixteenth century," who was "forced to flee Dijon when the peasants and villeins working his lands revolted" (*Book of the Dead,* pp. 237-238). Given what we know of Aunt Cornelia and the mob that burned down Rochenoire, the clan seems to have a pretty negative history with the lower classes, though Diogenes tells Constance that it was the branch of the family "left without favor, title, or money" that "fled to America." Yet their perusal of the portraits also reveals how strong the Pendergast genes are. The painting of the son of the Dijon landholder, a man who must have died between three and four hundred years before, features "full and sensual lips" that "seemed almost the mirror of Diogenes' own." It is this particular ancestor that started the line of Pendergasts/ Prendregasts that settled in Venice, and Diogenes tells Constance that he "sank into idleness and dissipation, and for several generations his descendants followed suit. For a time, in fact," Diogenes continues, "the lineage was sadly reduced. It did not regain its full flower for another hundred years, when the two family lines were reunited by marriage in America."

When Diogenes adds "even that, of course, proved a fleeting glory," he is preparing to inform Constance that "the Pendergast family has been in a long, slow decline. My brother and I are the last." Never one to miss a chance to cast Aloysius in a negative light, Diogenes notes: "Although my brother married, his charming wife … met an *untimely* end before she could reproduce." On the heels of this, he makes sure that Constance is aware that he himself is unattached: "I have neither wife nor child. If we die without issue, the Pendergast line will vanish from the earth" (*Book of the Dead,* p. 238).

After giving a few more examples from his illustrious family tree, and listening to Constance muse upon the fact that Antoine Leng Pendergast had not provided her with any of these names and histories, Diogenes makes the observation that it is also "clear my brother never spoke much of the family to you, either" (*Book of the Dead,* p. 239). He is making plain another contrast between himself and Aloysius when he tells her: "I know a great deal about my family, Constance. I have taken pains to learn their secret histories." Diogenes is on this point utterly truthful. Though the damage done to him was caused by members of his own family— Great Uncle Comstock and, to his mind, his own brother, Aloysius—Diogenes still values the sense of identity he has in being a Pendergast. He also feels that understanding his family will help him understand and cope with what The Event has done to him. In embracing his ancestors' eccentricity, he embraces his own. Diogenes, again, is completely truthful when he says to Constance: "I can't tell you how happy it makes me to be able to share this with you. I feel I can talk to you … like no other." The only catch is that he is determined to make her a sacrifice to his burning desire to cause his brother pain, no matter the pleasure inherent in her companionship.

Similarly, Diogenes is sincere when he assures Constance: "You deserve to know it," meaning all of the Pendergast family history. "Because after all," he adds, "you're a member of the family, too—in a way." Though Constance protests that she is "only a ward," Diogenes implies with his phrasing that she has the unique advantage of being the only other person aside from his brother to have been raised and educated by a Pendergast, without the disadvantage of a blood relationship that would render her unsuitable as a romantic object. Under another circumstance that did not involve his older brother's having responsibility for her safety and mental well-being, Diogenes might well rejoice in Constance's being like a long-lost cousin. If there were anyone on the face of the earth that would tempt Diogenes into a sincere romantic partnership, it would be someone exactly like Constance. Again, he is truthful in telling her: "To me, you are more than that—much more" (*Book of the Dead*, p. 239). Unfortunately, a large portion of that "much more" is as a tool in his revenge scheme.

At this point, Diogenes switches focus from the Pendergast ancestry to his introduction of absinthe to Constance. No doubt he is counting on its relatively high alcohol content to help make her tipsy and impair her judgment as well as on its fanciful, romantic reputation among rebellious artists and writers. When she protests its illegality (a more recent issue when *Book of the Dead* first saw print), Diogenes admonishes: "We should not be concerned with such trifles. It is powerful, mind-expanding: which is why great artists from Van Gogh to Monet to Hemingway made it their drink of choice." Absinthe is something Diogenes actually believes in. We have already seen in *Dance of Death* that despite his staggering intellectual capacity, Diogenes is prone to certain forms of superstition and magical thinking, as with the tarot cards; his attitude towards absinthe is similar.

Once more, however, Diogenes seeks to deceive Constance on the issue of his ability to see color. I do not think this is particular to Constance, or forms any crucial part of his overall design upon her, but rather it continues to be a point of pride with him, a subject on which he would try to deceive anyone. If anything, Diogenes could use his colorblindness as something to make Constance feel pity for him, but he disdains this, preferring to win her on his own terms. He tells her, referring to the absinthe: "Look into it, Constance. Have you ever seen a drink of such a pure and unadulterated color? Hold it up to the light. It's like gazing at the moon through a flawless emerald." Even though it is possible Diogenes has simply read literary raves about the green tint of the liquor, this makes me believe he has seen someone drinking it during his childhood, and the color stayed sharp in his memory. Though both Great Aunt Cornelia and Aloysius condemn absinthe early in the series, some Pendergast family member probably consumed it as Diogenes quietly witnessed.

After replying to Diogenes' query about how the absinthe makes her feel—probably part of an attempt to gauge the timing of his seduction efforts—Constance brings the subject back to the Pendergastian penchant for reproducing the ancestral New Orleans home, "including these paintings." Diogenes recounts how Antoine Pendergast worked with an artist "for five years" to re-create the portraits "from memory and a few faded engravings and drawings." He then tells Constance that 891 Riverside is "almost identical to the original, save for his choice of volumes in the library." Diogenes concludes with another jab at Aloysius: "After my brother took over this house, a great many changes were made. It is no longer the place Uncle Antoine called home. But then, you know that all too well."

Next, Diogenes moves to "a long, backless settee" which is

"cushioned in plush velvet" (*Book of the Dead,* p. 240), and gestures for Constance to sit next to him upon it. Here the conversation turns to the music, which has been present from the beginning of the chapter, "dense, lush, and demoniacally complex" (*Book of the Dead,* p. 237). By this time, the authors tell us, "the shimmering piano scales [...] freighted the air" (*Book of the Dead,* p. 241). Diogenes is more than happy to teach Constance about his favorite composer, and again I have the sense that this is something he would find pleasurable outside the circumstance of seduction and fraternal revenge. He calls Charles-Valentin Alkan "the forgotten musical genius of the nineteenth century," and assures Constance that she "will never hear a more luxuriant, cerebral, technically challenging artist—never." I am almost certain Diogenes is not just saying "never" because he believes Constance will not live much longer, but because he truly believes in Alkan's merit. Though certainly the details he provides about Alkan and his music enhance the mood he is trying to create for her seduction, Diogenes is actually enjoying a rare chance to reveal his true feelings to another human being. If telling Constance that "even now Alkan's music inspires strange behavior in listeners" and that "some think they smell smoke while listening; others find themselves trembling or growing faint" will help make her more willing to acquiesce to him, Diogenes still does not need to go as far in his Alkan appreciation lesson as he does. "This fugal passage, for instance," he points out, noting: "if you count the octave doublings, it has more parts than a pianist has fingers! I know you must appreciate it, Constance, as few do." Though, of course, the last line is meant to flatter her, it is also probably true. Diogenes might be the first to admit that if anyone could truly appreciate Alkan besides himself, it would be a woman who had lived over one hundred years without physically aging, and whose sanity had been compromised by the things she had to accept in order to have the privilege. Though in some ways Diogenes' declaration: "And thank God the greatest musical philosopher was a romantic, a decadent—not some smug Mozart with his puerile false cadences and predictable harmonies" is a dig at his brother, who favors the mathematical precision of Bach, it is also sincerely himself.

In the words and actions that follow, however, Diogenes returns to carefully following the principle that the truth is the safest lie. He mingles the truth with lies in such a way that he is utterly believable to Constance without letting her see his deepest actual vulnerabilities. When he tells her: "I can think of few pastimes more rewarding than to make you happy," Diogenes is reserving as one of those few the pastime of making his brother miserable. He probably needs all of his acting skill, however, to lose his smile when Constance answers: "You seem to be the only one." Though she does not blame his brother, she does something even more encouraging from the standpoint of Diogenes' ultimate aim with her—she blames herself. Yet again, I believe he is sincere when he protests: "You are a beautiful and brilliant young woman," though they both know that Constance is not chronologically "young." Then Constance utters the phrase that Diogenes will ultimately turn against her in his bid to urge her to self-destruction: "I'm a freak" (*Book of the Dead*, p. 241).

Diogenes is physically very gentle with her after she declares this, taking her hands "with exceptional tenderness" (*Book of the Dead,* p. 242). Even though he is already planning to use her own arguments against her, he is completely honest when he assures her: "Not at all. Not to me." This is true. He does not find her the least bit physically repulsive, and he has no difficulties of this nature to overcome in accomplishing her seduction. If anything, because of how very nearly she has approached biological immortality, Diogenes probably finds her far *less* repulsive than the average female bags of guts, blood, and bones of his acquaintance.

I would argue that all of the eloquent things Diogenes tells Constance about her unique condition on the night of her deflowering are far more true to him than the harsh phrases he leaves for her in his farewell letter. (In fact, he has probably already written this letter, and has it stashed, along with the giftboxed scalpel, in his Chapman bag. It was merely his best, accurate guess that she would call herself a freak at some point during the evening.) Diogenes recognizes—and would value, were he not completely focused on vengeance—that Constance has "acquired the gift of experience without the awful cost of age." He acknowledges to her: "You are a pearl beyond price. You have all the beauty and freshness of a woman of twenty-one, yet you have a mind refined by a lifetime . . . no, *lifetimes* . . . of intellectual hunger."

Yet, when it comes to Diogenes' final trick of the evening, causing Constance to give in to his amorous overtures by showing her his fake wrist-slashing scars, it is almost as though he is protecting his own deep vulnerability. He has no need to lie to her, no need to fake a suicide scar. All Diogenes would have to do is command her to look at his milky blue eye once more and tell her how it actually happened—that what his brother had done to him had been so unbearable that he had turned a gun on himself in hopes of escaping it. He truly *has* shared her experience *oBoof* desiring self-annihilation, just not her choice of method. Diogenes could even have disclaimed the reality of the injury in his letter, as he does with the wrist scar, by saying he had only been wearing a milky contact. It is not as though Aloysius would have been there to tell Constance otherwise. The very fact that Diogenes has created a fake wrist scar for himself proves that he has had time to contemplate all of this; he must have spotted Constance's own marks on a previous occasion of which she was unaware. To have gone with his own true story instead, however, would have been to reveal far too much of himself to Constance—a revelation that might have rendered him unable to sacrifice her to his overall goal. Still, Diogenes is able to draw on his actual experience for verisimilitude. Again, he can be sincere in saying to Constance: "It is true—we are alike, so *very* alike. I understand you. And you, Constance—you understand me" (*Book of the Dead,* p. 243). What Diogenes miscalculates, of course, is just how alike they are.

In any case, Diogenes goes on to have sex with Constance right there on that backless settee, with an audience of Pendergast family portraits. As he caresses her breasts, he quotes the poetry of Giosué Carducci in its original Italian; this quotation will eventually lead Constance to his true lair. It says something that Diogenes cites a poem that has helped him choose the place he calls his true home at this moment, but it could be attributed to the importance of said moment to his overall revenge scheme. Similarly, that his eyes were "wet with lust and triumph" does imply satisfaction in "triumph" over his brother in seducing his protected ward. Though the lust may also be partially a result over a perceived victory over Aloysius, I still maintain that it would not be real lust if Diogenes did not actually find her desirable.

Chapters Forty-Two through Forty-Five return to the adventures of Aloysius Pendergast as he attempts to escape prison. In Chapter Forty-Six, however, Viola Maskelene confirms for Bill Smithback that Menzies was indeed the one who suggested her to fill the late Wicherly's shoes. Soon afterward, Diogenes himself arrives in costume as Menzies for the opening gala. He is "magnificent in white tie and tails" (*Book of the Dead,* p. 265), and promises not to "inflict a long speech on" his audience, "because we have far more interesting entertainment planned." Menzies' enthusiasm is surely a milder version of Diogenes' own anticipatory excitement. He reads the assembled celebrants an e-mail allegedly sent by the fictitious Count of Cahors, expressing his regret that he is too old to travel and see the opening of Senef's exhibit in person. Then he moves on to introduce the performance from *Aida.* This, of course, is part of Nora's plan to replicate the original opening of the Tomb of Senef in 1872, which had also featured arias from that opera.

The tableau of Diogenes-as-Menzies in white tie and tails introducing an operatic performance can be seen as Preston and Child deliberately giving readers a subtle echo of a scene from the first book in the Diogenes trilogy, *Brimstone.* Fosco, the true villain of *Brimstone,* invites Agent Pendergast to attend an opera with him, and Pendergast agrees, only to find out more about a leading figure in the case. Though Fosco's white tie and tails are described at length, we have only a hint implying that Pendergast himself is similarly attired. Fosco greets him: "My dear Pendergast, I was *hoping* you'd come in white tie!" (*Brimstone,* p. 101). The authors describe their borrowed, corpulent antagonist as "rejoicing" as he speaks, so we must assume Fosco has gotten his wish in that respect. Fosco eventually discovers that confirmed opera-hater Pendergast is also wearing earplugs, though Aloysius assures him that they "merely attenuate the sound" (*Brimstone,* p. 102). He goes on to explain: "My hearing is exceptionally acute, and any volume above a normal conversation is painful to me." Ironically, it will later be discovered that Diogenes/Menzies is equipped with earplugs for his evening of opera as well, but for somewhat different reasons.

I cannot help wondering if Diogenes, unlike his elder brother, actually *enjoys* opera. Such an enjoyment would fit in with the romanticism he has been championing to Constance; seemingly Diogenes would endorse opera for the very reasons his brother hates it. Possibly, Diogenes associates opera with his mother; after all, one of his earliest memories is of weeping from the sheer beauty of her voice. She sang to him in French rather than Italian in the one example we have, but she may well have known arias and used them for her youngest son's lullabies. Even if Diogenes does not actually enjoy opera, he is surely aware of his brother's hatred of it, and thus finds it a perfectly fitting ornament to what he anticipates will be his greatest triumph.

In Chapter Forty-Seven, we find a freshly-escaped Pendergast in Eli Glinn's office recovering from his ordeal. Much of interest is spoken about Diogenes, however, and Aloysius is shocked to learn that his brother has destroyed the diamonds he stole from the Museum. "Once again," Pendergast admits, "his actions were beyond my ability to predict or comprehend" (*Book of the Dead,* p. 270). The psychiatrist, Krasner, offers up the opinion: "By destroying the very diamonds he had spent many years planning to steal, diamonds that he both desired and needed, Diogenes was destroying a part of himself. It was a suicide of sorts. He was abandoning himself to his demons" (*Book of the Dead,* p. 271). To a certain degree, Krasner is correct; the diamonds were also a link for Diogenes to his mother, the one remaining person or memory who could have influenced him in the direction of compassion or mercy.

According to Glinn, Diogenes' destruction of the diamonds caused the realization that "our preliminary psychological profile was woefully insufficient." Glinn offers to "spare" Pendergast "the details," because "it boils down to one thing." Which is, as the head of Effective Engineering Solutions puts it: "The 'perfect crime' which Diogenes spoke of was *not* the theft of the diamonds. Nor was it the outrage he perpetrated on you: killing your friends and then framing you for the crimes. Whatever his original intent was we are in no position to speculate. But the fact remains that his ultimate crime *has yet to be committed.*"

Glinn's summations are very useful to readers at this point; the authors intend for us to take his profiling skills seriously, even if they play some of Krasner's insights for comedic effect. When Pendergast brings up Diogenes' original messages about the date of the diamond heist, Glinn responds: "Another lie, or at least diversion. The theft of the diamonds *was* part of his plan, but their destruction was apparently a more spontaneous act." If Krasner is correct about the depth in mood that was necessary for Diogenes to destroy the diamonds, however, it was a sign of a quick recovery and resolve for him to send the dust in a package to the Museum. I also cannot help liking Glinn's capacity for being impressed by Diogenes: "I must say," he tells Pendergast, "the depth and complexity of your brother's plan is quite breathtaking."

After Glinn states that "all indications are that this crime [Diogenes' ultimate] is imminent," Pendergast sulks a little, saying: "I fail to see how I can be of any help," and adding: "As you see, I've been wrong at every turn" (*Book of the Dead,* p. 271). This brings Glinn to the crux of the matter; he has concluded, correctly, that Diogenes is "motivated by a powerful feeling of victimization, the sense that a terrible wrong was done to him" (*Book of the Dead,* p. 272). Further, he insists to a disbelieving Pendergast: "*You* are the person who inflicted this pain on your brother—at least, that's how he perceives it."

In short, the rest of Chapter Forty-Seven consists of Eli Glinn persuading Pendergast that whatever he did to Diogenes is a repressed memory locked inside his mind, and that he must attempt a memory crossing to access the buried recollection. Eventually, of course, Pendergast agrees. Chapter Forty-Eight finds us with Captain Laura Hayward on guard at the Museum gala, thinking far too much about Diogenes Pendergast. Though she does not think about how tall Dr. Menzies is when she is contemplating the master criminal having an alter-ego on the staff, her foreboding about the evening does increase even more when she recognizes Viola Maskelene is now part of the tomb's opening celebration.

Chapter Forty-Nine takes us back to Aloysius Pendergast, who is having the most difficult time he has ever had getting to the memory palace of his mentally re-created Rochenoire. He has to achieve "the state known as Sunyata" in his meditation, having first mentally removed all of the objects surrounding him in Dr. Krasner's cozy study, and progressing to all countries and features of the earth itself before "at last, the ancient mansion on Dauphine Street began to materialize in his mind" (*Book of the Dead,* p. 281). Even so, Pendergast continues to have difficulty with this memory crossing. "Normally," Preston and Child tell us, "entering into this palace of memory was a tranquilizing, calming experience: each drawer of each cabinet of each room led some past event, or some personal reflection on history or science, to be perused at leisure. Today, however, Pendergast felt a profound unease, and it was only with the greatest mental effort he was able to keep the mansion cohesive in his mind" (*Book of the Dead,* p. 282).

As from within the memory crossing Pendergast approaches Diogenes' room, in connection with Glinn's deductions readers begin to realize that perhaps the reason the door is "sealed in lead and covered with a sheet of hammered brass" (*Book of the Dead,* pp. 282-283) has less to do with the actions of the younger brother than with those of the elder. After all, Aloysius Pendergast is all too familiar with the evil deeds of serial and mass killers, and some have even been members of his family. He sealed the door to "the one room into which he had promised himself never again to enter" long before Diogenes murdered Torrance Hamilton, Charles Duchamp, or Michael Decker. Surely Pendergast could not have valued his pet mouse more than his young cousins that Aunt Cornelia killed, for instance. Not to mention the fact that he lives part time with Constance in the mansion inherited from Great-Uncle Antoine despite the horrors that must have taken place there before those he himself experienced. What could possibly be so bad about Diogenes that Special Agent A. X. L. Pendergast cannot face it?

Unfortunately, readers hoping for a glimpse inside Diogenes' boyhood room are to be sorely disappointed. When Pendergast finally removes the brass and lead, and kicks the actual door open, there is "nothing visible. The mellow light of the hallway did not penetrate the infinite gloom. The doorway was a rectangle of blackness" (*Book of the Dead*, p. 284). As Pendergast attempts to cross the threshold, "the house began to wobble, the walls evaporating as if made of air, and he realized he was once again losing the memory palace." Even after he pulls everything back together, what he sees, with the aid of a mental flashlight, is "not the room he expected to find. Instead, he was at the top of a narrow stairway of undressed stone, winding down into the living rock, twisting deeply into the earth."

Preston and Child tell us that upon seeing this stairway, "something dark stirred within Pendergast's mind: a rough beast that had slumbered, undisturbed, for over thirty years." This is their literary evocation of William Butler Yeats' famous line from his 1920 poem, "The Second Coming": "And what rough beast, its hour come round at last,/Slouches towards Bethlehem to be born?" It is a fitting allusion, because though the poem is titled "The Second Coming," which is, of course, a reference to the second coming of Jesus predicted in the New Testament, Yeats is more concerned with the coming of the Beast or the Antichrist that the Book of Revelations claims will precede the Christ. Pendergast, seeing in his memory palace the scene of his crime, has the sudden intuition that he has created the Beast that was born there, that what Diogenes became is his doing, his fault.

La Pièce de la Résistance

Chapter Fifty chronicles Aloysius Pendergast's repressed memory of The Event, and Chapter Fifty-Two consists of Eli Glinn drawing the facts from him because Pendergast is unable to bear reformatting them into a simple recitation. The chapter in between is simply back to the prison in the aftermath of Pendergast's escape.

Perhaps the most striking realization to be had from reading this scene of seven-year-old Diogenes and nine-year-old Aloysius exploring the subterranean family crypt and competing at Latin translation of the tombs' inscriptions is that the two boys are very companionable. Yes, they have an extremely normal sibling rivalry, but they are fairly comfortable with each other, immediately putting the lie to Aloysius's and Great Aunt Cornelia's assertions to D'Agosta that they never got along.

As Aloysius views this long-repressed memory, he recalls how he and Diogenes both loved Latin, but that Diogenes, though younger, quickly overtook him in prowess with the ancient tongue. "Diogenes, Pendergast remembered, had always been the better Latin student: his teacher thought him a genius" (*Book of the Dead,* p. 286). As the scene unfolds, Diogenes bests Aloysius at interpreting a particularly complex inscription, and is fairly arrogant about it, responding to his older brother's attempt "with a sarcastic snicker," and judging, "That doesn't make any sense" (*Book of the Dead,* p. 287). Aloysius is understandably annoyed at his little brother, and argues that Diogenes' translation "makes no more sense than mine." Yet he knows that it does, and he feels as though the only superiority remaining to him is that natural to being the elder of the two. Being older, he is less fearful of the creepy environment of the crypt and the darkness; being younger, Diogenes retains relatively more fear of these matters. Too, their attitudes toward the situation in which they find themselves seem illustrative of the brothers' most innate personality difference: Aloysius is cold, analytical, and purely interested in hard facts; while Diogenes tends toward superstition, intuition, and emotion. Thus, Aloysius resorts to lording his relative lack of fear over his little brother, pushing Diogenes to do things that frighten him just to prove his worthiness to share this adventure with his older brother.

Before venturing much further in my discussion of The Event, however, I wish to clarify that I do not "blame" Aloysius. He and Diogenes are both acting like perfectly normal siblings, neither doing anything out of the range of typical brotherly ribbing and rivalry. Despite both of their precocious intellects, they are both still young children with very little idea of the possible consequences of their actions. Despite my deep sympathy with Diogenes over the ways in which The Event shaped him, and my understanding of *his* blaming Aloysius for all that happened, I do *not* hold him even as much responsible as he himself does. Yes, he did have a critical role in "creating" Diogenes the sociopathic serial killer, but he certainly did not do anything with the intent of actually harming his little brother. If anyone is truly to be blamed it is the supposedly responsible adults involved—Great Uncle Comstock for actually creating the device in which Diogenes suffered, and Linnaeus Pendergast either for not having a thorough knowledge of what his subbasements contained, or for not ridding himself of the device if he knew about it. Isabella, the boys' mother, probably takes a lesser share of blame than her husband, since she was not born a Pendergast and probably did not have nearly as clear a picture of what dangers might be lurking beneath her home.

Further, The Event was a tragedy and a trauma for *both* Pendergast brothers, Aloysius as well as Diogenes, even if Diogenes suffered the most damage. Aloysius was so severely traumatized that he blocked the memory of it entirely, compounding the damage his brother suffered by not being able to acknowledge and apologize for his part in it. Perhaps the biggest tragedy is that both boys lost *each other*—they each lost a loving sibling to share in and reminisce about the experience of growing up a Pendergast, a commodity that becomes even more valuable after they lose their parents. A commodity so valuable that in secretly longing for it and subconsciously remembering the days of companionship and rivalry, neither can bring himself to kill the other and place it forever out of reach.

When the boys discover what turns out to be the crypt containing Great Uncle Comstock's devices, Aloysius at first speculates: "Maybe it's empty" (*Book of the Dead*, p. 287).

This prompts Diogenes to offer up the possibility: "Maybe it's meant for *us.*" I have no way of knowing, but I suspect he means their parents as well as himself and his brother. Aloysius in the memory crossing notes "a goulish gleam appearing in his eyes," but I do not believe this is anything more than the normal sensation of a little boy to some degree willingly scaring himself by walking through a cemetery, even if he is doing it partly to save face with his older brother. I do not believe we can take it as evidence of Diogenes' being disturbed from birth.

As they explore the machinery and signage left over from Comstock Pendergast's act, Aloysius knows more about the family history and tells Diogenes: "We've found all the stuff from Great-Grand-Uncle Comstock's magic show" (*Book of the Dead,* p. 289). Diogenes even has to ask who this ancestor is, and Aloysius replies: "Only the most famous magician in the history of the world. He trained Houdini himself." We are probably witnessing the beginning of Diogenes' obsession with his own family history. He probably believes that if he had known as much about Uncle Comstock as Aloysius did at that moment, he would have broken away from his brother and run upstairs, his psyche and color-vision intact, if not his dignity.

When the boys discover a man-sized box with spikes on the inside, Aloysius claims, "There's dried blood on those spikes." Whether he really believes this, or he is just trying to frighten Diogenes is anyone's guess. Diogenes has already noted the contraption "looks more like torture than magic." On the one hand, readers may wonder how a seven-year-old boy knows about torture, and give credence to the assertions that Diogenes was predisposed to darkness from the beginning. On the other, perhaps he inflected the words with scorn and disappointment, wanting to see something imbued with real magic. Or those in the camp believing in Diogenes' original evil may point to the fact that he "peered closely" at the alleged bloodstains, "fear temporarily overcome by a strange eagerness." Perhaps he did have an inclination towards blood, but without this incident, this Event, it could have been channeled into something like surgery, or medical research. Diogenes' subsequent judgment, "That's just paint," and his assertion, "I know dried blood when I see it," have also been used as justification for the argument that Diogenes was already torturing animals before The Event. If the average young boy's skinned knees and other potential mishaps are not enough to provide a knowledge of dried blood, Preston and Child later wrote a short story, "Extraction," which goes a long way toward giving Diogenes a perfectly innocent (yet also traumatic) reason for knowing what dried blood looks like. (This story will be addressed in its proper place in this work.)

By the time the brothers approach Comstock's "Doorway to Hell," Aloysius has decided he will admit his own fear of the situation in order to force Diogenes to go in first. Seemingly, Aloysius's knowledge of his own family history and of Comstock in particular, has made him cautious. Diogenes' caution and outright fear, on the other hand, are more instinctual. It is as if he knows something terrible is going to happen, and despite the companionship noted at the beginning of the chapter, his distrust of his older brother is palpable. ("Extraction" will cast further light on this as well.) Though

Diogenes protests his unwillingness at nearly every turn, Aloysius shames him into entering the contraption: "I admitted I was scared. If you're scared, say so, and we'll go back upstairs and forget all about it" (*Book of the Dead*, p. 291). Unfortunately, Diogenes does not take this last out that Aloysius offers him, although perhaps in addition to not wanting to admit his fear to his older brother he has reason to believe that even if he does, Aloysius will shift tactics and *still* not allow him to avoid the situation. In fact, once Diogenes has entered the first part of Comstock's box, Aloysius "crowded in behind him, blocking his retreat." Granted, prior to this Aloysius has told Diogenes, "I'll be right behind you, I promise" (*Book of the Dead*, p. 290), and at this point, he is trying to keep his promise—*and* prevent Diogenes from escaping. Again, urging Diogenes up the ladder into the second story of the Doorway to Hell, Aloysius promises, "I'll be right behind" (*Book of the Dead*, p. 291).

Aloysius does follow Diogenes up the ladder, but the next transition is through "a circular porthole in the far wall of the crawl space," and "Diogenes hesitated at the entrance to the porthole." Of course, Aloysius tells him to go through it. Preston and Child state: "The little boy glanced back once at his brother, a strange expression in his eyes. Then he crawled through the porthole and disappeared." I can only speculate about the "strange expression." It probably consisted of many elements—fear, distrust, hope, pleading, and foreboding, to name a few; an intuition of momentousness. Aloysius looks into the portal, but is hesitant enough in actually following his brother that Diogenes has time to ask, "Aren't you coming?" and remind him: "You *promised* you would stay right behind me" (*Book of the Dead*, p. 292). Aloysius assures Diogenes he is indeed coming, and to be fair, perhaps he did ultimately intend to follow his brother. He takes too long to actually move, however, and Comstock's device takes the option from him forever: "With a swift *thunk!* the porthole snapped shut, blocking his view" (*Book of the Dead*, p. 292). In the memory crossing, Pendergast continues to hear the young Diogenes' screams as he suffers, and he remembers everything that he has blocked from himself for over thirty years.

Later, when Glinn is dragging the story from Pendergast, we learn that Aloysius has even forced the route to the subbasement's crypt from Diogenes. Pendergast admits: "I made him tell me" (*Book of the Dead*, p. 302). Further questioning from Glinn reveals that in addition to the psychology Pendergast used on his younger brother, he also feels that he "used force" (*Book of the Dead*, p. 303) in getting Diogenes to enter Comstock's box first. He explains his reasoning and motivation to Glinn: Diogenes "had been sarcastic, as usual. I was angry with him. If there was something a little frightening … I wanted him to go first" (*Book of the Dead*, p. 303). Pendergast does give the impression in talking to Glinn that he did at least intend to follow his brother throughout his tour of the Doorway to Hell. Further, he provides more information about what Diogenes experienced, though we must extrapolate to have any real idea of it. Pendergast also spells out what Comstock's intentions must have been in the creation of the device to which he and Diogenes fell victims. Glinn asks what its purpose was, and Pendergast replies: "To frighten someone to death" (*Book of the Dead*, p. 304).

As the head of EES presses the agent to describe the infinitesimal portion of Comstock's horror show that he saw, "suddenly Pendergast moaned—a moan of such anguish, such long-repressed suffering, that Glinn was for a moment left speechless" (*Book of the Dead*, p. 305). To those of us who have followed Pendergast from *Relic* to this novel—and even beyond to the subsequent stories—it is staggering to even try to imagine what could elicit such a sound from this extremely stoic and emotionally reticent character. And whatever we imagine, we must multiply it at least a thousand times over to arrive at what Diogenes experienced.

"But for a moment," Glinn clarifies, "you saw what Diogenes saw." Pendergast affirms: "Only for a moment. But I *heard* all of it." Again, Pendergast provides a clearer picture of the means by which Comstock destroyed his brother's life. He calls it "a magic-lantern show," and provides the reason it still works by the time Diogenes triggers it: "A phantasmagoria. Operated by voltaic cell." Glinn presses Pendergast once more about what he actually saw, but the agent still denies him, replying: "I beg you, *do not ask me that.*" When readers think about what Pendergast *has* seen during the course of his casework, it is again staggering. Again, it is an example of Preston and Child's using the technique of withholding information for greater effect—i.e., "it is so bad we cannot even tell you what it is," so that each reader can imagine the thing that is the worst for him or her.

What Pendergast has heard, however, is quite bad enough. He tells Glinn: "Diogenes shrieked and screamed from within the inner chamber. Again and again … and again. I heard a terrible scrabbling as he tried to claw his way out—I could

hear his nails breaking" (*Book of the Dead,* p. 305).
Eventually, though Pendergast is not sure how much time
passes, he hears a gunshot. He explains to Glinn that
"Comstock Pendergast had furnished his … house of pain
with a single-shot derringer. He gave his victim a choice. You
could go mad; you could die of fright—or you could take
your life" (*Book of the Dead,* p. 306). While Pendergast goes
on to relate how his parents had disguised Diogenes' recovery
from a self-inflicted gunshot wound as a dangerous bout with
scarlet fever, which he could not dispute because he
consciously remembered nothing of The Event, Glinn reflects
upon Diogenes' suicide attempt. His thoughts express
perfectly my own feelings about what Diogenes suffered:
"The thought of something so awful, so utterly terrifying, that
a *seven-year-old* could possibly be induced to …"

That the young Diogenes actually picks up the old derringer
and tries to end his own life is for me the greatest single piece
of evidence that he was not born evil and did not wish to
become that way. He tried desperate measures to keep this
from happening. By the time Diogenes awakened, on the road
to physical recovery from the bullet wound, he had already at
least subconsciously experienced the rest of Comstock's
program. Plus, he had also discovered a reason not to attempt
suicide again—the idea of revenge.

Once Glinn has extracted as much from Pendergast as he can,
including the detail that it may have been up to a day before
the boys were rescued from their separate but unequal
chambers of Comstock's device, he lays out the pertinent
facts for his client. He tells Pendergast that his younger
brother "never realized that you had repressed the memory"

(*Book of the Dead,* p. 306). "As a result," Glinn concludes, "you never apologized to your brother, tried to make it up to him. You never even mentioned it, because you had utterly blocked out all memory of the Event" (*Book of the Dead,* pp. 306-307). Elaborating, Glinn continues: "But to Diogenes, your silence meant something else entirely. A stubborn refusal to admit your mistake, to ask forgiveness" (*Book of the Dead,* p. 307).

Leaving Pendergast for a time to his own thoughts, Glinn ruminates further upon what the memory crossing has revealed. Still accepting some of the family lore that Diogenes was different from the beginning, Glinn reflects: "Almost from birth, Diogenes had been a strange, dark, and brilliant creature, as had many Pendergasts before him." The only evidence for innate darkness we have, however, is a possible over-interest in blood; one that could have been produced by another early misadventure we have not yet examined in "Extraction." Yet Glinn is correct in guessing, "he might have swung either way, if the Event had not occurred. But the person who emerged from the Doorway to Hell—ravaged emotionally as well as physically—had turned into something else entirely" (*Book of the Dead,* p. 307).

Okay, Back to le Troisième Course

Chapters Fifty-Three and Fifty-Four involve Captain
Hayward rushing over to EES, seeking D'Agosta's help
because she feels something is up involving the Museum's
gala, and discovering Pendergast has escaped from prison.
We do not learn much new about Diogenes, except that
Pendergast finally names Menzies as his brother's alter-ego.
Chapter Fifty-Five returns us to the Museum, where
Diogenes/Menzies is introducing Nora and Viola to the
mayor and his wife, so that they can escort them through
Senef's tomb. Menzies' face is described as "florid" (*Book of
the Dead*, p. 317), and I am guessing that this is Diogenes'
own coloring from his genuine excitement as his moment
approaches, rather than make-up he has applied because he
thinks the old Museum curator he has created would be
flushed under the circumstance of an opening gala. He leaves
Nora and Viola's foursome to match other Museum staff to
other VIPs, but eventually the entire first group of three
hundred guests are gathered at "the first stop on the sound-
and-light show" (*Book of the Dead*, p. 320) and it begins.

Chapter Fifty-Six returns us to Hayward, D'Agosta, and
Pendergast as they arrive to find that Diogenes' sound-and-
light show has already started. After they win the power
struggle with Museum guard Manetti, he confirms for them
that "Menzies is in the tomb with the rest" (*Book of the Dead*,
p. 323). Presumably, Diogenes has known all along that
Menzies will have to accompany at *least* the first grouping of
guests through the tomb, if not the second as well.

Presumably he will be able to protect himself from any potential damage, unless he feels that the damage his pain factory is inflicting is identical to that he has already suffered. We learn, however, that like Comstock, Diogenes has tried to make sure his trap is inescapable. The computer program will not allow his brother and his friends to get the doors to the exhibit to reopen.

In Chapter Fifty-Seven we are returned to Nora and the first tour of the tomb. As suspected, Nora's reflections confirm for us that "Hugo Menzies had guided the overall project with a subtle and sure hand, while proving equally clever with the nuts and bolts of bringing the show together" (*Book of the Dead*, p. 325). From the details of the show provided, we also learn that Diogenes is a far more subtle artist than his ancestor Comstock. He is presenting a show that uses just enough lurid detail at first to enthrall his audience while slowly building an atmosphere of creepiness. The detail Nora observes, that "a cry rang out as one of the figures slipped from the bridge, plunging with a hideous scream into the darkness of the pit—cut off suddenly in a sickening smack of meat hitting stone" (*Book of the Dead*, p. 326), is pure Diogenes. Nora notes: "Initially, she had been against that little piece of drama, but she had to admit that—judging by the excited murmurs and gasps of the audience—it had been effective." Interestingly, however, Diogenes has either fudged or allowed his underlings to fudge some of the details about Senef's tomb. Though the program at first mentions that Senef was a grand vizier and regent rather than a pharaoh, as the narration progresses it refers to the great power of the deceased pharaoh and the destruction the tomb robbers must cause in order to break that power. This can be seen as a generalization to any powerful ancient Egyptian figure who has been mummified, and as an attempt to further enhance the spooky environment of Diogenes' pain factory; it can also be seen as a gesture of contempt on Diogenes' part to the *vulgus mobile*—the assumption that none of these common meatbags will notice the distinction. The chapter ends, however, before any deviation from the official script has begun—before the parts of the program that so affected Lipper and Wicherly are unleashed upon the wider audience.

For Chapter Fifty-Eight, we come back to Pendergast, Hayward, and D'Agosta in their desperate attempts to shut down Diogenes' show. They discover how many backups he has put in to guarantee the sound-and-light show both continues to receive power and continues to be carried to television viewers. Pendergast is able to locate the computer program that Diogenes has labeled *confundo;* as the special agent explains, "*Confundo* in Latin means to trouble, distress, throw into confusion. It's no doubt a system routine added by Diogenes to hijack the show" (*Book of the Dead*, p. 331). Through means of monitors, Pendergast also manages to catch a glimpse of Diogenes himself within the exhibit, and calls his helpers' attention to it: "They all watched as the man slipped a hand inside his dinner jacket, casually extracted a black eye-mask, and put it on. A pair of earplugs followed" (*Book of the Dead*, p. 330). Diogenes is not taking any chance on suffering any further damage that might interfere with his plans to leave the scene after finally pulling off his ultimate crime. No doubt he is counting on the crowd being completely enthralled with his presentation, so that they do not notice these important adjustments to his couture. Hayward confirms the man observed is Menzies; Pendergast recognizes him as his younger brother. By the end of the chapter, Pendergast has determined that the tomb must be penetrated through an outside wall of the Museum, because Diogenes has done such a superb job of preventing any more conventional access.

Naturally, Chapter Fifty-Nine puts us back in the Tomb of Senef just as the regularly scheduled presentation begins to jump the tracks. Nora notices immediately when the strobe lights go out of synch, though the gala guests think it is just part of the script. Interestingly, her experience of the diabolical sound-and-light show is valuable not only for the insight it provides into Diogenes' own imagination, but because it is the best clue Preston and Child give us to what Diogenes himself may have experienced in Comstock's box. For instance, I would wager that the horrific effects of the mummy come straight from Comstock himself. He may not have used the Egyptian themed-device of the mummy, that fits so well with Diogenes' opportunity with the tomb, but there was surely some kind of ghastly corpse involved. Nora notices that "somehow the mummy didn't look right," and that "it was bigger, darker, somehow more menacing. Then a bony arm broke free of its bandages—something not even in the script—and, clawing and twitching, reached up to its own swathed face" (*Book of the Dead*, p. 339). In addition to the probability that this is an image Diogenes himself may have experienced during The Event, there is also an echo of Torrance Hamilton's death here.

Nora goes on to observe: "The arm was distorted, as

elongated as an ape's. The bony fingers sank into the linen wrappings and ripped them away, revealing a visage of such horror" that it caused her to gasp. Diogenes would be tickled to know that she at first attributes this change in the program to "some joke of Wicherly's" (*Book of the Dead*, p. 339), and Menzies does not even enter her mind. Eventually, the digital image of the mummy's mouth "became a sinkhole of black slime, which began to seethe and wriggle," and Nora watches as "it morphed into a swarm of greasy black cockroaches, which began rustling and crawling their way out of the ruined orifice" (*Book of the Dead*, p. 340). A few minutes later, it "looked as if the mummy were vomiting blackness—the swarm of insects had taken flight, the cockroaches morphing into fat, lubricious wasps, their mandibles clicking like knitting needles as they flew toward the audience with a horrible believability" (*Book of the Dead*, p. 340).

Again, I believe Diogenes saw images very much like these during The Event. I may not be giving Comstock enough credit when I say that he probably did not have the strobes and sound equipment available to Diogenes, but I think Diogenes took a certain amount of pride in using technology to best his ancestor's effects. He was surely able to enhance the detail of his imagery with digital video recording, so that his mummy, roaches, and wasps were more horrifying to his victims. Diogenes, however, also proves less merciful than Comstock in one crucial way—he does not provide the Museum guests with any means of putting themselves out of misery, such as the derringer he turned on himself as a child. Given that his actual physical brain damage was probably caused as much or more so by the bullet rather than

Comstock's phantasmagoria, Diogenes needs to use lasers and sounds his ancestor probably had no access to, although light and sound was definitely a part of the Doorway to Hell. Nora's thoughts give the readers some idea of the effectiveness of Diogenes' devices: "The malfunctioning strobe lights kept flashing, flashing, *flashing* in her peripheral vision, so very brightly, and Nora felt a real twinge of dizziness. Another gut-twisting low note sounded" (*Book of the Dead*, p. 339). A few moments later, her reactions continue: "Those sounds—she had never heard anything like them. They were like the sounding of the last trump, full of dread and horror, so loud it seemed to violate her very being" (*Book of the Dead*, p. 339). Later, of course, readers learn that Nora does not even suffer the full effects that Diogenes had planned; again, we are left to extrapolate the worst from the initial details that Preston and Child have provided. We also learn later that trampling actually kills a few of Diogenes' victims, but again, death is not the object of his sound-and-light show, which is probably the biggest reason he does not provide the guests with easily accessible means of self-annihilation. Diogenes wants the first visitors to the reopened Tomb of Senef to go forth from the Museum and deepen the world's misery in whatever ways occur to them, much as he has wished to do since the tender age of seven. If the members of the television audience can add to this, so much the better.

In Chapter Sixty, however, readers are given the privilege of waking up with Constance after her night of debauchery with Diogenes. When she awakes, Wren informs her that it is 8:30pm—she is waking in the midst of the Museum gala, though she has no particular awareness of this fact. That Constance is waking up in her own room implies that she and Diogenes retired there after whatever took place on the settee; that she is waking up so late implies several different possibilities or mixtures of them. It is probable that she and Diogenes entertained each other until the earliest hours of the morning, and it is possible that the absinthe and all the physical activity combined to contribute to her sound sleep. Despite having been a virgin, Constance was probably able to climax, another factor that would have contributed to her deep relaxation. Of course, it is also quite possible that Diogenes gave her some kind of sedative as well, to ensure she would not wake as he strategically placed his parting gifts and left.

Constance also awakes with a hearty appetite, and amidst the several substantial items she asks Wren to bring her for breakfast is that well-known home remedy for too much sexual activity, cranberry juice. She also seems happy, again indicating Diogenes (at least with her) was a reasonably attentive and skilled lover. Preston and Child tell us "Constance stretched languorously—deliciously—then sat up in bed" (*Book of the Dead,* p. 341). After Wren has gone to fetch her breakfast, "a private smile flitted across her face, vanished, then returned again, as if prompted by some recollection" (*Book of the Dead,* p. 342). When she discovers the envelope and package Diogenes has left under her pillow, "Constance smiled, then flushed deeply." Obviously, Diogenes believed that her heart would break more effectively if she actually enjoyed her first sexual experience. His purpose has been overall nefarious, yet it still says something that he was able to complete this incredibly intimate time span with Constance and leave her with extremely positive feelings to destroy. One cannot help wondering how much practice Diogenes has had and whether or not there are any survivors. I would like to think that, as a gentleman, he let them live. The only reason Diogenes wishes Constance to be an exception is for his brother's sake.

There is no reason to believe that Diogenes disguises his handwriting for Constance, since it is later confirmed that he did not disguise his physical appearance with her. Again, he does not expect her to live to reveal anything to his brother, though of course his letter could be found after her predicted demise. So I think it is safe to assume his handwriting really is "dense" and "elegant." Of course, as soon as Constance opens the letter (again, it says something about both her *and* Diogenes that she chooses the letter first rather than the gift package), she is brought up to speed on Diogenes' game. He does, however, begin innocuously enough by expressing the hope that she has slept well, but starts dropping hints that he means to upset her almost immediately: "There is a good chance it will be your last such sleep for some time" (*Book of the Dead,* p. 342). Though he follows this up with a quick foreshadowing of his ultimate advice to her, within a few lines Diogenes has broken what he feels is the most pressing news to Constance—that Antoine Pendergast murdered her sister, and used her body, as well as those of other victims, to perfect the serum that prolonged both his and Constance's life. I must fault Diogenes—or, more likely, his creators— somewhat for writing: "that Antoine killed and vivisected your sister" (*Book of the Dead,* p. 343). It would, of course, have been impossible for anyone, even a Pendergast, to do it in that order. Diogenes compounds whatever shock this news might bring Constance by accusing her of having known it all along: "Perhaps at first it was just a supposition, a strange twinge of dark fancy. No doubt you ascribed it to your own perverse cast of mind. But over time—and you two had so very *much* time—it must have come to seem, first a possibility, then a certainty." He does not let up on this theme: "Yet no doubt this was all subconscious, buried so deep as to be almost undiscoverable. And yet *you knew it:* of course you did."

To reinforce the effect of putting this secret into words, Diogenes assures Constance that "before he died, *Uncle Antoine told me so himself.*" With Diogenes, however, there is always the chance that he is blatantly lying. He must have realized during the writing of the letter that even Constance would be aware of this possibility by now. This is precisely what makes me believe Diogenes is telling the truth here; in fact, I cannot help wondering if Antoine Pendergast himself brought up being worried about Constance having suspicions on exactly this point. How else can Diogenes be so sure that his words about her sister Mary will have the desired effect? Diogenes goes on to reveal (again, I believe, factually): "Oh yes: I had several chats with the old gentleman. How could I not seek out a dear relative with such a colorful history, with a worldview so similar to my own?" With what we know about Diogenes' feelings about the Pendergast family, this seems entirely logical.

At this point in the letter, Diogenes takes a purely confessional turn, and it is evidence of how ambiguous his attitude toward Constance truly is. It is completely unnecessary to his overall purpose to tell her: "The very possibility that he might still be alive after all those decades added excitement to my search, and I did not rest until I at length tracked him down." It is a relief to him to tell someone how he actually feels about something, and he allows himself the luxury because he believes Constance will be dead soon. Diogenes also admits his own nefariousness, saying that Antoine "quickly sensed my own true nature, and naturally became most anxious that your path should never cross mine" (*Book of the Dead,* p. 343). True, Constance's knowledge of Diogenes' real self can be calculated to add to her shame in betraying Aloysius's trust, but I think Diogenes has also become comfortable with her and is at least somewhat loathe to give this comfort up.

In fact, I think Diogenes uses the whole first portion of his letter—the part about Constance knowing that she gained longevity at least in part through the murder of her own sister—to help work himself up into believing she deserves what he is attempting to do to her. The reason she deserves him goading her to suicide is that she has been a bad sister to Mary, just as Aloysius has been a bad brother to him. Even more fitting, therefore, to use another bad sibling to cause his own bad sibling further pain. In the midst of laying out his accusations against her, Diogenes turns her own language of despair upon her, calling her a freak.

Diogenes' next tactic is to try to make Constance's time with his ancestor even more shameful than merely benefiting from the man who killed her sister. He hints: "Together, alone, in this house: was it possible that you even grew to become, shall we say, on *intimate terms* with Antoine?" (*Book of the Dead,* p. 344). Of course, he knows there was no sexual activity—or at least none involving vaginal penetration—and he quickly admits as much. The tone of his accusation, however, remains romantic when he says: "But you loved him—no doubt *you loved him.*" Diogenes is guessing, probably correctly, that Constance's feelings for Antoine were more complicated than that of a grateful adopted daughter towards a father figure. Why else did she so quickly fall in love with Aloysius, and then so quickly transfer her affections to Diogenes himself, but their similarities in looks and temperament to the man she had lived with so many years? Even if she never let herself put it into words, even in her own mind, Diogenes senses that it dwells in her subconscious and that she will recognize it and be made uneasy now that he has dredged it up for her. To reinforce his meaning, he calls her "consort to your sister's murderer," "consort" having the nuance of a sexual/marital partnership.

Diogenes goes on to tell her that no one would mourn her, and this is where he gets personal—yet his words are still, in many ways, ambiguous. He concludes: "*I* shall not mourn you: you were a toy; a mystery easily solved; a dull box forced and found empty; an animal spasm" (*Book of the Dead,* p. 344). These are certainly words meant to hurt, but in some ways they say much more about Diogenes than they do about Constance. A person ravaged by Comstock's Doorway to Hell and his own self-inflicted brain damage, who sees everyone as bags of meat and blood is not going to be able to see orgasm with *anyone* as much more than "an animal spasm." Also, to Diogenes, "a toy" is not necessarily a bad thing, given how much he enjoys playing with his victims. In a way, he pays Constance a compliment by implying that it is her mind he found wanting rather than her body—he knows this is the aspect of her being that she cares most about. Too, there is a certain air of trying to convince himself with his insults as much as he is trying to convince Constance. Plus, he has already somewhat contradicted himself by referring to the time he spent with her as "pleasant hours" (*Book of the Dead,* p. 342), though he could mean they were made pleasant by the thought of her ultimate deception.

Thus, when Diogenes writes: "So let me give you a piece of advice, and please believe this to be the one honest, altruistic thing I have ever told you" before commanding, "Do the noble thing. End your unnatural life" (*Book of the Dead,* p. 344), there is truth mingled with a fair share of self-pity in his words. It is "honest" and "altruistic" because Diogenes *really is* a nihilistic existentialist who believes human life is meaningless and filled with suffering. I do not think he feels, however, that Constance's life is that much more "unnatural" than his own, except in that she has benefited by harm done to her sibling, as he believes his own brother has. Diogenes' own life is unnatural as well, what with the lack of inhibition he must constantly fight (or discreetly give into) and the lack of recognizable sleep, to name just a few examples. He might be tempted to end it, were he not so fixated on fraternal revenge. I cannot help wondering if signing himself "Ever your Diogenes" (*Book of the Dead,* p. 344) is merely another example of his warped sense of humor, or if it also expresses an unconscious desire—albeit one that he never believes he will give into.

In a final act of distancing himself as well as attempting to make sure he has pushed Constance over the edge, Diogenes leaves a postscript. He calls her previous attempt at wrist-slashing "juvenile" (*Book of the Dead,* p. 345), and provides better instructions for the next attempt he believes she will make. Further, Diogenes reveals that the scar that he showed her on his own wrist was made "with a bit of greasepaint and wax." Again, he made a false creation rather than let Constance in enough to tell her of his real attempt at the tender age of seven. Perhaps Diogenes' greatest error in reading Constance was assuming her previous wrist-slashes were "juvenile." The slashes made horizontal to the length of the arm probably did not bespeak a lack of anatomical knowledge as much as an unconscious desire to live in spite of the gesture.

In any case, the package accompanying Diogenes' letter contains, first: "a hinged box of beautifully polished rosewood." Then: "Within, nestled on purple velvet, rested an antique scalpel" (*Book of the Dead,* p. 345). Diogenes has a penchant for wooden boxes, with hinges, lined with velvet—he will have one for Margo, later—because this, in essence, is what Comstock's Doorway to Hell was. Back in the chapter in which The Event is described, wood is mentioned, hinges are mentioned, and when they first look into the Doorway to Hell, they see "a dim, stifling interior, lined with what looked like black velvet" (*Book of the Dead,* p. 290). The scalpel, however, is chosen for Constance in particular. Its age suggests that Diogenes may have lifted it from Antoine Pendergast's own collection; he hopes that Constance will find it fitting to end her life with an instrument that may have been used to harvest her own sister's cauda equina nerves for the life extension serum.

Chapter Sixty-One is seen through the perspective of Bill Smithback, who is trying to figure out what is going on with the activities of Hayward and D'Agosta, while Chapter Sixty-Two follows the latter pair out of the Museum. We return to Smithback in Chapter Sixty-Three, as Pendergast drafts him to help make nitroglycerin for the purpose of broaching Diogenes' trap from an outer wall of the Museum. In Chapter Sixty-Four, however, readers are taken back to Nora in the Tomb of Senef, and through her we experience some of what Diogenes has created in his paean to Comstock's torture box. He leaves off the hideous insects to concentrate harder on the effects of strobes and extreme sound vibration, increasing the general sense of panic by filling the rooms of the exhibit with fog. Nora notices that "with each flash" of the strobe lights, "she seemed to feel stranger, heavy … almost drugged" (*Book of the Dead*, p. 362). Then Nora is aware that "a new sound cut in over the deep booming—a high, keening at the threshold of audibility, rising and falling like a banshee. The razor-sharp shriek seemed to riddle her consciousness like a shotgun blast, increasing the strange sensation of alienness."

Yet Nora is faring better than most of the rest of the group: "People were squeezing through, fighting and clawing, ripping at one another's clothes, forming a bloody bottleneck of insanity and panic." Nora is attacked by one man, and trapped by Collopy, who is suffering the same leg-drag as Lipper did. After Viola finds her and helps her escape the Museum head's grasp, Diogenes launches something he surely borrowed from Comstock's original: "And then a swirling image appeared above them—a huge, three-dimensional spinning spiral" (*Book of the Dead*, p. 365). Within a few moments, with excruciating audio accompaniment, "the spiral began to rotate faster. Nora stared at it, instantly mesmerized. It was a holographic projection, it had to be. And yet it was *real*... it was like nothing she had ever seen before." Even though "it drew her forward, sucking her in, pulling her down into a maelstrom of insanity," Nora still manages to break its hold upon her by not looking at it, and manages to save Viola from it by blindfolding her with a piece of her gala gown. The two women determine to block their eyes and ears from as much as they can, but before she blindfolds herself, Nora "caught a glimpse of a man standing in an alcove in the far corner, dressed in white tie and tails, utterly calm, an eye-mask over his face, head tilted up, hands clasped in front, standing stock-still, as if waiting" (*Book of the Dead*, p. 365). She recognizes him as Menzies, but wonders if seeing him is just another illusion.

It amazes me that Diogenes can simply wait for the full effects of his pain factory to be inflicted. I suppose it is possible, however, that he sneaks careful glimpses of the growing chaos, just not necessarily at the moments when others see him. Also, considering how many years Diogenes has waited to perpetrate this grand scheme, perhaps a few more minutes in the name of his own safety are easy to bear.

Chapter Sixty-Five returns to the viewpoint of Smithback as he and Pendergast succeed in breaching the tomb's outer wall. It does not tell us much that truly relates to Diogenes, except that finally Aloysius has come to a full grasp of his younger brother's purpose and methods. He tells Smithback:

"Stop the show—rip out wires, rip down screens, smash lights, but *stop the show.* We must do that before we do anything else—even before we help the people" (*Book of the Dead,* p. 369).

In Chapter Sixty-Six, however, the confrontation comes. First, though, Pendergast shoots out the strobe lights and finds that his brother has hidden electrical cables behind false moldings in the wall. Ultimately, he discovers that Diogenes has sequestered an entire generator inside "a large XX Dynasty chest, gilded and intricately carved" and placed this "within a glass display case" (*Book of the Dead,* p. 372) to protect it even further. Whether this coincides with his planned stopping point, or he is able to sense that something has gone wrong with his sound-and-light show, Diogenes "reached up and pulled off his mask" (*Book of the Dead,* p. 373) as his brother and Smithback are staring at him. Diogenes is apparently recognizable to Aloysius the minute he unmasks, though it is a few moments before Smithback can identify him as Menzies. While Smithback notices Pendergast's intense reaction to the man, he observes "that the tuxedoed figure's reaction was even stronger." As Diogenes instantly recognizes his brother, despite the still-dyed brown hair from his prison escape, his first impulse is to go "into a sudden, instinctive crouch, like a man poised to spring." This is his natural reaction to Aloysius—fight or flight. Yet Diogenes is no stereotypical, cowardly villain. Even though he is incredulous that his brother is standing before him rather than safely ensconced in a federal prison, "he gathered himself together and slowly rose to his full height," facing Aloysius with dignity—if dignity can be mixed with fury. Diogenes simply utters: "*You!*" Then, according to Smithback, "with a long, spidery hand—he removed the headphones and earplugs, and slowly and deliberately dropped them to the floor." I am not sure if Diogenes is preparing for hand-to-hand combat with his brother, or if he is preparing to surrender to him, figuring that if somehow Aloysius has been freed from prison, he may also have been restored to agent status. I am not sure at this point if Diogenes really even knows what he is doing. Clearly, he never anticipated that he might want a firearm with him on this evening he felt would be his ultimate triumph; otherwise he would either have drawn it or dropped it on the floor in surrender. Smithback observes of Diogenes, whom he is just then recognizing as Menzies: "His eyes were flaming red, his limbs quivered. His face was flushed as deeply as Pendergast's was—he was filled with rage" (*Book of the Dead*, p. 373).

Fortunately for Diogenes, his brother not only falters between the necessity of apprehending him and the enormity of the guilt he now feels towards him, but is distracted by the sudden appearance of Viola Maskelene. The moment Aloysius turns toward the woman he loves, Diogenes recognizes that escape is the only way he will ever be able to complete any future revenge scheme against his brother. Smithback, still thinking of him as the head of the anthropology department, notes that "Menzies darted to one side with incredible speed and vanished into the darkness" (*Book of the Dead*, pp. 373-374). Diogenes knows his brother will stay with his damsel in distress rather than pursue.

Chapter Sixty-Seven takes us right into Diogenes' mind, as he sits in a private train car approximately thirty minutes after his escape from the Museum. As the chapter begins, he is attempting to mentally distance himself from what has just taken place. After ordering ice, water, and sugar cubes from the porter, Diogenes looks out the window and sees several people on the train platform, including one who will turn out to be Constance in disguise. She is the last thing he is looking for, however. "Diogenes saw them all, yet he paid them little heed. They were simply visual ephemera, a distraction for his mind … to keep it from drifting toward other, more maddening thoughts" (*Book of the Dead,* p. 377). He has cooled off enough from his "anguish, disbelief, and white-hot rage" to realize that "under the circumstances he had managed quite well: he always had multiple exit plans in place, and this evening he'd followed the most appropriate one to the letter." This one phrase, "multiple exit plans in place," has long been my mantra in opposition to those who said Diogenes could never have survived the volcano, and at this writing, I am looking forward as much as anyone to reading just how he managed.

One of the things Diogenes is using to cheer himself up, however, is that he is planning to finally finish off Margo Green during one of the train's stops. He reflects that "the hypo was already filled and lovingly nestled in its gift box, beautifully wrapped and beribboned." No doubt the gift box is wooden, hinged, and lined with velvet, much like the one containing Constance's scalpel. In noting that the package in turn is "tucked safely away in his valise," Diogenes allows readers a generalized inventory of this carrying case for "his most precious items—his scrapbooks, his personal pharmacopeia of hallucinogens and opioids, his ghastly little trinkets and playings of which nobody who'd ever caught sight had been permitted to live." I am not sure if "personal pharmacopeia" means only those drugs he uses on victims or bystanders, or if it implies that he uses some of them himself for either recreational purposes or, for instance, to come as close as possible to normal sleep. It is interesting, too, to contemplate past incidences of people who might have taken a glimpse at the contents of Diogenes' valise—who might they have been, what tempted them to peek, and in what manner were their punishments measured out? I also wonder, regarding the scrapbooks (one of which surely contains the clipping about the diamond heist he showed to Viola in *Dance of Death)*, how many of the news stories match those that Pendergast left for D'Agosta to aid his search?

Diogenes returns to the contemplation of Margo Green, and we learn a few things about his attitude towards her, and towards his psycopathological pastimes. He sees her as "the only carryover from the earlier stage of his plan," and "a sitting duck, to be played with and dispatched with little risk, time, or effort" (*Book of the Dead,* p. 377). He wonders: "What about her, in particular, had drawn him back—more than say, William Smithback, Nora Kelly, Vincent D'Agosta, or Laura Hayward?" (*Book of the Dead,* p. 378). Well, one reason is that whole "little risk, time, or effort" thing he has just cited. Any of those others at this point would definitely involve far *more* risk, time, and effort. Also, I feel Diogenes is just using these names for rhetorical purpose, except, perhaps, for Smithback. Although he would be loathe to admit it to himself, his sense of fair play would eliminate

D'Agosta and Hayward from the list of preferred victims—as previously mentioned, D'Agosta for the debt of killing Fosco and Hayward for the debt of helping him frame his brother. Hayward would also prick his sense of chivalry, as would Nora, even though the latter would have been a victim of his sound-and-light show. It is interesting that Diogenes does not include Viola Maskelene on this list, especially given her value to Aloysius; again, perhaps he now feels he owes her a debt because of her unwitting role in his most recent escape.

Though Diogenes ultimately pins his continued pursuit of Margo on "her long connection to the museum," I honestly believe he is using this just to work himself up into actually finishing her off. She may have been connected to the Museum longer than Nora, but if one cannot precisely say that Diogenes likes her better than the vast majority of people he encountered there, it can be said he dislikes her less than most of the rest. Yes, Diogenes reflects that "it had pleased him […] keeping her on the brink of expiration, teasing out her widowed mother's pain to the greatest possible extent," but he had never actually crossed the line and killed her. In the final analysis, thanks to Constance, we will never know (barring future unknown developments in *The Obsidian Chamber*) if he ever would have.

Diogenes mentally moves on to an enigmatic place—in reference to Margo and her mother's situation, he thinks: "It was a brew of suffering from which he drank deep, and whose astringent taste renewed his own thirst for the living death that was his life." These are pretty harsh terms in which to cast one's own existence-- "living death." Does Diogenes really view his own life since The Event in this way? If so, he must be subconsciously relieved that he has the opportunity—or necessity—of rethinking and re-plotting the ultimate revenge on his brother. If he had succeeded, what would he have had left to sufficiently motivate him to keep living? It might also mean that on some level he hates what he has become, while still embracing his role as an agent of pain. It is possible, though, that Diogenes may have only meant "living death" in the context of what he endured while masquerading as Menzies. He feels the experience has been "an insufferably extended torture" amongst "the pontificating, pedestrian, whoreson, didactic, beggarly, jejune, ossified, shit-encrusted minds" he had to work with daily.

Once the porter delivers the requested supplies, Diogenes turns his attention to the flask of absinthe he has in a pocket of his suit. Given all that he has been through in the matter of an hour, it is not surprising that he would want a drink to help steady his nerves. Besides the flask, however, Diogenes has brought another special element with him for the preparation of his favorite libation, and he has packed it in his valise. The item is "a silver spoon with the Pendergast family crest stamped on its handle," and we may deduce from the fact that the crest is "somewhat melted at one corner" that Diogenes managed to retrieve the spoon from the fire that destroyed Rochenoire. That he has this spoon at all is another indication that he values his identity as a Pendergast; his attitude toward it is indicative of even deeper feeling: "He handled it as one might handle one's newborn child. Carefully, lovingly, he laid the spoon across the top of the glass."

As he did with Constance, Diogenes thinks about the color of the absinthe at its various stages of mixing with ice water and sugar, and wishes he could see it. He first notes the "brilliant green liquid" from the flask, "which to him looked pale gray." Then with the addition of water and sugar, it becomes "first a milky green, then a beautiful opalescent jade—if his eyes could only see in color" (*Book of the Dead*, p. 378). Again, I cannot help but think he watched someone in his family—probably someone he loved, possibly his mother—preparing and drinking absinthe while he still had his color vision.

After Diogenes has a few sips of absinthe, readers are first treated to his opinions about passenger trains. Noting that the train he was on "was one of only two luxury passenger trains still operated by Amtrack," he reflects: "It was a criminal disgrace the way politicians had allowed America's passenger train system, once the envy of the world, to fall into insolvency and disrepair" (*Book of the Dead*, p. 379). Then we are let in on his immediate future plans: "But this, too, was a passing inconvenience: he would soon be back in Europe, where people understood how to travel in dignity and comfort." It is interesting, however, that Diogenes has no qualms about having a good stiff drink of a fairly strong alcohol before getting off the train to finish off Margo. Clearly he is used to its affects, and trusts his own ability to act competently under its influence.

He feels he has needed to imbibe, however, in order to further examine the frustration of his most ambitious plot. This is where Diogenes reveals just how long he has been in hatching this particular scheme: "Fifteen years of planning, careful disguise, artful intrigue, ingenious contrivance … all for naught" (*Book of the Dead*, p. 380). This does seem at odds, however, with the fact that Diogenes appears to be bidding his brother farewell as he drives away from the diamond heist in *Dance of Death*. Perhaps, even though he has apparently had this sound-and-light show project in reserve for a long time, Diogenes would have been content with simply framing his brother and killing Viola if he had actually managed to obtain Lucifer's Heart. Perhaps he had qualms about damaging that many people in a way similar to what had happened to him, even though he had already done "the meticulous medical research into how one could contrive to transform ordinary people into murderous sociopaths using nothing more than sound and light." When Pendergast tricked him out of the red diamond *and* Viola as victim, any possible misgivings on Diogenes' part disappeared.

In addition to the medical research, for which Diogenes would have needed knowledge comparable to that of a neurologist or brain surgeon, he also obtained the training required of an anthropologist, and utilized the skills of a top computer programmer. In this plot alone, Diogenes displays such brilliance in sufficiently different areas of study to prove his elder brother's contention of his genius. Incidentally, in reflecting on testing his program, Diogenes lets us know his opinion of Wicherly. He mentally refers to him as "that ass." Even though Diogenes will soon move to the pleasurable contemplation of his own ill-intentioned seduction of Constance, he obviously does not approve of the late Egyptologist's predatory attitude towards women.

More importantly, Diogenes' musings reveal that he believes the absolute worst with regards to his brother and The Event. He thinks of him thus: "Aloysius, who—as the less gifted brother—had always taken grim pleasure in tearing down those things he himself lovingly constructed. Aloysius who, realizing he would always be bested intellectually, had taken the ultimate step of subjecting him to an Event that would ensure . . ." Diogenes cuts his thoughts off, because "the hand holding the glass began to shake" (*Book of the Dead,* p. 380), but one might assume they end in at least "ensure that he (Aloysius) would be the more successful brother." He may even believe that Aloysius intended his death, given what the young Diogenes attempted to do to himself with the derringer. In short, Diogenes thinks that Aloysius was so jealous of his higher IQ that he attempted to damage or kill him through The Event. One wonders, not about Aloysius's actual intent, which was not anywhere near this level of ruthlessness, but about whether Diogenes' intellectual ability actually did suffer from The Event. If so, what might he have been capable of otherwise? Or was it only Diogenes' capacity for normal, socially constructive behavior that suffered— along, of course, with his color vision.

Among the thoughts with which Diogenes comforts himself is that his beautiful scheme would indeed have worked if his brother had not escaped from prison. After another sip of absinthe, he manages to remind himself: "He *had* succeeded, at least in part. He had hurt his brother terribly. Aloysius had been publicly humiliated, charged with the murders of his own friends, sent to prison" (*Book of the Dead,* p. 381). I can only assume that since coming face to face with his brother in the Tomb of Senef, Diogenes has either heard news reports of an escape at Herkmoor, or deduced the facts from his brother's dyed hair. Diogenes contemplates his brother's fate:

"He might be free, temporarily, but he was still a wanted man: the prison break would only deepen the hole he was in." I feel certain that during all the aforementioned fifteen years of planning, and even before, Diogenes has kept a close watch on Aloysius; he still knows his brother intimately. "For somebody so private," Diogenes realizes, "the prison ordeal must have been mortifying." Again, in keeping with Diogenes' astonishment in *Dance of Death* that Aloysius was willing to give himself up to authorities, we can almost detect a note of relief at the idea of his brother being at large. While true in Diogenes' mind that Aloysius "could never rest, never take an easy breath," he was also evading execution—which Diogenes does *not* want his brother to suffer.

Diogenes apparently retains every confidence that he can locate Aloysius, even while his brother is a fugitive. He has begun to tell himself that "he was still relatively young. He had many years left, more than enough to develop a plan—a *better* plan." Presumably Diogenes would need to know his brother's whereabouts for such a plan to give him true satisfaction. Interestingly, he ruminates over developing the new plot in the place toward which he is heading, the place he considers his true home. "Just the thought of being back in his library, among his treasured possessions, within the embrace of a structure lovingly designed to spoil his every whim, helped restore his equanimity." That Diogenes has such a place seems to contradict his conceptualizing of "the living death that was his life."

As Diogenes contemplates one last blow he believes his brother will have time to face before hitting the road as a fugitive, he also gives evidence that some of the lies he has told Constance were in his last letter rather than in person. Seducing her was "an abominable, delicious pleasure." True, Diogenes is also gloating that "every cynical lie he had told, had been a joy" (*Book of the Dead*, p. 381), but "delicious" is not a word one uses in connection with "a dull box forced and found empty" (*Book of the Dead*, p. 344). There is also the tinge of wonder in his musing: "Remarkable: a hundred years of childhood ... and yet still so fresh, so innocent, and naive" (*Book of the Dead*, p. 381). Again, "innocent" and "naive" are to be exploited for Diogenes, but "fresh" is still a positive word. He is proud of his "long and windy disquisitions on color," chief among his lies, but I still maintain that part of that pride was keeping his lack of color vision from Constance. Indeed, Diogenes is ultimately able to be heartless, imagining Constance "lying in a pool of her own blood"--although blood, for him, is something of an aphrodisiac. His greatest pleasure, however, is his mental picture of "his brother standing over the dead body of Constance, reading the letter" (*Book of the Dead*, p. 381). Yet all of the words he has formed in thinking about her reflect at the very least an ambiguity in his feelings toward Constance.

Diogenes is utterly unprepared for what happens next, and yet, even under the influence of the absinthe, his intuition and reflexes are enough not only to keep him from being shot, but to escape the train before his cover is blown. Constance, disguised as an elderly woman, enters his train car. Diogenes does not recognize her at first, at least not on a conscious level. Yet, as she approaches him, "some sixth sense abruptly screamed danger" (*Book of the Dead*, p. 382). Preston and Child go on to tell us that "then, as the woman reached into her handbag, he realized what it was: these were no longer the slow, hesitant movements of an old lady. They were lithe and quick—and they seemed to have a dreadful purpose." It is not until after she pulls the gun out of her purse that Diogenes "recognized the bottomless, expressionless eyes that looked back at him from beneath the wig. Recognized them well" (*Book of the Dead*, p. 382). Of course, Diogenes' cause is aided by Constance's gun being old and rusty, and by her being unfamiliar with its use. Still, he manages to duck or flinch away from three shots before realizing he must flee the train. It is not so much that Diogenes fears dying by her hand; he contemplates grabbing her and taking the gun away, but realizes the gunshots have already attracted too much attention from the staff and passengers of the train. He takes advantage of the fact that one of Constance's bullets has broken the window of his private car: "Instantly, without conscious thought, Diogenes whirled around and dived out through the shattered window, landing heavily on the concrete platform, rolling once, twice, a confused welter of dust amidst bits of safety glass" (*Book of the Dead*, p. 383).

To those who have read all the novels in the Pendergast series, and are familiar with Aloysius's long-lost son Alban and the manner in which he was genetically enhanced, I posit that this scene between Diogenes and Constance suggests that Diogenes possesses even more of the preternatural instinct the Nazis valued in Aloysius. If Alban's genes had come from Diogenes rather than Aloysius, he might still be around for readers to enjoy.

Diogenes, master of escapes, manages to make his way relatively unnoticed from the train platform—except, of course, somehow Constance is able to follow his trail. Chapter Sixty-Eight finds him in Boston's Logan Airport, about to board a flight for Italy. Fortunately having carried his various passports and other documents in his suit pocket, rather than in the valise Constance forced him to abandon, Diogenes is now disguised as an Australian businessman in his mid-sixties. Later we learn it is the day after the Museum gala; Diogenes purchases a copy of the *New York Times* along with a James Rollins novel, and sees an article in the paper about the shooting on the train. If he sees anything about the strange occurrences at the Tomb of Senef, it does not register in the portion of Diogenes' thoughts the authors allow us to see. Perhaps Smithback is too busy taking care of his wife to file a report? I cannot help wondering if Diogenes actually likes reading Rollins, or whether he merely thinks the novel a good addition to his new alter-ego. (If he does enjoy thrillers, for whom does he root?) Though his brother claims not to like popular fiction, Aloysius did seek out D'Agosta's novels and offered the author a positive opinion of them.

Apparently, Diogenes is able to camouflage his emotions well. The description of the Australian businessman, Gerald Boscomb, whom he is pretending to be is that "his face" was "open, ruddy, and cheerful" (*Book of the Dead,* p. 384). He says "G'day" to clerks and airline workers, and smiles over the *Times* sports section. Preston and Child note, however, that "the pleasant, somewhat vacant expression on his face was no more than skin-deep. Inside, his head was a boiling stew of fury, disbelief, and savage self-reproach" (*Book of the Dead,* p. 385). In addition to Diogenes' prior upset over his brother spoiling his large-scale version of Comstock's phantasmagoria, he now added his astonishment not only at Constance's continued existence, but her determination to end his own. "With her, he had miscalculated disastrously," he admitted inwardly. Though "everything he knew of human nature indicated that she would take her own life," and Diogenes had judged her to have lived her many years "uncertain what she was intended for, confused about the meaning of her life," he "now saw that he had cleared up her confusion and given her the one thing no one else could have: something to live for." On Preston and Child's pages Diogenes does not explicitly make the connection, but I would argue that if Aloysius "created" Diogenes through The Event, then similarly Diogenes "created" Constance through his seduction and abandonment of her. If Diogenes allowed himself to see this parallel, however, it might render him too sympathetic to Constance and render him unable to effectively dispose of her. He is already unwillingly impressed by her, both in her resistance to his urging her to suicide, and in her ability to track him.

As Diogenes ponders the situation, readers learn that Constance is not the first to set malignant sights on him. Other such occurrences hardly fazed him, apparently. "Those who interfered with him—there had been several—hadn't survived long enough to make a second attempt. He had washed away his sins in their blood" (*Book of the Dead,* p. 385). Already, however, Diogenes is beginning to think of Constance as a unique case: "he could see that she was not like the others. He could not understand how she had identified him on the train—unless she had somehow physically followed him from the museum" (*Book of the*

Dead, pp. 385-386). We learn later, of course, that Constance has indeed followed him from the Museum. Not to mention that after this feat, "she had forced him to leap out a window, flee in undignified panic, abandoning his valise with its treasured contents" (*Book of the Dead,* p. 386). Yet, while these achievements set her apart from those Diogenes has killed previously, they also lead Diogenes to conclude that "as long as *she* lived, he would never be safe." Thus, "Constance Greene had to die."

Part of Diogenes' reasoning in this is based on either a mistake in his thinking or in that of the authors: "Constance Greene alone could identify him." Though Viola Maskelene eventually tells Pendergast that she has seen Diogenes in two different disguises, and neither was Menzies, she did see his true appearance when he picked her up at the airport in *Dance of Death.* He wanted Viola to be sure to notice the resemblance to his brother. Too, Aloysius seems able to penetrate Diogenes' disguises, and he and D'Agosta have seen him as himself on videotape. Perhaps Diogenes figures his brother will be too busy escaping recapture to pose much of a problem. Or perhaps he means that "Constance alone"-- aside from a preoccupied or imprisoned Aloysius—could recognize him even in his most clever disguises.

In any case, Diogenes decides that killing an adversary as worthy as Constance "would require a finely tuned plan." While musing upon the Cape buffalo and its "peculiar strategy when hunted," he comes up with an idea to lure Constance into a trap. In order to do this, Diogenes must actually hope that she has managed to pursue him to the Boston airport. As he wanders into a Starbucks in the international terminal in search of her, we learn that he shares his brother's taste for green tea—although he is willing to settle, at least in this instance, for some that costs less than Aloysius's favorite brand. Diogenes does, of course, see Constance in disguise in the bookstore where he had purchased the *Times* and the Rollins book. He reaffirms his commitment to his entrapment scheme, recognizing that "he could kill her here—it would be easy—but he would not be able to escape the layers of airport security" (*Book of the Dead,* p. 387). Until he boards the plane without incident, Diogenes is unsure whether Constance shares his caution, wondering: "Did she care enough about her own life to take greater care—or was her sole aim to end his?" (*Book of the Dead,* p. 387).

Chapter Sixty-Nine returns us to Pendergast and D'Agosta at 891 Riverside, bringing each other up to speed—Pendergast revealing Constance's disappearance and Diogenes' letter, and D'Agosta providing police details from the shooting on the train. It is from D'Agosta, then, that the reader learns a little more about Diogenes and his valise; of it, he reports: "They brought it into an evidence room, and when the warrant came down, they opened it up. Apparently, the evidence officer took one look and, well, whatever happened next, he had to be sedated" (*Book of the Dead,* p. 389). D'Agosta adds that after this, "a hazmat team was called in, and the stuff is now under lock and key—nobody seems to know where" (*Book of the Dead,* p. 389). Once more, Preston and Child are enhancing the fearsomeness of those valise contents by being vague about just what they are. Did the evidence officer have to be sedated because of how horrifying some of Diogenes' treasures were, or were some of the vials of drugs broken, causing some inhaled effect? Would the latter be the reason the hazmat team was called in, or were there traces of leftover diamond dust/anthrax found? Was a container of human blood broken and spilled, and precautions against blood-borne pathogens taken? Perhaps the most intriguing question is posed by the last portion of D'Agosta's report—that no one seems to know the present location of the contents of Diogenes' valise. One wonders if somehow even in his fugitive state, Pendergast still has some pull with a strategically placed person in the NYPD, or perhaps Glinn has arranged to spirit them away? I am tempted to mention the possibility that Diogenes himself had perhaps blackmailed such an authority on the force, and may in the future be reunited with his valise and some, at least, of his treasures.

One final point of interest in this chapter is that after D'Agosta expresses the hope that Constance succeeds in her aim of killing Diogenes, Pendergast replies: "The thought of their meeting again is too terrible to contemplate" (*Book of the Dead,* p. 390). Logic would decree that he fears for Constance's safety in the clutches of a brilliant psychopath, but knowing Constance has already tried to shoot Diogenes and considering Pendergast's follow-up line of "I must catch up with her—and stop her" makes me wonder if he actually fears for his younger brother's life as well. Again, Pendergast expresses the ultimate faith in his brother's cleverness and ability to evade law enforcement, if not Constance: "Diogenes has been preparing for this escape for years, and we have no hope of tracing him" (*Book of the Dead,* p. 390).

In Chapter Seventy, readers are returned to the labyrinthine twists and turns of Diogenes' viewpoint. By now, both he and Constance have arrived in Florence, and he is attempting to lure her into a narrow, medieval alley that he feels is perfect for his ambush. Though Diogenes is fond of Florence, his mood is still bleak due to the frustration of his plans. He is walking along the Arno River, famously featured in Dante's *Divine Comedy*. As he notes "the perfect curve of the arches of the Ponte Santa Trinità, designed by Ammanati: curves that had confounded the mathematicians," and "the statues of the four seasons that crowned both ends," he feels: "None of it gave him pleasure anymore. It was all useless, futile" (*Book of the Dead*, p. 392).

Diogenes has already reflected again upon the fact that Constance had forced him to flee without his clothing and his valise, but the shopping and snacking he does while making sure she is following him gives readers further insight into his likes and dislikes. True, he is taking his time and trying to be seen, but he still chooses some items rather than others. One of the first things Diogenes buys is stationery; on the one hand, perhaps his trademark cream laid has run low. On the other hand, one wonders to whom he writes, other than to his victims? Perhaps he plans to pen a letter to Aloysius after he has killed Constance? He also buys luggage, presumably for the clothing he intends to buy later. He has these first two items sent over to his hotel, but purchases an umbrella and raincoat for more immediate use, partially because "the sky was threatening rain" (*Book of the Dead*, p. 391).

His next stop is at the famed Florence delicatessen, Procacci. The truffle sandwich he orders there is one of the place's specialties, and he has "a glass of vernaccia" (a Tuscan white wine) to accompany it. Though the truffle sandwich is a popular feature there, this, a croissant, and hard candy (the last item provided to Viola during her captivity), are the only food items mentioned in conjunction with Diogenes thus far in the series. It could be a coincidence, but it does make me wonder if perhaps, ironically, he is a vegetarian. Perhaps his years of gory experimentation with mammals, both human and otherwise, and his tendency to view people as sacks of guts, blood, and bones, prone to decay, have left him unable to find meat appetizing? If Diogenes is a vegetarian, he is a very careful one who makes sure he gets enough protein to maintain the strength of his powerful, lanky frame. Yet, being too particular about one's dietary requirements would tend to attract attention and scrutiny he would rather avoid. At this point, we can only speculate.

From Procacci, Diogenes goes into a designer store and comes out with "two suits, one in silk and the other a black double-breasted *completo* with a broad pinstripe, which he favored because of its faint thirties gangsterish flavor" (*Book of the Dead,* p. 392). Though his taste is similar to that of Aloysius, Diogenes is a little flashier; also, he somewhat enjoys identifying with the wrong side of the law. He then—after finally sighting Constance entering a church—buys two pairs of shoes at Ferragamo; obviously he has quite a line of credit in Mr. Boscomb's name. From there he moves on to more mundane necessities like underwear and socks. No doubt these, too, are expensive, but Preston and Child do not disclose any tantalizing details such as boxers or briefs. Apparently, however, our would-be gangster wears a nightshirt. This has got to be some old-fashioned, eccentric

Pendergast family habit, although Aloysius does not seem to favor it. The purchase that most intrigues me, however, is that of a bathing suit. Diogenes believes, rightly, that he is on his way home; surely he has one in his villa on Stromboli? He also believes, not so rightly, that he will have disposed of Constance by the end of the day—is he planning on relaxing in the hotel pool afterward? Given the styles of men's bathing suits popular in Europe, and the fact that Preston and Child do not say "swimming trunks," I am guessing it only covers the essentials.

Purchases made, Diogenes pretends to look in the back windows of antique shops until he sees Constance's reflection in one of them. He notes that she, in her disguise, "for all the world looked like one of the swinish American tourists who visited Florence in mindless shopping herds" (*Book of the Dead*, p. 393). This phrasing, along with some of his other ruminations on train travel and absinthe, lead me to think that Diogenes tends to see Europe as far more cultured and civilized than his native United States. Once he does spot Constance, however, he uses the fact that the rain and the many pedestrians have caused a "sea of umbrellas" that will block her view of him. Diogenes runs and doubles back in such a way that he will enter the Via dei Coverelli from the opposite end than the one he believes Constance will expect. He is apparently willing to chance the attention he might attract by running, though according to the authors Diogenes is "sprinting silently" (*Book of the Dead*, p. 393). This is further proof that he shares Aloysius's oft-described feline grace. Diogenes knows the Via to be "one of the darkest, narrowest streets in Florence" (*Book of the Dead*, p. 394), partially because "the medieval buildings on both sides had been built out over the street on arches of stone, which blocked the sky and made the alley, even on a sunny day, as dim as a cave." Interestingly, Diogenes is counting upon "Constance's intelligence and her uncanny research abilities," knowing "she would have studied a map of Florence and considered deeply" where and when "to launch her attack." He believes she will try to use that same dark street to ambush him, but that "his flanking dash in the other direction would turn the tables. He would now be approaching her from behind, instead of from the front" (*Book of the Dead,* p. 394).

Chapter Seventy-One returns the reader to Pendergast, who is accompanied by D'Agosta on his ride to catch his own plane to Florence. In trying to explain what happened to people in the Tomb of Senef, Pendergast puts defining words to his younger brother's purpose there: "Diogenes wanted to inflict on the world the pain that had been inflicted on him. He wanted to re-create the ... the terrible Event that ruined his life" (*Book of the Dead,* p. 395), he tells D'Agosta. Pendergast spells it out even further for his friend: "You recall I mentioned he had been victimized by a sadistic device, a 'house of pain'? The Tomb of Senef was nothing less than a re-creation of that house of pain. On a grand and terrible scale" (*Book of the Dead,* p. 395). Incidentally, Pendergast also confirms: "There was no Count of Cahors. Diogenes fronted the money for the restoration of the tomb" (*Book of the Dead,* p. 396).

When D'Agosta expresses his disbelief over the sheer reach of Diogenes' plans, Pendergast contradicts him. "No. Utterly logical. His aim was to re-create the terrible, unforgivable

Event … for which I was responsible." D'Agosta tries to dissuade him on the last point, but Pendergast is firm. "I *am* my brother's creator" (*Book of the Dead*, p. 396), he insists. "And all this time, I never knew it—I never apologized or atoned for what I did" (*Book of the Dead*, pp. 396-397). If only Diogenes could have heard this. We can only wonder what his reaction might have been to finally receiving this acknowledgment from Aloysius. Further, I am not sure that D'Agosta's assertion that "there's only one way to take care of Diogenes" (*Book of the Dead*, p. 397) adds anything to the reader's insight about the younger Pendergast brother. If Pendergast shares this belief (and I do not think he does), it would place him in an extremely difficult position, feeling morally unable to kill the brother he knows he has wronged unless another life immediately depended on it.

Chapter Seventy-Two takes us back to Diogenes as he is attempting to sneak up on Constance. He makes his approach to the place he believes she will wait to ambush him carefully, "flattening himself against the ancient *sgraffito* facade of some long-forgotten palace. With enormous caution, he peered around the corner" (*Book of the Dead*, p. 398). Apparently, despite the teaming number of tourists and citizens with umbrellas on the main thoroughfare, the street Diogenes has chosen for his next encounter with Constance is deserted enough not only for this suspicious behavior but to actually kill her and slip away without being noticed.

Right after this, however, readers are presented with something of a conundrum. "His hand slipped into his pocket and removed a leather case, from which he took an ivory-handled scalpel identical to the one he had left beneath her pillow" (*Book of the Dead,* p. 398). Has Diogenes had this leather case and scalpel in his pocket since he left the Museum and boarded the train? It seems more likely that in between jumping out the train window and arriving at the Boston airport, he managed to visit one of his boltholes and assume the identity of Boscomb (the police report on the train incident cited his name as Eugene Hofstader), along with a different suit. Surely the one he wore on the train was torn or at least abraded in his landing on the concrete platform? Even if Diogenes did have the identical scalpel in his pocket on the train—it *is* possible he might have wanted to hold it in his hand as he contemplated Constance's supposed suicide—he would have had to transfer it to the new suit. He would also have had to take two scalpels from the beginning, planning to keep one—again, possibly from his Great-Uncle Antoine's collection. I doubt Diogenes could have acquired this while shopping the streets of Florence, unless this was where he had purchased the first, before launching his initial campaign described in *Dance of Death.* In any case, I believe Diogenes having two such scalpels, and being determined that Constance should die by this special means, indicates a special feeling towards her on his part—one that has only been enhanced by her stubborn will to live and seek revenge.

Another indication that Diogenes has real feelings for Constance, twisted though they may be, is his visualization of her death at his hands. He imagines that after he slashes a major artery below her collarbone, "he would then hold her while she died; he would cradle her; he would allow her blood to flow over him as it had done once before … under very different circumstances" (*Book of the Dead,* p. 399).

There is a warped tenderness here, although it is also mixed with the knowledge that Constance would hate suffering this indignity in her final moments. Diogenes further anticipates that "he would leave both her and his raincoat in the alley." Though he would need to abandon the raincoat because of the theoretical bloodstains Constance would leave upon it, it is a well-known profiling truism that leaving a protective garment or blanket with a body is an indication of feelings of pity or regret about the victim.

Constance, however, is not finished increasing Diogenes' admiration for her. She is indeed waiting in his ambush spot, but she has climbed up above it, and drops down upon him with her own scalpel. Before Constance strikes, she even manages to induce in Diogenes "a twinge of panic" (*Book of the Dead,* p. 399) by not being where he expects her to be. Yet even as she manages to wound him, Diogenes demonstrates his seemingly native Pendergastian agility. First, again with the intuitive quality that will be his stronger nephew's trademark later in the series, "he instinctively threw himself sideways even as a shadow dropped upon him" (*Book of the Dead,* p. 400). He "twisted around, and—even as he fell—drove his own scalpel in a glittering arc toward her, aiming for the neck." The authors go on to tell us that "His greater experience with the blade, combined with superior speed, paid off."

Diogenes has only managed to wound Constance, but she has both managed to wound him and once more upend his worldview. "He fell hard onto the cobblestones, his mind swept clean by astonishment." Diogenes realized that Constance's "poor disguise had been no accident. She had been showing herself to him, just as he had been revealing himself to her." Further, "she had allowed him to lead her to a point of ambush, and she had then used it against him. She had countered his countermove." In his thoughts, Diogenes pays her the compliment: "The simple brilliance of it astounded him" (*Book of the Dead,* p. 400).

Once Diogenes realizes both that Constance has already fled the scene and that she cannot immediately come back at him because she, too, is bleeding, he turns his attention towards his own injury and towards escape. He is likely as stoic as Aloysius in tending his wounds, though fortunately he does not have the necessity of stitching up his own abdominal arteries as his brother did in *Cabinet of Curiosities.* Initially, Diogenes "dared not open his coat and inspect" because he cannot "afford to get blood on the outside of his clothing" (*Book of the Dead,* pp. 400-401). So as a temporary fix, "he belted his raincoat as tightly as possible, trying to bind the wound." It is difficult to determine whether the wooziness Diogenes appears to feel is from blood loss, or from the sheer shock of Constance outsmarting him. The sentence, "He took a step, staggered" (*Book of the Dead,* p. 400), could mean that he physically staggered, or that he was psychologically staggered by the turn of events. Diogenes does, however, feel "a wave of faintness" (*Book of the Dead,* p. 400). He remedies this like countless blood donors the world over—he orders "a *spremuta*" (*Book of the Dead,* p. 401), which is Italian for juice—in the cafe he enters to tend his wound.

In the cafe's bathroom, Diogenes removes his raincoat to find "the amount of blood was shocking. He quickly probed the wound, confirming that it hadn't pierced his peritoneum." He cleans himself up with paper towels, and tears up his shirt to bind the wound closed and stop the bleeding. Raincoat back in place, and no visible signs of his encounter with Constance remaining, he takes a taxi to the train station. Diogenes believes this is his opportunity to throw Constance off his trail, and he has every confidence that his ultimate destination will protect him from her. "She would never find him there— never" (*Book of the Dead,* p. 401). Note that he has, at this point, completely abandoned the idea of killing her. As he slides into the backseat of the taxi, Diogenes finally gives into the onslaught of voices in his head, quotations from poetry in several languages, including the seemingly ever-present lines from Eliot's "Wasteland" that he has been fighting the whole time he has been matching wits with Constance.

Chapter Seventy-Three gives the reader Constance's thoughts after their Florence encounter, but of course there are details to learn about Diogenes in these thoughts. The first thing is that he was correct that Constance would need to retreat somewhere and clean up her own wounds before renewing her pursuit. The second we learn because of Constance's musings upon his disguises, and how she could penetrate them: "But there were two things he could not alter. His stature was the first" (*Book of the Dead,* p. 405). By this we know Diogenes has not been attempting to de-emphasize his height as Menzies (for instance, by stooping a little, as a somewhat elderly man might), adding to the mystery of why the head of the anthropology department was not an immediate suspect once the theory of his having an alter-ego on the Museum's staff was proposed.

Constance also reveals that Diogenes has a "peculiar scent," which she mentally describes as "strange and heady, like a mixture of licorice underscored by the keen, dark smell of iron." I am not prepared to speculate on the iron component, but perhaps the licorice element is a by-product of habitual absinthe-drinking? In Constance's quest for clues to find Diogenes' ultimate lair, she forces herself to remember every detail of her time with him. She hopes she can take his assertion that he lived by the sea as factual—and in hindsight, of course, we know that she can. In dredging up the lines from the Carducci poem that Diogenes whispered to her during their most intimate moments, in hopes that the poem itself will contain further hints, Constance admits to us that the experience was "exquisite" (*Book of the Dead,* p. 406).

Chapter Seventy-Four is extremely brief, but readers are returned to Diogenes' viewpoint for a few paragraphs. We learn he has had his wound stitched in Switzerland during the course of two days' worth of train and boat travel, zig-zagging throughout Europe under different identities to be sure Constance has lost his trail. Though we do not yet learn Diogenes' ultimate destination, we do find him on the deck of a boat, "heading north, toward the Aeolian islands, the most remote of all the Mediterranean islands" (*Book of the Dead,* p. 408). Perhaps more importantly, we are treated to his meditations on where he is heading: "*Home.* He rolled the bittersweet word around in his mind, wondering just what it meant. A refuge; a place of retreat, of peace." The prospect of returning home, together with Diogenes' surety that his latest maneuvers have made him untraceable, have soothed him. "She would not find him. Nor would his brother. Five years, ten years, twenty—he had all the time in the world to plan his next—his final—move" (*Book of the Dead,* p. 409). On the one hand, again, Diogenes is not thinking specifically any longer of killing Constance, but on the other, it is impossible to conclude that "his final move" will not include this.

An incidental finding from this short chapter is that Diogenes smokes cigarettes, but we can conclude that he is not addicted, since "he had not smoked in more than a year—not since he had last returned home" (*Book of the Dead,* p. 408). The smoking, too, "helped calm his agitated mind" (*Book of the Dead,* p. 408), and by the chapter's end, Diogenes is standing "at the rail, inhaling the breath of the sea, feeling a modicum of peace steal over him" (*Book of the Dead,* p. 409). Even the voice in his head, "for the first time in months," becomes "almost inaudible amid the sound of the bow plowing the sea" (*Book of the Dead,* p. 409).

In Chapter Seventy-Five we are back with Pendergast, following Constance's trail. Registering surprise that Constance had an encounter with Diogenes in Florence and survived it, Pendergast's thoughts confirm that "normally, those who came within Diogenes' orbit did not leave it alive" (*Book of the Dead,* p. 412). More importantly, he, as has Constance before him, has deduced the location of Diogenes' home. Pendergast reads the same Carducci poem that Constance apparently spent hours staring at in the Italian national library, and knows enough of the obscure legend at its heart to put the puzzle pieces together: "A holy hermit, living alone on one of the Aeolian islands off the coast of Sicily, swore that in the very hour of Theodoric's death, he witnessed the king's shrieking soul being cast into the throat of the great volcano of Stromboli, believed by the early

Christians to be the entrance of hell itself" (*Book of the Dead,* p. 415). Pendergast makes the connection between an "entrance of hell" and Great Uncle Comstock's Doorway to Hell, and, after looking at the same atlas that Constance viewed, concludes that his brother lives in or near the one village that exists on the volcanic island of Stromboli. Constance, not having the actual story of The Event to inform her, must have just found it a suitable location for the diabolical man who betrayed her.

To me, however, Diogenes' choice of Stromboli as his home bespeaks a fitting defiance on his part. It is as if he is saying to his brother and the world, "So, you push me through the Doorway to Hell? Very well, I will seek shelter there in its shadow and make it my home; I will thrive there, in spite of your actions."

For Chapter Seventy-Six, we actually join Diogenes in this home. It is a villa, the highest on the slope of the volcano. He is relaxing on his terrace with a glass of sherry, looking down at the small village of Piscità below him. "Here," Preston and Child tell us, "at the very edge of the world, he felt safe" (*Book of the Dead,* p. 416). We learn that Diogenes has had this villa for twenty years; with the vagueness surrounding both his age and that of his brother, I am not sure if Diogenes purchased it soon after the fire at Rochenoire with some of the money he demanded from his brother, or after he came into his inheritance and faked his death. Diogenes tries to make it back to his villa every year, "always arriving and departing with the utmost care," presumably so that none of his crimes are traced back to the identity he keeps here—that of "an eccentric and irascible British professor of classics who came periodically to work on his magnum opus—and who did not look with favor on being disturbed." Indeed, Diogenes keeps very closely to this identity, considering that he contemplates starting work on a "translation of *Aureus Asinus* by Apuleius that he had always intended" (*Book of the Dead,* p. 418). *Aureus Asinus* is Latin for "The Golden Ass"; it is the first surviving novel in Latin, chronicles the misadventures of a man who studies magic and accidentally turns himself into a donkey while attempting to turn himself into a bird, and contains more than a few lurid scenes as well as inset stories. Interestingly, the narrator is only able to return to his human form by becoming a devotee of the great mother-goddess Isis. The picaresque tale suits Diogenes' absurdist leanings, yet it is revealing that the psychopathic serial killer is capable of finding relaxation in such a scholarly pursuit. Surely, were it not for Comstock's box, he would have turned out to be a fairly respectable member of society, if a bit cynical and misanthropic.

Readers also learn, with regards to his chosen home, that Diogenes "avoided the summer and the tourists." This was an extra precaution on his part, because the island of Stromboli was "sixty miles from the mainland and inaccessible for days at a time due to violent seas and the lack of a port" (*Book of the Dead,* p. 416). Yet Diogenes has plainly been rattled by Constance's pursuit. He is still trying to assure himself that "*She* could not follow him here." With the emphasis given to the pronoun, we can already see that Constance has taken on a very special status to him. Too, when Diogenes begins to realize that the noise of the three-wheeled motorbike that serves as a taxi on the island is coming far too close to his villa, Constance is the first thought to come into his mind. "The tinny whine drew still closer, and for the first time Diogenes felt a twinge of apprehension" (*Book of the Dead,* p. 417). He tries to dismiss it: "He chuckled at himself. He had grown too wary, almost paranoid. This demonic pursuit—coming hard on the heels of such a huge failure— had left him shaken, unnerved" (*Book of the Dead,* p. 418). When he hears the vehicle "stop at the bottom of his wall," however, Diogenes secures himself as best as he can within his home, turning all of his lights off. Though "the villa, like most on the island, was built almost like a fortress" with "masonry walls … almost a meter thick," Diogenes has still "made several subtle improvements of his own" (*Book of the Dead,* p. 418). A few paragraphs later, though, readers learn that "he had seen no need to arouse local suspicion by making it as secure as the Long Island structure" (*Book of the Dead,* pp. 420-421).

Even after taking the somewhat drastic step of barricading himself inside his house, Diogenes tries to talk himself out of the conviction that Constance has come for him. "Once again, he had the feeling he had reacted out of sheer paranoia. Just because he'd seen a boat, heard the taxi" (*Book of the Dead,* p. 419). After reasoning that "there was simply no way for her to have found him—certainly not this quickly," Diogenes "began to breath easier." He concludes that "this business had unnerved him even more than he realized."

Of course, Constance really *has* come for him, but even after she causes the key he has balanced on the door handle to fall, Diogenes worries that "he might have just killed some hapless burglar or delivery boy" with the shots he has fired through the door in response. Though part of his concern is that he wants to keep his home free of any form of trouble with the authorities, Diogenes does seem to have a sense of justice in not wanting to harm an innocent bystander. Constance eventually returns fire, however, and the two engage for awhile in a battle of wits and bullets. Diogenes only survives by his good physical reflexes and his uncanny intuition. Readers do learn during the course of this skirmish that Diogenes shares at least some of his brother's knowledge of ballistics. "He stared at the holes her rounds had torn in the woodwork. She had managed to get her hands on a mid-caliber semiautomatic, a Glock from the sound of it" (*Book of the Dead,* p. 420). This is just another example that adds to my impression that throughout his years of keeping Aloysius under observation, Diogenes has tried to make sure he was knowledgeable in all of the same areas in which his brother had expertise.

Diogenes is not merely stunned and amazed at Constance's cunning and audacity, however. After his shock begins to wear off, it is replaced with "a rush of limb-trembling rage. She had invaded his home, his bolt-hole, his ultimate refuge" (*Book of the Dead,* p. 421). In this spirit, Diogenes decides he cannot merely wait for Constance to shoot her way into his villa. "He *had* to get outside—and not only outside, but up the mountain" (*Book of the Dead,* p. 422).

From the moment Diogenes has the inspiration to incorporate the volcano of Stromboli into his battle with Constance, clues are dropped that can be construed as pointing to his survival of their encounter. At the time the novel ends, Constance, Pendergast, and most readers believe that Diogenes has fallen to his death in the Sciara del Fuoco, a gash in the volcano that spews lava into the sea. At the end of the 2015 novel *Crimson Shore,* however, it appears that Diogenes has survived fairly intact. In this context, lines such as: "The Sciara del Fuoco. A perfect solution to his problem. A body that fell in there would virtually disappear" take on a whole new meaning. Perhaps Diogenes does hope to push Constance to her death, but perhaps he has a back-up escape plan as well. The authors tell us that Diogenes "knew every switchback of the steep and dangerous trail" and that "on the mountain, every advantage would be his." Yet Diogenes also "reminded himself that he had underestimated her at each turn. That could not be permitted to happen again. He was up against the most determined, and perhaps most deadly, adversary of his career" (*Book of the Dead,* p. 422). All the more reason he would plan an escape route, even from this, just in case he needed one. Diogenes took a metaphor from big game hunting when he was planning his ambush on Constance in Florence, that of the Cape buffalo. Surely he also knows that people have escaped predators by pretending to be dead? If Constance will not stop until she has killed him, the best tactic might well be to let her believe that she has.

Chapter Seventy-Seven returns the reader to Pendergast's perspective. Through his eyes we see Diogenes' "lush and extensive garden of tropical plants, birds of paradise, and giant exotic cacti" (*Book of the Dead,* p. 425). The plants must either require very little care in the island environment, or else Diogenes must employ a caretaker when he is away. Granted, by this time night has fallen and he may not be able to distinguish them, but Pendergast does not specifically mention any plants commonly used as poisons. Diogenes may actually have a garden for reasons of aesthetics, but I would like to think he grows some of the substances he uses on his victims. Pendergast also notices that his brother's terrace facing the Mediterranean is "colonnaded with old marble columns"; no doubt this appeals to Diogenes' love of Latin. As previously mentioned, it is from Pendergast's examination of his brother's house that we learn Diogenes probably lied about the color of his library to Constance, although, as I said, it was a quick glance under inferior lighting.

Chapter Seventy-Eight marks the last time, in the trilogy, that we experience Diogenes' viewpoint. He pushes himself up the slope of Stromboli as quickly as possible, counting on his superior strength and speed to get far enough ahead of Constance that he can take a few minutes to figure out a likely spot from which to ambush her. After Diogenes settles on a place, his thoughts confirm that he does indeed plan to "throw her body into the Sciara, where it would vanish forever" (*Book of the Dead,* p. 429). His following thought is that "he would once again be free," and of course the surface meaning is clear—he would be rid of this great adversary that Constance has become. Perhaps it also means, however, that he would "be free" of a woman he cannot stop thinking about.

Preston and Child tell us: "The fifteen minutes that passed next were the longest of his life." After thirty minutes, "Diogenes found his mind racing with speculation" (*Book of the Dead,* p. 429). Thinking that because Constance does not know the trail, because "no map could convey the steepness, the danger, the roughness of the trail" (*Book of the Dead,* p. 428), she cannot possibly be planning to ambush *him,*

Diogenes begins to think perhaps she has finally reached her physical limits. "He had assumed her hatred would carry her far past the point of normal exhaustion. But she was only human; she had to have a breaking point" (*Book of the Dead,* p. 429). The tone of Diogenes' thoughts seems pitying, almost tender: "She had been following him for days, hardly eating and sleeping. On top of that, she would have lost a fair amount of blood. To then climb almost three thousand vertical feet up an unknown and exceedingly dangerous trail at night … maybe she just couldn't make it."

When Diogenes also entertains the possibility that Constance may have injured herself, or "perhaps even been killed," he wonders, almost maternally: "Did she have a flashlight? He didn't think so" (*Book of the Dead,* p. 429). Yet, of course, he is still prepared to do her in: "If she was lying there with a broken ankle, or collapsed in exhaustion, killing her would be simple" (*Book of the Dead,* pp. 429-430). Then Diogenes realizes that this could be Constance's strategy: "to make him believe she'd been hurt, to lure him back down—and then ambush him" (*Book of the Dead,* p. 430). He tries to be patient, on the theory that "eventually her hatred would force her up the mountain," but it is not long before wild speculation begins anew. It occurs to Diogenes that Constance might have "gone back to town and was lying low, planning something new."

While Diogenes' inability to handle suspense in this situation is understandable, especially in light of the impulse control problems to which his brain injuries make him prone, the language used to describe his feelings is reminiscent of romantic passion: "He couldn't bear the thought that this might continue. He could not go on in this manner. It must end *this very night.* If she would not come to him*B*, he had to force the issue by coming to her" (*Book of the Dead,* p. 430). When Diogenes eventually realizes that Constance has outfoxed him by taking a different trail up to the Sciara del Fuoco—a trail he was not even sure existed—he is not stingy with his mental compliments: "She was a consummate researcher; she had gotten hold of some old atlas of the island. She'd studied it, memorized it…. He could see the breathtaking subtlety of her plan" (*Book of the Dead,* p. 431).

By the time Diogenes sees Constance, "silhouetted against the horrid lambent glow, a figure in white, *dancing*" (*Book of the Dead,* p. 431), he can no longer control himself. On the one hand, it is in "a convulsion of fury" (*Book of the Dead,* p. 432) that he probably emptied his gun in Constance's direction; on the other, he has wasted a large amount of ammunition with "the bright flashes blinding his own night vision." Yes, Diogenes wants this over with, but it is also as though he cannot stay away from Constance. The language of his thoughts is riddled with fatalism: "It was now or never. The end was upon them." With the pronoun "them," Diogenes is acknowledging Constance as an equal, admitting that they share a bond, a destiny entwined. If he had thought the end upon *himself,* that would have implied she was just a victim to be easily dispatched. He has come a long way from thinking he could get her to kill herself.

As Diogenes rushes towards Constance on the ridge, he feels "there was only one possible outcome. One of them would walk back down the mountain; the other would be thrown into the Sciara" (*Book of the Dead,* p. 432). He does not believe Constance will be able to shoot him in the dark, and "thrown" implies anticipation of physical contact. Surely Diogenes believes his superior size and strength will overcome her? Or, again, does he have a possible escape route in mind, even from the Sciara?

Though Chapter Seventy-Nine returns the reader to Pendergast's viewpoint, it gives us the novel's climax, and one last glimpse of Diogenes. Pendergast sees "two figures, silhouetted against the dull glow of the volcano. They were locked in a curious, almost passionate embrace" (*Book of the Dead*, p. 435). He is quick to correct himself in his perception, noting "these were not lovers—these were enemies, joined in mortal struggle, heedless of the wind, or the roar of the volcano, or the extreme peril of the cliff edge on which they stood." I would argue that the two perceptions are not mutually exclusive. That Diogenes and Constance were "each raking and clawing at the other, each pulling the other into the abyss" is again indicative of great passion. Yes, there is hatred involved on Diogenes' part, and desperation, but he has also come to admire Constance. That Constance survives to be hauled back up the edge of the cliff by Aloysius means that Diogenes wanted her dead less than she wanted him dead. That Diogenes has apparently survived, too, leaves readers with a multitude of questions we can only hope will be answered in *The Obsidian Chamber*.

Interestingly, the image of two beings locked in "mortal struggle" on the edge of the volcano is an echo of the climax of Tolkien's *The Lord of the Rings*. In the third book of the trilogy, *The Return of the King*, Frodo and Gollum struggle over the One Ring of Power on the edge of Mount Doom.

Ironically, it is only Gollum's inability to break the Ring's power over him that saves Middle Earth. Of course, with Constance and Diogenes, there is no Ring of Power but only the irresistible draw of one to the other that places each of them in such peril.

Chapters Eighty and Eighty-One provide only a few pieces of information relevant to Diogenes. Not knowing yet the events that transpired on Stromboli, Captain Hayward tells D'Agosta that "based on evidence retrieved from Diogenes Pendergast's valise, fresh warrants have been issued for Diogenes" (*Book of the Dead,* p. 439). Nora, while visiting a feeble but recovering Margo, reflects that because of Pendergast's interruption of his brother's sound-and-light show, "the prognosis was excellent for Collopy and the others" (*Book of the Dead,* p. 444). Not only has Diogenes failed in causing permanent damage to the Museum's staff, he has not managed to destroy it as an institution, either. Nora tells Margo: "Thanks to all the controversy, the Tomb of Senef is the hottest show in town" (*Book of the Dead,* p. 445).

Of course, we learn one last thing about Diogenes in Chapter Eighty-Two. He is not sterile. I do not think anyone can fault him for not protecting Constance from pregnancy, given that he did not believe she would live even long enough for a fertilized ovum to attach itself to the lining of her uterus.

Desserts

If Constance asserts that Diogenes is "gone" at the end of *The Book of the Dead,* he is definitely not forgotten. Even though the eighth book in the Pendergast series, *Wheel of Darkness,* has a completely different story to tell, the impact of Diogenes on both his brother and Constance permeates the novel's atmosphere. In pleading with the monks of Gsalrig Chongg to take Constance in, even though they have never had a female in their monastery before, Pendergast states: "She needs your help. *I* need your help. We are both ... *tired* of the world. We have come a long way to find peace. Peace, and healing" (*Wheel of Darkness,* p. 6). Though Pendergast does not realize it at the time, Constance is still pregnant by Diogenes; she is also deeply wounded by his treatment of her, and damaged by what she has become in seeking vengeance. She believes she has killed him. On his part, Pendergast has not only lost friends and mentors to Diogenes, and suffered incarceration and a possible death sentence hanging over him, but recently had the psyche-shattering experience of realizing his own role in Diogenes' development. It is not a stretch to imagine that when he and Constance stopped at the pile of prayer stones before they arrived at Gsalrig Chongg, and Pendergast "bent down, picked up an old stone, and added it to the pile" (*Wheel of Darkness,* p. 3), that he was making an offering not only for those Diogenes killed, but for the soul of his brother, as well as for the mental and emotional well-being of Constance and himself.

There is a thematic undercurrent in *Wheel of Darkness* of

undoing Diogenes. Pendergast attempts to talk to Constance about her visit to the Feversham Clinic, where she supposedly went to have an abortion (though later readers learn she changed her mind). This, of course, would have been a basic, very literal way of "undoing" something Diogenes had done. Even with Constance eventually giving birth to Diogenes' child, allowing it to be raised by the monks as the reincarnation of their Rinpoche is a way of "undoing" him as well—taking the offspring of someone perceived as quintessentially evil and making him into a holy person. Constance also tries to "undo" Diogenes by demanding Pendergast promise never to speak of him in her presence again. He makes the promise but does not keep it.

More symbolically, when Pendergast is summoned to the inner monastery at Gsalrig Chongg to investigate the disappearance of the Agozyen, he is ushered into a room filled with Buddhist cultural treasures, including incredibly ancient scrolls, paintings, and tapestries. One of the monks tells him: "The 'incense' you note is the resin of the *dorzhan-qing* plant—burned ceaselessly to keep the worms at bay—ravenous woodworms indigenous to the high Himalayas that seek to destroy everything in this room made of wood, paper, or silk" (*Wheel of Darkness*, p. 13). "Woodworm" is the transposed verbal opposite of "wormwood," which Diogenes claims as his favorite food in Pendergast's imagined encounter in Dr. Krasner's office in *Dance of Death*, and is a valued ingredient in the absinthe he drinks. Similarly, as Constance is tutored in the discipline of Buddhist meditation, she is taught to concentrate on the image of a particularly complex Tibetan knot, and then mentally untie that knot. At the first session described in the novel, she falls into meditation for five hours doing this. The knot is akin to the ones Diogenes tied in the rope used to hang Charles Duchamp in order to frame Aloysius; thus, once more, we have the symbolism of "undoing" Diogenes. Later, on board the *Britannia* when Constance joins in meditation with Pendergast, we learn she has been gifted with another such knot, "to be used in a particular kind of meditative exercise to expunge attachment, to rid oneself of evil thoughts or influences, or to aid in the joining of two minds" (*Wheel of Darkness,* p. 311). Further, "in Constance's case, the knot was to be used for cleansing herself of the stain of murder" (*Wheel of Darkness,* p. 311), a stain for which Diogenes bears much of the responsibility in provoking her to such a degree.

Also, the monk who is attempting to explain to Pendergast just how dark and powerful an object the Agozyen is tells him that the box it was kept in "has been passed down, from Rinpoche to Rinpoche, always sealed" (*Wheel of Darkness,* p. 17). Interestingly, this means that Diogenes' son, viewed as the reincarnation of the Rinpoche, will be the guardian of something meant to be unleashed to "cleanse" the world when the world has sufficiently deteriorated to deserve it. Depending on how one feels about the idea of the Agozyen, and the concepts of good and evil, this could be taken as Diogenes' son being in charge of something that will destroy a world populated by evil beings such as his father—or as Diogenes' son being responsible for something that could bring an end to billions of relatively innocent lives. The first interpretation would be an "undoing" of Diogenes as well; the second is just plain scary.

The next time that Diogenes is relevant to *Wheel of Darkness* is once Pendergast and Constance are on board the cruise ship *Britannia.* Constance returns to their shipboard suite to find its door open when she knows Pendergast to be out. Her mind goes immediately to Diogenes. "Instantly, her heart began to beat furiously, as if it had been waiting for just such an event.... *It can't be him,* she thought. *It can't. I saw him fall. I saw him die*" (*Wheel of Darkness,* p. 81). The last sentence, of course, is a lie, or at least incorrectly worded. Constance did indeed see him fall, into something that definitely should have been his death. But she certainly did not witness his last breath. In any case, she has misgivings about what she has witnessed, or her thoughts would not have leaped to him. Diogenes has been such a forceful presence that he haunts the stage long after his supposed exit.

Readers quickly learn that Constance is still carrying the scalpel Diogenes gave her, complete with its lovely gift box, in her purse. She takes it out, apparently still believing he could be the one invading their lodgings, almost as though she is disappointed that she did not get to end him with it and had to rely upon a volcano instead. Ironically, the person actually responsible for leaving the suite door open has tarried in Constance's room due to the allure of another object associated with Diogenes. The maid who cleans their suite, a former professor from Belarus fallen upon hard times, is reading the volume of Akhmatova's poetry that Diogenes gave to Constance. Preston and Child tell us: "Constance was not quite sure why she had brought this book along. Its history—and its legacy—was painful to her. Just to look upon it now was difficult. Perhaps she'd carried it as a penitent carries a cilice, hoping to atone for her misjudgment through pain" (*Wheel of Darkness,* p. 83). Or perhaps she had not been ready to let go of it until that moment, subconsciously realizing that some of Diogenes' argument on behalf of the sensual had merit, even though he had betrayed her. Constance does, however, make a gift of the book to the woman, in exchange for her help as an observer among the ship's employees.

The next time Diogenes becomes relevant in *Wheel of Darkness* is in the passage already discussed in which Pendergast, under the influence of the Agozyen, discourses on the brothers' agreement about anthropology's lack of merit as a field of academic study. Aloysius is too far gone to care that he has broken his promise to Constance not to mention his brother in her presence, and apparently she is too shocked at the change in him to register any protest over this. In continuing his argument for the futility of preserving human life, Pendergast also mentions one of Diogenes' crimes—the murder of Michael Decker—but he seems to have glossed over his brother's important role in this. Instead, he states: "Thanks in part to my own incompetence, my only friend in the Bureau died a most unpleasant death" (*Wheel of Darkness,* p. 288).

Of course, exposure to the Agozyen has brought Pendergast's mindset much closer to that of his younger brother. He tells Constance that the ancient mandala "has *liberated* my mind. Swept it clean of jejune and hidebound conventions of morality" (*Wheel of Darkness,* p. 296). Pendergast's choice of the word "jejune" is an echo of Diogenes' inner rant in *Book of the Dead* about all the less-than-brilliant people he had to deal with on a daily basis during his years as Menzies in the anthropology department.

Diogenes also plays a large part in the shared meditation between Constance and Pendergast, after Pendergast has looked at the Agozyen and the tulpa is stalking him. It is difficult to discuss this meditation and the subsequent experience Pendergast has in a scientifically objective way; though later Pendergast and the authors attempt to write everything off as explainable in terms of the science of the human mind, there remains—in my view, at least—an air of inexplicable mysticism surrounding them. It is as if the Agozyen is an ancient Buddhist version of Comstock's phantasmagoria and Diogenes' own sound-and-light show, altering viewers' brains and removing their inhibitions so that they, in turn, may unleash further evil upon the world. That Pendergast experiences this puts him that much closer to understanding what happened to Diogenes in The Event, except that he has the advantage of an adult's perspective over that of a young child.

During the shared meditation, Constance is able to see Pendergast's memory palace of Rochenoire. On one level, this is not too surprising; she has learned from Diogenes that Antoine Pendergast modeled 891 Riverside on the old family home, so her mind can supply certain details. Constance would not know, however, about Aloysius's mental sealing—and recent excavation—of Diogenes' room in that house. Certainly he has never discussed this, nor The Event, with her. Constance nevertheless sees that "not quite halfway down the long hall, one door was open—battered open, the doorframe smashed, splinters of wood and twisted pieces of lead scattered about the floor" (*Wheel of Darkness,* p. 314), and that "the yawning black opening exhaled a cold, cellar-like stench of mold and dead, greasy centipedes" (*Wheel of Darkness,* p. 314). Constance's own memories, however, inform the temptation that the Kalazyga demon behind Pendergast presents her with during the shared meditation. Meaning Diogenes, Constance "remembered him at the very edge, the two of them locked together in a macabre caricature of sexual union, struggling … the expression on his face when he realized they were both going over" (*Wheel of Darkness,* p. 316). She admits to herself that his expression "was the most horrifying, most pitiful, and yet most satisfying thing she had every seen—to revel in the face of a person who realizes, without the shadow of a doubt, that he is going to die." This description by Constance casts quite a bit of doubt on the notion that Diogenes might have had an escape route planned from the Sciara, although readers already know him as an extremely good actor. Not to mention that part of what Constance may have seen was Diogenes' dismay at how willing she was to give her own life as long as his was forfeit.

Further, Constance acknowledges that she would no longer need Diogenes' great wronging of her "as an excuse: she could simply murder, whoever and wherever, and again and again revel in the hot blood-fury, the ecstatic, orgiastic triumph" (*Wheel of Darkness,* p. 316). That this last tempts Constance reveals that she has more in common with Diogenes than she would wish. If, on some level, this meditation is being controlled by Pendergast, it also implies that he has guessed this about her, and that to some small degree he holds her responsible for killing his brother.

Constance is able to resist the temptation and break the meditation, but probably only because she herself has not looked upon the Agozyen.

Right after the end of the shared meditation, a tulpa, created by the man who brought the Agoyzen aboard the *Britannia,* attacks Pendergast with the aim of not only killing him but destroying his very soul. I cannot help finding it interesting that Pendergast perceives this powerful evil entity as "overwhelming his senses with the cloying odor of a damp, rotting cellar, of slippery insects and sagging corpses" (*Wheel of Darkness,* p. 341). This sounds precisely like the environment in which The Event took place. After trying many mental exercises from the realms of philosophy, art, and mathematics, Pendergast flees in thought to his memory palace refuge of Rochenoire, and particularly to his own room. "It was the one place in his memory construct so well defended that nobody—even his own brother, Diogenes— could ever penetrate" (*Wheel of Darkness,* p. 345). I find it strange that Pendergast thinks about Diogenes at this moment. The way in which he thinks of him is peculiar as well—on the one hand, Diogenes is perceived as a potential threatening invader of his protective psychic construct; on the other, the phrase "even his own brother" implies that Diogenes shares an innate closeness second only to Pendergast's own self.

Given this, and given the novel's previously mentioned themes of "undoing" Diogenes, it is even more fascinating that it is apparently Diogenes who "undoes" the tulpa—or at least, his brother's mental and emotional construct of him helps defeat it, or re-orient it. Even if the presence of Diogenes in this memory crossing is purely a product of

Pendergast's imagination, it is still instructive to examine it. In any case, it is the first of several such appearances in the novels between *Book of the Dead* and *Crimson Shore.*

Pendergast blacks out as the tulpa manages to attack him even in his room in Rochenoire, and wakes again to the sound of Diogenes' voice asking, "Don't you think it's time we spoke?" (*Wheel of Darkness,* p. 354). When he dares to examine his imaginary surroundings, Pendergast realizes he is in "their hideout, the tiny room they had fashioned beneath the back stairs in the old house: the one they'd called Plato's Cave. Its creation was one of the last things they had done together, before the bad times began" (*Wheel of Darkness,* p. 356). Now that Pendergast has remembered The Event, he has freed his mind to be able to remember that there actually *were* good times with his brother before it, that Diogenes had *not* simply been evil from birth. Pendergast needs some kind of reconciliation with his brother, now that he has allowed himself to remember these things, almost as much as he needs to escape destruction at the smoky hands of the tulpa. In describing the boys' clubhouse, Preston and Child state that "weak afternoon light trickled through the lattices, revealing dust motes floating lazily in the air and giving the hidden space the otherworldly glow of an undersea grotto" (*Wheel of Darkness,* p. 355). This is reminiscent of Diogenes' description to Constance of his library on Stromboli, and I suspect unconsciously Diogenes had somewhat re-created one of the last good memories he shared with his brother.

When Pendergast looks at his brother, I assume he sees Diogenes as an adult, because of the mention of "the sharp contours of his face," despite the fact that "both his eyes were still hazel … as they were before the Event" (*Wheel of Darkness,* p. 355). Looking at this as purely a construct of Pendergast's mind, it reflects a need for Diogenes to be restored somehow to his true self, to what he would have been if The Event had never taken place. If we look at this as more of a supernatural/spiritual phenomenon—allowing for a belief that something of Diogenes' essence actually did come to his brother's rescue, even though he was not, in fact, dead—it would represent a spiritual aspect of Diogenes whose eyes remained unharmed. When Pendergast remarks to Diogenes that he is dead, his younger brother's response is informative: "'Dead.' Diogenes rolled the word around, as if tasting it. 'Perhaps. Perhaps not. But I'll always be alive in your mind. And in this house'" (*Wheel of Darkness,* p. 356). The "perhaps, perhaps not" is, I think, a clue to just how early Preston and Child wanted to reserve the right to bring Diogenes back if they wished. The part about being alive in Pendergast's mind and in his memory palace is a way of providing him with at least a sense of the reconciliation he feels he can never have.

Diogenes retains much of his warped sense of humor in the memory crossing. When he broaches the subject of the threat Aloysius faces from the tulpa, he states his brother's troubles are "perhaps more dire than any I've seen you in before. I'm chagrined to admit that, this time, they are not of my devising" (*Wheel of Darkness,* p. 355). "Any I've seen you in before" implies that Diogenes has, as speculated in discussing the trilogy, been watching Aloysius for a long time. That Diogenes is able to remind Aloysius of teachings he has received from a lama that will help him turn the tulpa towards another victim lends credence to this too, and to my theory that Diogenes has frequently studied what Aloysius has studied, just to be sure he can use this knowledge against his brother. Of course, it could just be that this Diogenes is merely a mental construct and therefore can access anything Aloysius himself can access. In either case, the strategy Diogenes helps Aloysius recall is basically another version of "playing dead," which may also be what he has done with Constance at the volcano. Once Aloysius grasps what his brother is trying to tell him, Diogenes quips: "Now, go forth and sin no more" (*Wheel of Darkness,* p. 356), paraphrasing Jesus' words to the woman he saves from being stoned for adultery. This simultaneously fits with our concept of Diogenes' blasphemous sense of humor, and tells us just how guilty Aloysius now feels about The Event—that he would put the words of the most holy figure of Christianity in Diogenes' mouth.

Once the tulpa has moved on, Pendergast tries to get Diogenes to stay, and to answer more questions. Diogenes refuses to tell Aloysius whether or not he is dead; that Aloysius doubts this after what Constance has said—that Constance herself occasionally doubts it—is another testament to how wily and brilliant they believe Diogenes to have been (or to be). Pendergast is more successful in getting an answer when he asks Diogenes why he helped him. "I didn't do it for you," his brother answers. "I did it for my child" (*Wheel of Darkness,* p. 358). One could interpret this logically as Pendergast subconsciously registering signs that Constance was still pregnant. Then again, Pendergast under the influence of the Agoyzen was able to untie Constance's cleansing knots with only his mind, so who knows exactly what is supposed to be real within the context of this novel? Whether something of his brother, or his own subconscious, Pendergast does not believe or recall either, and expresses great surprise when Constance is revealed to be still pregnant at the end of the novel.

The first mention of Diogenes in *Cemetery Dance* is a cursory one; Pendergast is performing a Japanese tea ceremony in memory of his friend, Bill Smithback. The memories of Smithback he reviews, of course, include the late journalist's helping him blast open the Tomb of Senef, and being abducted in a taxi for his own protection from Diogenes. The second and subsequent mentions of Diogenes, however, are far more interesting. These come when Pendergast drags D'Agosta along to visit Great Aunt Cornelia to talk about incidents of Vôdou and Obeah among the servants that might give him some insights into the circumstances surrounding Smithback's murder. With Cornelia, one never knows if she is genuinely confused, or if she is playing mind games with her visitors. On this occasion, she insists that Pendergast is really Diogenes, and addresses him that way throughout the conversation. This certainly raises the possibility that Diogenes visited her during his time in New York.

Speaking to Aloysius as if he is Diogenes, Aunt Cornelia gives us a different perspective on her feelings towards her great-nephews than previously. The last time readers saw Cornelia, however, it was when D'Agosta and Hayward were visiting her, masquerading as her brother Ambergris and his wife. Ironically, on this visit in *Cemetery Dance,* she at least pretends to recognize D'Agosta as Ambergris. On the prior visit, when D'Agosta sought information about Diogenes in Pendergast's absence, Cornelia painted the almost obligatory dark portrait of him—that of a child evil almost from birth. We cannot be sure if she meant it at the time, if she is giving Ambergris what she thinks he wants to hear, or if she is seeing through D'Agosta. At this most recent visit, she is delighted to see Diogenes, or at least is pretending to Pendergast that she is delighted to see his younger brother. As they are leaving, Cornelia even tells "Diogenes": "You were always my favorite, you know" (*Cemetery Dance,* p. 118). Whether she actually means this, or if it is the kind of thing she would tell both brothers individually, or if she is deliberately trying to upset Pendergast, is anyone's guess.

In between the greeting and the effusive yet odd farewell, Cornelia reveals that Diogenes knows a great deal about Vôdou and Obeah. "Certainly more than your brother does, eh? Though he is no stranger to it either—is he?" (*Cemetery Dance,* pp. 116-117). Leaving aside our interest in what Pendergast knows and how he came to know it in favor of the subject of this book, when Pendergast remarks on the breadth of Cornelia's knowledge of Obeah, she scolds "Diogenes." She tells him, "that's a fine thing to say, coming from *you.* Do you think I've forgotten your little—*experiment,* shall we say?--and the unfortunate reaction it provoked from the *mobile vulgus--*" (*Cemetery Dance,* p. 117). Cornelia flips the order of the Latin words, but the meaning is the same as when Menzies uses the phrase twice in the Museum. The fact that the destruction by fire of Rochenoire is so often credited to "a mob" makes one wonder if Diogenes played any role in inciting this fire. No one has ever said the Pendergasts only had trouble with a mob just that one time, however, so we still do not know. One would think Cornelia would be less light-hearted about something that led to Rochenoire's destruction and the death of her nephew; she has expressed great sorrow over the incident on other occasions. Of course, the context also invokes memories of the stories she told Pendergast about his ancestor Antoine Leng Pendergast, of how he supposedly tried to bring an old Vôdou woman back to life; this could all be part and parcel of either Cornelia's confusion or her playing with Aloysius.

When Pendergast asks Cornelia the purpose of an *oanga* in Obeah, she further incriminates Diogenes (again, assuming we can credit her): "To extract the dead person's soul, make him a slave. A zombii," Cornelia replies. "You of all people know all this, Diogenes" (*Cemetery Dance,* p. 117). Though this is consistent with Diogenes' well-known interest in the occult, one tends to think Cornelia is not just referring to books she saw him reading as a child or adolescent. One wonders what Diogenes might have tried to resurrect, and whether he started with animals, or went straight to human corpses.

When Cornelia bids farewell to "Diogenes," she says something very strange. "I'm glad you finally did something about that horrid eye of yours" (*Cemetery Dance,* p. 118). Again, we do not know whether she is just messing with Pendergast, but his silvery-gray eyes would be closer in appearance to Diogenes' bad eye than his good one. Not to mention that, if she really believes she is talking to Diogenes, this is an incredibly tactless thing to say. It is also possible that Cornelia, assuming her confusion is legitimate, is responding to some subconsciously-sensed difference she perceives in Pendergast since his encounter with the Agozyen. This would mean that his exposure to the dangerous mandala has somehow made him more like Diogenes.

Cornelia's assertions about Diogenes' knowledge of Vôdou and Obeah are somewhat supported a few chapters later in *Cemetery Dance* when Pendergast calls in his old teacher, Monsieur Bertin. Interestingly, Cornelia had mentioned him in the conversation in the context of employees who brought scandal upon the Pendergast family. The dead woman Pendergast had inquired about was someone Cornelia felt to be among the worst in that category, except for "that dreadful, *dreadful* Monsieur Bertin" (*Cemetery Dance,* p. 116). When Bertin arrives at the airport, Pendergast tells D'Agosta that "he was our tutor when we were youths" (*Cemetery Dance,* p. 205). By "we," Pendergast means he and Diogenes, and he further explains to his friend: "Monsieur Bertin taught us zoology and natural history," but "unfortunately, he had to leave the family employ." D'Agosta's questions elicit that the circumstances that caused Bertin's exit involved "the fire," but Pendergast refuses to comment further on whether Bertin had something to do with it. He does, however, admit that "while Monsieur Bertin was hired to teach us natural history, he was also extremely knowledgeable about local lore and legend: Vôdou, Obeah, rootwork, and conjure" (*Cemetery Dance,* p. 205). Pendergast adds: "The fact is, Monsieur Bertin knows as much about the subject as anyone alive" (*Cemetery Dance,* p. 206). Thus, Diogenes would have had access to this knowledge in his childhood and adolescence.

As long as we are skimming near the subject of the fire that destroyed Rochenoire, *Cemetery Dance* provides us with yet another inconsistency in the time scheme. The Obeahman Pendergast visits to obtain an *arrêt* for Nora, Monsieur Ravel, asks Pendergast if Rochenoire is "the one that was burned back in '71?" (*Cemetery Dance*, p. 127). Given that *Dance of Death* posited Diogenes' age at the death of his parents in the fire at about seventeen, and given that Pendergast's session with Dr. Krasner in the same novel showed us Diogenes at age ten in 1972, this makes no sense whatsoever. Perhaps this is why Pendergast does not answer this query by Ravel directly, because the date is off?

Returning to the subject of Monsieur Bertin, however, he is interesting not only because of his role in Diogenes' education (and possibly in the loss of his parents and home), but because of his role in setting up the tale told in "Extraction." "Extraction" is a short story that Preston and Child published as a Kindle single in October, 2012. Though it came out two months prior to the novel *Two Graves,* I will discuss it here because of Bertin's presence. The timing of the story is hard to place, because Constance is in it also, and she does not return to 891 Riverside until the end of *Two Graves.* The frame of "Extraction" is that Monsieur Bertin is visiting 891 Riverside, and is about to have dinner with Pendergast and Constance. The first attempt by the cook is spoiled—the pasta has gone beyond the point of al dente, and new pasta must be boiled, putting the dinner off for thirty minutes. Bertin, famished and exasperated, suggests to Constance: "Ask your guardian about *'dents.'* Now, there's a story to pass the time while one is dying of hunger" ("Extraction").

He is playing on the similarity between the words for teeth in both Italian and French; Pendergast eventually explains to Constance that the tale in question is one about the local New Orleans legend that takes the place of the tooth fairy myth. When he and Diogenes were young, it seems, the tooth fairy in New Orleans was actually a creepy old recluse named Dufour. It was the custom that when a child lost a primary tooth, he or she would leave it in a special container on Dufour's porch at the next full moon; word was that if this duty was not carried out, Dufour would come to the child in the middle of the night and take "his due" ("Extraction").

At the time the story Pendergast tells Constance opens, he is nine and Diogenes has just turned six. Pendergast has already warned Constance that she might not really wish to hear the narrative, given how much part his brother plays in it, but despite earlier insisting he never mention Diogenes again in her presence, she admits: "That only whets my interest more" ("Extraction"). Pendergast tells us that at the age of six, "this was before various, shall we say, *aberrant* interests had taken possession of" Diogenes. In other words, The Event had not yet taken place. Again, this is more evidence that Diogenes was not born evil. Yet Pendergast also tells us that Diogenes "had somehow gotten into our great-grandfather's locked library cabinet, and he'd been reading a lot of old books he shouldn't have—tomes on demonology, witchcraft, the Inquisition, deviant practices of all imaginable sorts, [and] alchemy" ("Extraction"). Though Pendergast offers the opinion that these volumes "had a deleterious effect on him in later life," it was, of course, not the contents themselves that changed Diogenes. I feel the subject matter of these books, though dark, was perfectly in keeping with the character of the precocious little boy who liked to wander about exploring the curious objects he found in the various rooms of Rochenoire, as his memories in *Dance of Death* showed us.

Though Pendergast also notes that Diogenes, "even at six," was "a secretive, devious little boy" ("Extraction"), the reader soon learns he had good reason to be. When the nine-year-old Aloysius discovers "Diogenes hovering suspiciously around the back door, clutching something in one hand," and his little brother refuses to tell him what he has, Pendergast admits: "I seized his hand and tried to pry it open. We tussled. He was only six and lost the struggle" ("Extraction"). Further, when the object turns out to be one of Diogenes' baby teeth and he learns he plans to offer it up to Dufour, Pendergast "scoffed at his fear." Pendergast explains to Constance: "I argued with him. I told him that he would not bring the tooth to Dufour's place, but instead do what normal children his age did and leave it under his pillow, even if I had to force him to do so" ("Extraction").

Pendergast admits: "I was a terrible older brother to Diogenes" ("Extraction"). So, given the examples above, is it any wonder Diogenes had already become "secretive" and "devious"? If these are the things that happen every time Aloysius finds out what you are doing, it stands to reason that you would try to make sure he does not find out. Not to mention that when Diogenes, despite being only six to Aloysius's nine, manages to get his tooth back and escape his older brother, said brother goes to extreme lengths to assert his will. Pendergast recounts how he waited, hiding in the decaying palmettos on Defour's property, until Diogenes came to deposit the tooth in the designated receptacle under the requisite full moon. He noted how quietly Diogenes slipped away after performing the task: "Looking back upon it today, I find myself amazed that one so young could move with such deliberate stealth. In later life he would improve on that talent immeasurably" ("Extraction"). It seems apparent that Pendergast had a role in "creating" Diogenes even before The Event—his stealth was first developed to escape the interference of his older brother. Then again, of course, both brothers are frequently described as cat-like in their movements—this seems to be a Pendergast family trait. It also seems odd that Pendergast feels the need to remark upon Diogenes' improvement in the stealth department to Constance, who, after all, has seen him virtually appear in the library at 891 Riverside at will.

Pendergast retrieves the tooth from where Diogenes has placed it. Angry at what to him is an embarrassingly superstitious belief on the part of his little brother, and fearing that if he places the tooth under Diogenes' pillow, he will wake, find it, and take it back to Dufour, Pendergast throws "the tooth down a storm drain" ("Extraction").

Despite the fact that it was approximately 10:30pm when Diogenes left his tooth at Dufour's, he is waiting up when Aloysius returns home. (Their parents are absent, and they are being very loosely watched over by an avuncular family member who lets them do as they please for the most part.) Pendergast tells Constance that Diogenes' "young face" was "creased with wariness and distrust." Again, with good reason, because Pendergast continues: "In triumph, I told him what I'd done and why. I chastised him again for his ridiculous and childish superstitions" ("Extraction"). Yet Pendergast is not so harsh as to be unmoved by Diogenes' reaction. His little brother "alternated between juvenile paroxysms of rage and spells of crying—the only time that I can remember ever seeing him cry." Aloysius finally realizes he has done something wrong, and apologizes. He also promises to protect Diogenes from Dufour—whom, of course, he still does not believe knows anything about the matter. Yet nothing he says or does seems to comfort Diogenes, who knows better. Pendergast admits to Constance that his own behavior up to that point "was quite awful, and I'm ashamed even today to think of how I behaved. The tragedy of how Diogenes turned out must partly be laid on my shoulders" ("Extraction"). There is, of this writing, no record of Aloysius ever telling Constance about The Event, and his role in it. This is not entirely his fault, however, since Constance is so rarely in a mood to discuss his brother. Given the occurrences narrated in "Extraction," and the way in which they played out, it is almost unbelievable to me that Diogenes' relationship with his brother was sufficiently repaired afterward for them to walk together companionably in the family crypts competing at Latin translation. I can only conclude this is because Aloysius actually apologizes for his actions in "Extraction," and wonder what they both might have been spared had he been able to apologize for The Event. The distrust Diogenes displays in the face of Aloysius's pushiness encountering Comstock's box, however, is all the more understandable with the knowledge readers gain from "Extraction."

When Diogenes disappears the next day, Aloysius at first

believes he has done it of his own volition, and "he was off hiding in a closet with one of his forbidden books or indulging in some childish experiment in the vast basement of our home" ("Extraction"). When Diogenes has not been located by the next day, and his Uncle Everett has not only called the police but is "agitating to have the waterfront dragged," Aloysius finally tells his relative what he did concerning Diogenes' tooth. Even though Uncle Everett thinks it is a crazy story, he is willing to investigate every avenue to find Diogenes, so he goes off to talk to Dufour. He returns four hours later, with Diogenes. Pendergast tells Constance: "My brother was ashen, stone-faced. He immediately and wordlessly went up to his room, closed and locked his door, and did not come out for several days." In addition, Uncle Everett "looked terrible. Hideous in fact.... His face looked all wrong, somehow: his jaws sunken, his cheeks hollow, his lips trembling as if palsied, but the lower portion grossly swollen, as if he were carrying water in his mouth" ("Extraction").

Of course, Uncle Everett's condition is due to the fact that he has traded all of his teeth to Dufour in exchange for Diogenes' freedom. If Diogenes was witness to this bloody and painful procedure, it would certainly have provided him with an experience for knowing "dried blood when" he sees it, as he stated in Pendergast's memory of The Event. Even if not, the simple bit that remained on his own baby tooth was sufficient. It certainly does not mean he had already started hurting animals. Nor does the reference in "Extraction" to Pendergast's finding a dead cat "in a dark corner of our garden" mean anything of the sort, either, especially since he has already asserted to Constance that this was before Diogenes' interests became "aberrant." There are several things that could prove fatal to a cat outdoors without assuming that Diogenes at age six was one of them.

Interestingly, when describing to Constance the use to which Dufour has put all of the children's teeth over so many years, Pendergast makes the comparison of the flashlight beam on the teeth murals to "some nightmarish magic-lantern show" ("Extraction"). Both traumatic incidents from his and Diogenes' childhoods are thus linked, given the most crucial component of Comstock's box.

The only other thing about Diogenes that "Extraction" casts light on comes from its denouement. Pendergast tells Constance that three years later, Dufour's house, now abandoned, burned to the ground. "No one was particularly surprised by it; abandoned houses did have a tendency to burn. But I, for one, long wondered if my brother Diogenes was somehow responsible." Pendergast adds: "Later, it came to my attention that he enjoyed fires very much; the larger the better" ("Extraction"). If this is true, it would mean Diogenes was committing arson at the age of nine. Of course, this would have been after The Event, and I think it is quite probable. The statement carries with it, however, another hint that Diogenes may have been somehow involved in the fire that destroyed Rochenoire. Again, I feel that either it was to a great degree accidental, or that he at least regretted it terribly, given the fate of his mother and the family silver.

We learn only a few things relevant to Diogenes in *Fever Dream.* One is that his name comes from that of his grandfather, Louis de Frontenac Diogenes Pendergast, whose grave Pendergast must visit every five years in order that he not be disinherited from the family fortune. Another is contained in yet another good memory that seems to have been released since the unblocking of The Event in Pendergast. He is at the family's old country home of Penumbra, with the old butler, Maurice, investigating the suspicious circumstances he has recently discovered surrounding his wife's death. "I remember the day that my brother and I were reenacting the Roman assault on Silvium," Pendergast recalls for the family servant. "The siege engine Diogenes built proved rather too effective" (*Fever Dream*, p. 76). Whatever he launched with that engine destroyed a set of Wedgewood plates. "No cocoa for a month," Pendergast adds. The boys played together, plotted together, and got punished together, prior to The Event.

Meanwhile, it is in *Fever Dream* that Constance arrives back on American soil. However, she is arrested on suspicion of throwing her baby—Diogenes' son—off the ship on which she has traveled home. When Captain Laura Hayward asks her why, she replies "Because he was evil. Like his father" (*Fever Dream*, p. 163). When asked by a psychiatrist what happened to the baby's father, she tells him, "He was precipitated into a pyroclastic flow" (*Fever Dream*, p.218). Because this is a ruse designed by Constance and Pendergast to protect both her and the child, however, we cannot even be certain that Constance truly believes Diogenes was evil any longer. It is probably reasonable to make the assumption, though.

Cold Vengeance also contains some bits and pieces about

Diogenes. In one instance, readers are introduced to a Dr. Beaufort, a forensic pathologist whom Pendergast learned from in his youth—on the occasion of Great-Aunt Cornelia's poisoning her family. Beaufort recalls of Pendergast that "the boy was an exceptionally *quick* study and possessed of a rare and powerful curiosity. *Too* powerful, and disturbingly morbid" (*Cold Vengeance,* p. 149). The pathologist goes on to note: "Of course, the boy's morbidity had paled in comparison with his brother's … But this reflection was too distressing and Beaufort forced it away" (*Cold Vengeance,* p. 149). This is another instance of Preston and Child ramping up Diogenes' reputation by not being specific about exactly what he has done or said. We are meant to wonder just what actions or words have made Beaufort too distressed to linger over Diogenes' memory. Did he actually wish to participate in his own cousins' autopsies, perhaps?

Diogenes also appears in another of Pendergast's memory crossings in this novel. Pendergast begins the Chongg Ran session to examine the question of whether his wife Helen is actually still alive, but instead of landing in his usual place in Rochenoire, he again finds himself in Plato's Cave, the childhood clubhouse he shared with Diogenes. There, Preston and Child remind us, the brothers "had gone to hatch childish schemes and plots … before the Event that sundered their comradeship forever" (*Cold Vengeance*, p. 198). Diogenes is there, waiting for him, but the vision is a curious one; Pendergast sees "his brother, aged about nine or ten, wearing the navy blazer and shorts that were the uniform of Lusher, the school they attended," but "strangely speaking in the adult's voice." Lusher, by the way, is an actual charter school in New Orleans; it is interesting that both brothers attending this school would seem to contradict Pendergast's memory in his exercise with Dr. Krasner, in which Diogenes at the age of ten attended a school called St. Ignatius. Possibly in the *Cold Vengeance* memory crossing, Diogenes is nine, and by ten he has done something to get himself kicked out of Lusher and sent to Catholic school? Diogenes' age in this vision is odd to begin with, because at nine The Event is already two years past, and they no longer shared Plato's Cave.

In any case, Diogenes is paging through an art book featuring paintings by Caravaggio, and the nine-year-old with the grown-up voice tells Pendergast he is "just in time" to help him try to "goad" a rabid dog that Maurice has sighted nearby "into entering the Convent of St. Maria" (*Cold Vengeance,* p. 198). Predictably, Pendergast does not accept this proposition, and Diogenes moves on to discuss one of the paintings in the art book, *The Beheading of St. John the Baptist.* He tells his brother this is one of his favorites; interestingly, it was another painting by Caravaggio with a similar subject that he claimed as his favorite when he was contemplating cutting Viola's throat twice. After describing one of the figures in the John the Baptist painting, however, Diogenes moves on to the next: "And the nobleman standing over John, directing the proceedings—such an air of calm command! That's just how I want to look when I …" (*Cold Vengeance*, p. 199). The authors tell us that Diogenes cuts off his sentence there; we are left to wonder if he is already envisioning delivering some future victim to his brother with a double throat-slash like Uncle Comstock's? Or perhaps he means the way Menzies was calmly overseeing the chaos at

Senef's tomb before his brother showed up? Surely Viola told Aloysius about his brother's plans to kill her, so both possibilities could be informing Pendergast's subconscious during this meditation.

Diogenes finally comes around to the subject of Helen, acknowledging Pendergast's reason for being there. He tells his brother: "I saw her once, you know." He goes on to add: "You two were in the gazebo in the back garden, playing backgammon. I was watching from behind the wisteria bushes." I do not doubt that this, or something similar, happened; we know that Diogenes kept a fairly consistent eye on his brother's whereabouts and doings. Pendergast probably realizes this, too; perhaps this was an occasion on which he felt a certain unease, as though being watched? Diogenes is gracious enough to compliment his brother's wife; either that, or Pendergast is so devoted to her that he cannot imagine anyone, not even Diogenes, not admiring her beauty.

After determining that his brother thinks Helen is still alive, and receiving his answer as to why, Diogenes gives his opinion about Judson's possible motivation for lying. "Motive? That's easy. He wanted to inflict the maximum amount of pain at the moment of your death. You have that effect on people." Diogenes mocks his brother for thinking Helen is still alive in the face of forensic evidence allegedly proving she is indeed in her grave, and he even taunts him: "The body must've been in quite a state. How terrible for you to have that image lodged in your mind—your *last* image of her." Pendergast's memory crossing versions of Diogenes are remarkably in character with what we know of him; even when he is helpful, he retains a certain perverseness, reflected in his warped sense of humor. Even if they are purely creations of Pendergast's imagination, and not imbued with some mystic ally-induced essence of Diogenes himself, they are faithful recreations, and worth examining on that premise. In any case, just after he inflicts the memory of Helen's mangled and decayed body on his brother, Diogenes offhandedly provides him with the essential clue: "Have you found the birth certificate yet?" (*Cold Vengeance*, p. 199).

Perhaps more important, Diogenes urges Aloysius to trust his own judgment because he is "the one who was—not to put too fine a point on it—in possession of her loins. You were her soul mate, were you not?" (*Cold Vengeance*, p. 200). Yet when Pendergast tells Diogenes that this line of thought leads him to believe "that she's alive," Diogenes laughs at him. He is delighted that "those bad old Pendergastian genes are finally rising to the fore in you. You now have a crazy obsession of your very own," he tells his older brother. "Congratulations and welcome to the family." On some level, of course, it is because this is Pendergast's greatest fear— going insane as several ancestors have before him—that the Diogenes of his subconscious taunts him in this manner.

When Pendergast tries to scoff at his brother by saying, "You're dead. What do you know?" Diogenes turns the question back upon him. "Am I really dead?" In part, it is a nagging doubt in Pendergast's mind that Diogenes is truly dead that keeps him popping up in his memory crossings. Even though Diogenes feeds this doubt, he anticipates a time when he and his brother are both dead: "The day will come when we shall, all of us Pendergasts, join hands in a great family reunion in the lowest circle of hell. What a party that will be!" (*Cold Vengeance,* p. 200). Even here, in Aloysius's memory crossing, Diogenes is proud of his identity as a Pendergast—even proud to claim kinship with the brother he blames for everything he has suffered since the age of seven.

Nothing specific to Diogenes is learned in *Two Graves,* though he is mentioned several times in its pages. Pendergast at first believes that the photos taken from security cameras near the crime scenes of the Hotel Killer are those of Diogenes in disguise. They are not, however, but rather those of a twin son Pendergast never knew he had. The respective resemblances between Diogenes and Alban, and Aloysius and Tristram, lead me to believe that, except for his blind eye, Diogenes is the physically superior specimen with regards to his brother. It is also interesting that Alban has an encounter with a volcano as well, though he survives more obviously than does his uncle. The only other pronouncements about Diogenes himself in this novel comes from D'Agosta. Contemplating what turns out to be Alban leaving small pieces of Tristram amongst his dismembered victims, D'Agosta notes: "Diogenes did not strike him at all as the kind of psycho to start dismembering himself and leaving the parts at the crime scenes" (*Two Graves,* p. 169). I am sure Diogenes would accept that as a compliment. D'Agosta also tells Laura Hayward that "a quick-and-dirty search of the databases indicates his brother really did vanish and is presumed dead" (*Two Graves,* p. 204). Though earlier in the novel, D'Agosta contemplates his strong faith in Constance as a witness to Diogenes' death, he still uses the word "presumed."

White Fire contains no mention of Diogenes per se, but when

Pendergast speaks with his contacts in the FBI and with Mime about any signs of Alban's resurfacing, we can certainly imagine that he has a similar watch set for his brother. The difference, of course, is that he knows Alban is still alive at this point in the series, and he has an even greater concern and feeling of responsibility toward his son than he does toward Diogenes. However, the way literary figure Oscar Wilde is portrayed in the set piece between himself and Arthur Conan Doyle—as realistically as Preston and Child can do so—reminds me a great deal of what Diogenes might have been like had he been born a Victorian and escaped The Event. Diogenes' sense of humor, when not toppling over the edge into the homicidally violent, is reminiscent of Wilde's. Neither should we forget that Wilde's letters to his gay lover are among the volumes Diogenes leaves with Constance as arguments for the sensual delights of living. Indeed, Wilde's own wife, with whom he had children, was named Constance.

Right before the publication of *Blue Labyrinth* in 2014, a rather strange collaboration between Preston and Child and the "Goosebumps" series' author R. L. Stine saw print in the short story anthology, *FaceOff*. Titled "Gaslighted," its premise was that through genetic and neuron-level manipulations, undesirable memories could be removed from a person's brain and other memories could be implanted. Pendergast, when caught investigating the scientists and doctors involved in this, is subjected to the process and made to believe—temporarily—that his entire F.B.I career has been a delusion. In particular, Constance Greene and her long lifespan are a bizarre figment of his imagination. In this story, however, we are presented with the idea of a kinder, far more normal Diogenes, who oozes with concern for his poor, demented older brother and is extremely hurt by his ravings about a plot to ruin his life. This Diogenes, though, is far more a product of Pendergast's fantasies than any that shows up in his memory crossings. Of course, Pendergast fights back from the brainwashing and reclaims his old life.

In *Blue Labyrinth,* the effects of countless readers begging for Diogenes' return are beginning to show in Preston and Child's writing. In this novel, I believe they have a little fun with readers when they introduce the new head of the anthropology and osteology departments at The Museum, Morris Frisby. They describe him as "wearing an expensive pin-striped suit" and "well over six feet in height" (*Blue Labyrinth*, p. 57). If this is not enough, Pendergast brings up his brother's alter ego at their first meeting: "Ah, yes. Promoted after the rather mysterious disapperance of Hugo Menzies, if I'm not mistaken" (*Blue Labyrinth*, p. 58). Presumably, those at the Museum who knew that Menzies turned out to be Diogenes have either gone elsewhere, like Nora Kelly Smithback, or are keeping very quiet out of a desire to forget all about it, like Margo Green. Speaking of Margo Green, Frisby also has a dramatic confrontation with her towards the novel's end. Yet, of course, Frisby is merely a red herring, and ends up being killed by the real villains of the tale. Besides, no one who was actually Diogenes would have accepted Pendergast's dressing-down, or survived his close scruitiny.

Diogenes does, however, show up in this novel; not in a memory crossing per se, but in one of his brother's moments of delirium after being exposed to their ancestor Hezikiah's elixir. In particular, it is when Pendergast has lost consciousness from pain after his morphine drip has been used up. He finds himself on the ridge of Stromboli, and notes that Diogenes' fall had occurred "just over three years ago" (*Blue Labyrinth,* p. 293). In this vision, Diogenes is sitting "on a deck chair set upon a fin of old lava that stood out precariously from the ridge above the smoking Sciara del Fuoco." Further, he is drinking lemonade and dressed in a floral shirt and Bermuda shorts, sunglasses and a straw hat. He greets Pendergast with his traditional *"Ave, Frater."* Diogenes goes on to discuss the irony of his brother's "present predicament" and both Alban and Hezekiah's roles in it. He laments his late nephew: "I should have liked to have met him: Alban and I would have had a lot in common. I could have taught him many things" (*Blue Labyrinth,* p. 294). Most pointedly, however, Diogenes tells Pendergast: "You, with your prudery, your hidebound sense of morality, your misguided desire to do right in the world—it's always been a mystery to me that you weren't tortured by the fact we've lived comfortably off Hezekiah's fortune all our lives." By the end of the novel, Pendergast has taken as much of this to heart as practicality will allow, and sells off his Louisiana holdings to establish a charitable foundation, though during the vision he argues with Diogenes until he gets frustrated enough to decline debating "with a hallucination." Diogenes' answer to this is most telling. He reveals he has severe burns on the left side of his face, and says: "Just keep telling yourself that, *frater*" (*Blue Labyrinth*, p. 295).

Just before the publication of *Crimson Shore* in November of 2015, Preston and Child put out an issue of their newsletter,

The Pendergast File, that they billed as a "prequel" to that novel. In it, we are given the musings of a "tall man with a scar on one cheek" who is wearing "an impeccably tailored suit." He also possesses "a hand-tooled valise of Italian leather." His name is never mentioned, nor is that of the woman in the photograph "with cropped dark hair" to whom he murmurs, "This time, my darling..."

Even in the epilogue of *Crimson Shore,* where this same figure appears, he is never mentioned by name. Pendergast, however, has spoken to Constance before he disappears, and warns her: "Someone's been here. Someone I fear that I—that *we* know only too well" (*Crimson Shore,* p. 324). Someone they both know could only be Diogenes; any possibility that Alban has not died and it is him instead is argued against by the fact that Constance was not really around when Alban kidnapped Tristram back from their father. Proctor, however, *was* involved in that incident, and it is curious that he recognizes the "strange, silky voice" (*Crimson Shore,* p. 336) of the man who surprises him from behind with a hypodermic needle.

Since *Crimson Shore*'s publication, and with the approach of that of the next novel, *The Obsidian Chamber,* Preston and Child have confirmed in many interviews that it is, indeed, Diogenes, and he has returned. We can only hope that *The Obsidian Chamber* answers many of our questions about Diogenes. First and foremost, how did he survive Stromboli? Was it a planned-out escape route, or happy accident? Does he know he has a son? Has he any better insight as to his brother's memory issues about The Event? Has the need to pay back Constance for pushing him into the Sciara overtaken his desire for revenge upon his brother? Have Preston and Child brought him back just to make sure they can show us a body this time, as they did with Helen? I hope the answer to the last question is a resounding, "No!" As for the rest, I am as anxious to find out as any of you.

THE END

Bibliography

Bunning, Joan. "El Gran Tarot Esoterico," *Learning the Tarot.* http://www.learntarot.com/fgdesc.htm.

Child, Lincoln. *Utopia.* Doubleday (New York), 2002.

Conrad, Joseph. *Heart of Darkness.* Dover Publications, Inc. (Mineola, NY), 1990.

Dean, Liz. *The Art of Tarot: A Complete Guide to Using Tarot Cards and Their Meanings.* Cico Books (London), 2001.

Hill, Kate. "Albano-Waite Tarot Reviews," *Aeclectic Tarot.* http://www.aeclectic.net/tarot/cards/albano-waite/review.shtml

Preston, Douglas, and Lincoln Child. *Relic.* Tor Books (New York), 1995.

Preston, Douglas, and Lincoln Child. *Reliquary.* Tor Books (New York), 1998.

Preston, Douglas, and Lincoln Child. *The Cabinet of Curiosities.* Warner Books (New York), 2002.

Preston, Douglas, and Lincoln Child. *Still Life With Crows.* Warner Books (New York), 2003.

Preston, Douglas, and Lincoln Child. *Brimstone.* Warner Books (New York), 2004.

Preston, Douglas, and Lincoln Child. *Dance of Death.* Warner Books (New York), 2005.

Preston, Douglas, and Lincoln Child. *The Book of the Dead.* Warner Books (New York), 2006.

Preston, Douglas, and Lincoln Child. *The Wheel of Darkness.* Grand Central Publishing (New York), 2007.

Preston, Douglas, and Lincoln Child. *Cemetery Dance.* Grand Central Publishing (New York), 2009.

Preston, Douglas, and Lincoln Child. *Fever Dream.* Grand Central Publishing (New York), 2010.

Preston, Douglas, and Lincoln Child. *Cold Vengeance.* Grand Central Publishing (New York), 2011.

Preston, Douglas, and Lincoln Child. "Extraction" (e-book). Grand Central Publishing (New York), 2012.

Preston, Douglas, and Lincoln Child. *Two Graves.* Grand Central Publishing (New York), 2012.

Preston, Douglas, and Lincoln Child. *White Fire.* Grand Central Publishing (New York), 2013.

Preston, Douglas; Lincoln Child; and R. L. Stine. "Gaslighted." *FaceOff,* edited by David Baldacci. Simon and Schuster (New York), 2014.

Preston, Douglas, and Lincoln Child. *Blue Labyrinth.* Grand Central Publishing (New York), 2014.

Preston, Douglas, and Lincoln Child. "A New England Mystery," *The Pendergast File* (newsletter), October 24,

2015.

Preston, Douglas, and Lincoln Child. *Crimson Shore.* Grand Central Publishing (New York), 2015.

"Utopia," *Stormhaven,*
http://www.prestonchild.yuku.com/topic/1874/John-Doe-Diogenes-spoilers#.VzPSKY-cHug.

Yeats, William Butler. "The Second Coming."
http://www.yeatsvision.com/SecondNotes.html.

\#\#\#

Made in the USA
Columbia, SC
13 May 2019